COASTAL
NAVIGATION
USING GPS

By the Same Author

Basic Coastal Navigation:
An Introduction to Piloting for Sail and Power

COASTAL
NAVIGATION
USING GPS

For Sail and Power

Frank J. Larkin

SHERIDAN HOUSE

Published by Sheridan House Inc.
145 Palisade Street
Dobbs Ferry, NY 10522
www.sheridanhouse.com

Copyright © 2003 by Frank J. Larkin

The publisher takes no responsiblity for the use of
any of the materials or methods described in the
book, nor for the products thereof.

Library of Congress Cataloging-in-Publication Data

Larkin, Frank J.
  Coastal navigation using GPS / Frank J. Larkin.
    p. cm.
  ISBN 1-57409-169-7 (alk. paper)
  1. Coastwise navigation. 2. Global Positioning System. I. Title.
  VK559.L3423   2003
  623.89'3—dc21   2003013613

Production/Design: Quantum Publishing Services, Inc., Bellingham, WA
Composition: Kathleen Weisel
Printed in the United States of America

ISBN 1-57409-169-7

Author's Note

The warning statements shown in this book can be found on every nautical chart and in
most navigational publications. They are not simple disclaimers, as the skeptic may
think. Instead, they reflect the reality of an environment that is hostile to human
habitation—the sea. Navigation is a flawed science that requires knowledge, skill, and
attention to many details while you pilot your boat. Read and heed these warnings.

CONTENTS

INTRODUCTION

We are living in an age where a single idea can change traditional methods, transform whole industries overnight, and open the door to possibilities that were beyond our dreams only a short time ago. Such is the case with the Global Positioning System (GPS). GPS has transformed navigation. Today, with an inexpensive little black box, in just a few seconds, you can determine your exact position on the earth's surface to within 35 feet or less. Sailors who navigated the seas over the centuries with only a few mechanical instruments and some crude charts would have perceived GPS as nothing less than a miracle. The tedious calculations associated with navigation are now reduced to the press of a button—and all of this power is available to every boat operator.

Currently, many boat operators are switching to GPS navigation. The available GPS systems range from large integrated setups costing in the thousands of dollars down to a simple handheld set for only a few hundred dollars. In Chapter 12, you will find criteria that will help you evaluate all of the different types of available GPS sets and options and make the best selection for your particular boating needs.

One of the unfortunate aspects of this GPS navigational trend is that few boat operators actually know how to use their sets safely and accurately. If you are one of these GPS owners, this book was written for you. It will help dispel much of the technical jargon and confusion that surrounds GPS. Most GPS sets come bundled with so many "bells and whistles" that it could take years to learn how to use all of them effectively—especially for users who have no prior experience with electronic navigation systems and basic navigation techniques.

Fortunately, only a few significant GPS functions provide 95 percent of the navigational benefits. By focusing on these basic navigation functions, you can learn to navigate your boat with GPS like an old pro in a very short time. Those other nice-to-have capabilities of your GPS can then be learned at your leisure at a later time.

GPS operating manuals can easily confuse a user because they assume so much prior knowledge of navigation. GPS manuals are not intended to be navigation texts. They show you how to press the right button, but not how to put the GPS functions together into a working navigational process. This book provides the necessary coastal navigation background information to help you quickly understand how to use a GPS set to navigate your boat effectively.

Written in an easy-to-understand style with many illustrations and examples that enhance your learning process, this book is a valuable text. Many chapters provide questions and answers that test your comprehension and progress, and a multiple-leg navigational exercise is threaded throughout various chapters to build up your navigational skills and confidence as you are exposed to each practical navigation technique and new GPS topic.

To get the maximum benefit, read this book chapter by chapter from the beginning. Don't jump ahead. Perform each requested task in sequence. Don't move on to the next chapter until you fully understand all of the information that has already been presented. (This is also true of your GPS operating manual. Stay focused on the one topic that you are directed to read in the manual.) Each chapter of this text is formulated to build on previous subject matter to form the steps for navigating safely and effectively with a GPS system. Complete all of the navigation practice exercises. Use the worksheets and logs for all of your computations. In doing so, in a short while, you will become a competent GPS navigator.

Teachers and Navigation Instructors

A set of 17 PowerPoint presentations are available on a CD. These presentations are coordinated to the chapters and exercises outlined in the book. A suggested syllabus and course announcements are included. For more information on the Coastal Navigation Using GPS CD, contact Sheridan House at 1-888-SHERIBK or check out their website at http://www.sheridanhouse.com.

Read This Warning Carefully

The sea is a hostile environment for the sailor so plan to use every care to safeguard your life. The aids to navigation depicted on nautical charts comprise a system of fixed and floating aids with varying degrees of reliability. Therefore prudent mariners will not rely solely on any single aid to navigation, particularly a floating aid. Read the introduction to the U.S. Coast Guard *Light List* and the *U.S. Coast Pilot* for the specific details of these problems. While the Coast Guard uses every modern technique to position buoys accurately, there are many reasons why a buoy may be off station. Sound signals may not function or lighted buoys may be extinguished. Charted depths can change due to shoaling, shifting of the seabed, and storms, or you may be using an out-of-date chart. The Coast Guard makes every effort to maintain aids to navigation in an operable condition. However, don't assume anything while on the water. Keep your charts updated to the latest Local Notice to Mariners, a free service offered by the Coast Guard. Double check everything when you transit unfamiliar waters—LORAN and GPS are not always infallible. Train yourself to become a rational skeptic about the sea.

Now that you have been warned, let's begin your journey to learn about coastal navigation using GPS.

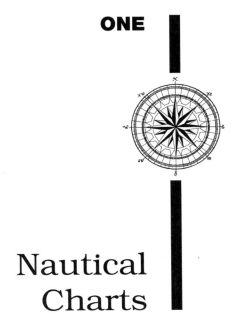

ONE

Nautical Charts

In the past, the only road map on the sea was the nautical chart. Without a chart, you were no better than a blind person. It takes only one little rock or shoal to spoil a beautiful boating day or put a large dent in your bank account or put your life and limb at risk. Thankfully, today we have electronic navigation tools—LORAN and GPS—to assist us. Columbus would have marveled at the power of today's navigational equipment. Small recreational boats have better navigation capabilities today than many naval ships had during the Second World War.

Electronic navigational equipment such as GPS can be very useful when operated correctly; unfortunately, this great tool often becomes a lethal weapon when the user is not properly trained. The word *lethal* is used intentionally. In this chapter, the importance of nautical charts is explained so that you can use the wealth of information that they contain to enhance your GPS experiences. GPS features and user tips are interspersed throughout each chapter of this book. Read them carefully to ensure that you are using your electronic navigation set correctly and accurately.

For the purpose of navigation, the earth is considered to be a perfect sphere (a ball). When creating a nautical chart, the cartographer or mapmaker faces the problem of presenting the rounded features of the earth on a flat surface—a chart. From a practical point of view, it is difficult to plot courses on a rounded surface. With the advent of computerized charts, this problem may soon be solved. Until then, the

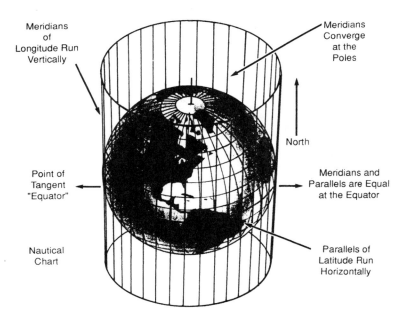

Figure 1.1   The Mercator projection *(F. J. Larkin).*

chart maker uses a technique called *projection* to accomplish the transition from the earth's sphere to the flat surface of a nautical chart.

THE MERCATOR PROJECTION

The charts used aboard small boats are usually Mercator projections with the exception of those used in the Great Lakes, which are polyconic projections. A Mercator projection is created by transferring the spherical surface of the earth onto a cylinder. The process is illustrated in Figure 1.1. A polyconic projection is made by transferring the earth's spherical surface onto a cone. In the northern latitudes, the polyconic projection is considered to be more accurate.

The vertical lines of a Mercator projection are called *meridians of longitude* and they are drawn as large circles around the globe, converging at the North and South poles. Because they *converge* at the poles, meridians of longitude project distance accurately at only one location on the earth's surface—the equator. One minute of longitude is equal to a nautical mile only at the equator. One minute of longitude is less than a nautical mile at all other locations on the globe. Refer to Figure 1.1 and observe how the meridians of longitude converge and meet at the North and South poles. Note that the meridians of longitude become distorted as they approach the poles. Because of this distortion, they cannot be used for measuring distance on a nautical chart.

Longitude is measured 180 degrees east and west from the *prime meridian*, located at Greenwich, England, for a total of 360 degrees. These longitude lines meet at a point called the *International Date Line* on the opposite side of the globe. Label longitude with a suffix to indicate whether your position is either east (E) or west (W) of the prime meridian. Each degree of longitude has 60 minutes and each minute has 60 seconds. *Remember, longitude is never used for measuring distance on a nautical chart.*

The horizontal lines on nautical charts are called *parallels of latitude* because they are equally distant to each other. Since parallels of latitude are not distorted like meridians of longitude, they are used to measure distance on a nautical chart. The parallel of latitude called the *equator* is labeled as zero (000) latitude. Parallels of latitude increase numerically northward and southward from zero (000) latitude at the equator to ninety (090) degrees at the poles for a total of 180 degrees for each hemisphere, which together total 360 degrees. Each degree of latitude has 60 minutes and each minute of latitude has 60 seconds. Label latitude with a suffix to indicate whether your location is either north (N) or south (S) of the equator.

Study the graphic in Figure 1.2 until you fully understand how the numbering system for latitude and longitude works. Understanding latitude and longitude is critical for the proper operation and use of GPS. Chapter 5 covers this material in greater depth.

THE NAUTICAL CHART

Nautical charts contain a wealth of information that is important for the safe operation of a small boat. Charts show the depth of the water referencing a vertical datum, usually feet or fathoms. Charts also reference a horizontal datum, lights, buoys, channels, lighthouses, prominent landmarks, rock shoals, reefs, sandbars, and much more information that is essential for the safe operation of your boat and your electronic navigation equipment. Use of the proper horizontal datum is critical when assessing the accuracy of data provided by your GPS set. Computerized charts are also available today. These can be stand-alone charts on a laptop computer or charts included as part of a GPS unit. You will find that the screens on many GPS units used on small boats are so small that operators may find them too small for practical use aboard their boats. In any case, GPS should never be used without reference to an up-to-date nautical paper chart. I contend that, in stormy conditions, when you and your boat are being tossed around by the waves, you will not be able to read those small screen charts on a GPS unit. Plus, you will have great trouble entering data into your GPS unit due to its small and limited number of keys. However, do not be deterred. There are many good navigation techniques that you can use

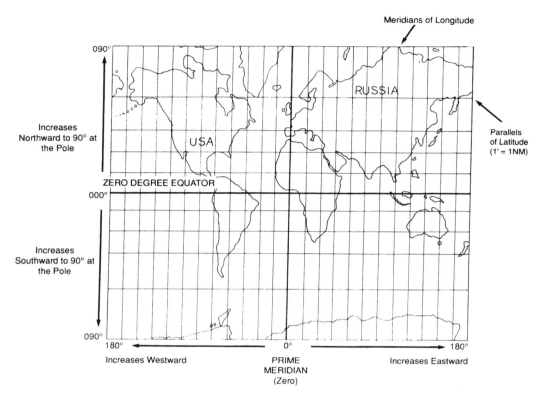

Figure 1.2 Latitude and longitude *(F. J. Larkin).*

to overcome these shortfalls. These techniques are explained throughout this book.

Chart Orientation

Normally, nautical charts are oriented with true north at the top, east at the right-hand side, west on the left-hand side, and south at the bottom of the chart. Review Figure 1.3, the Navigation Practice Chart, as an example of the design of a typical nautical chart. Make a copy of Form 1, Navigation Practice Chart, in Appendix 7 and increase its size to 11 × 17 inches. All of the navigation exercises provided in this book will be completed on a Navigation Practice Chart.

Small craft (SC) charts have a different orientation because they are designed to follow coastlines and coastal bays frequented by small craft. The charted area is more important on a SC chart than the orientation to true north. Figure 1.4 presents a sample section of a small craft chart. Note how true north is oriented to the northeast in this example, which is different from a standard nautical chart. If you are not sure about the location of true north, you can make very serious

Navigation Practice Chart

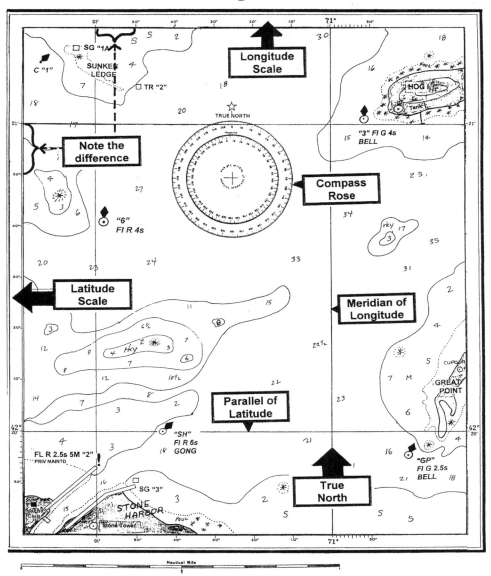

SOUNDINGS IN FEET

Figure 1.3 The Navigation Practice Chart orientation *(F. J. Larkin).*

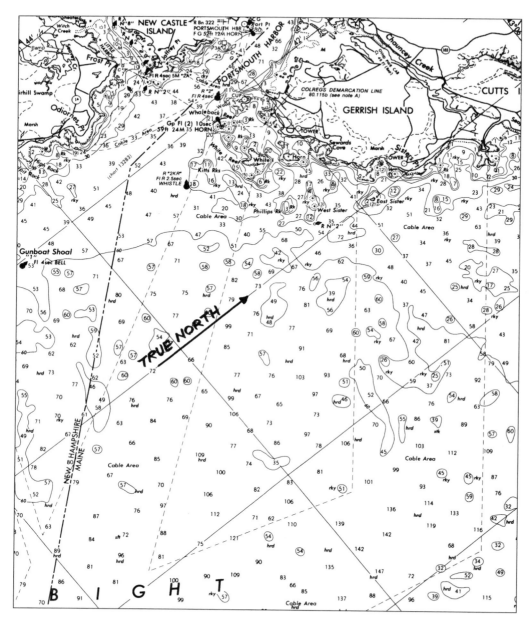

Figure 1.4   A small craft chart. Note the orientation of true north
(Source: NOAA nautical chart).

piloting errors. Look for the nearest compass rose for reference to the correct orientation toward true north when using a small craft chart.

As previously mentioned, the lines on a chart that run horizontally across the chart are called parallels of latitude. They are measured on the scales printed at the left and right of the chart. I find the phrase "LAT IS FLAT" to be a great memory aid.

One minute of latitude is equal to a nautical mile. The latitude scales on charts of the Northern Hemisphere number from the bottom toward the top of the chart since they portray the area that is north of the equator. Charts in the Southern Hemisphere number in the reverse— from top to bottom. Take another look at Figure 1.3 and observe the latitude scales at the right- and left-hand sides of the Navigation Practice Chart.

The lines that run vertically (up and down) on a nautical chart are meridians of longitude. They are measured from scales located at the top and bottom margins of the nautical chart. Note that these meridians are not as wide as the parallels of latitude scales. Stop here for a minute and measure the difference between a minute of longitude and a minute of latitude on the Navigation Practice Chart in Figure 1.3 until you convince yourself that a minute of longitude is smaller than a minute of latitude. *Never use the longitude scale on a nautical chart to measure distance.* A minute of longitude is smaller than a minute of latitude. They are equal only along the equator.

Every position on a nautical chart is expressed in terms of latitude and longitude. The data readout from a GPS unit displays positions in latitude and longitude expressions. Some sets show TD (time difference) data readouts. Most GPS units allow you to select LAT/LON or TD readouts. Always select the LAT/LON option. Review Figure 1.3 and study the numbering schemes for latitude and longitude shown in the margins. Each margin shows degrees, minutes, and seconds. Between the 20-minute and 21-minute lines on the latitude scale at the left-hand margin of the chart, note that 60 seconds are referenced in 10-second increments—10″, 20″, 30″, 40″, and 50″. Also note that just below the 20-minute latitude line is a scale for reading 10 individual seconds. In the United States, your LAT/LON position will always be north of the equator and west of the prime meridian.

In piloting, parallels, meridians, the equator, and the poles are used as reference points to determine your boat's position on the earth's surface. For example, Boston Light in Boston Harbor, Massachusetts, is positioned at 42 degrees, 19 minutes, 42 seconds North, and 70 degrees, 53 minutes, 24 seconds West. Coast Guard publications report LAT/LON in degrees, minutes, and seconds. However, most GPS sets come preset to degrees, minutes, and decimal minutes (for seconds). More about this potential source of GPS errors is explained in Chapter 5.

Magnetic Variation (example):   4° 15′ W 1985 (8′ E) *on magnetic north arrow means Magnetic Variation* 4° 15′ W *in* 1985, *annual change* 8′ E *(i.e., magnetic variation decreasing* 8′ *annually).*

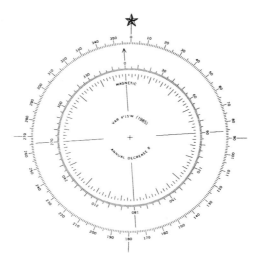

Figure 1.5   A compass rose   *(Source: Nautical Chart No. 1).*

The Compass Rose

Every nautical chart has at least one compass rose. Figures 1.3 and 1.5 show examples of a typical compass rose. Observe how the compass rose is similar to the card on your boat's compass. The star located at the top of a compass rose always points to the location of true north on a nautical chart. Each compass rose has two circles. The outer circle is oriented to true north; the inner circle is oriented to magnetic north. Course headings or directions can be measured using a compass rose on a nautical chart. Study the following characteristics of a compass rose in Figure 1.5:

- True directions are printed around the outer circle of the compass rose.

- Magnetic directions are printed around the inner circle of the compass rose. This inner or magnetic scale is oriented toward magnetic north.

- Local magnetic compass distortion, called *variation error*, is printed at the center of the compass rose.

- Note that true north on the outer scale and magnetic north on the inner scale point to different directions.

In the Boston area, magnetic north (inner scale) is located approximately 016 degrees to the west of true north (outer scale). This difference between true north and magnetic north is called *variation error.*

Variation error is different for each location on the earth's surface. However, this change is predictable, precalculated, and printed for you in the center of the compass rose. Always use the variation error from the compass rose nearest to your course line.

Find the variation error in the center of the compass rose shown in Figure 1.5. It reads 4 deg. 15' W, which is read as 4 degrees, 15 minutes West (of true north).

In piloting, variation error is used to convert a true course heading to a magnetic course heading or vice versa. The formula for converting a true course to a magnetic course and, eventually, to a compass course is explained in Chapter 9.

Soundings and Water Depth

Designations for depth of water are depicted on a nautical chart with numbers, color codes, contour lines, and a system of standardized symbols and abbreviations. The National Oceanic and Atmospheric Administration (NOAA) publication Chart No. 1 contains all of the symbols and abbreviations used on nautical charts. This publication is explained in Chapter 2. Many of the figures used in this chapter are taken directly from Chart No. 1.

Water depths or soundings are the numbers printed on a nautical chart. These depth numbers can be expressed in feet, meters, or fathoms. A fathom is equal to six feet. The baseline measurement against which a chart's depth is determined is called a *vertical datum.* The vertical datum used for a nautical chart is printed in the General Information Block on a nautical chart. Ordinarily this baseline reflects the average of the low water predictions, expressed as "Mean Low Water," or the more conservative average of the lowest low water predictions, which are indicated as "Mean Lower Low Water."

Figure 1.6 shows a sample General Information Block from a nautical chart. The vertical datum is "Soundings in Feet at Mean Lower Low Water." This means that the depths on the chart are measured in feet and represent the average of the lower water level predictions for the height of the tides in Boston Harbor. Use the vertical datum referenced on your nautical chart to set up the vertical datum on your electronic depth sounder. Check the depth sounder's operation manual for the proper setup procedure.

Depth soundings printed on a nautical chart are averages or means. This means that they can be higher or lower. Also, water depths are affected by the phase of the moon, the weather and by persistent winds.

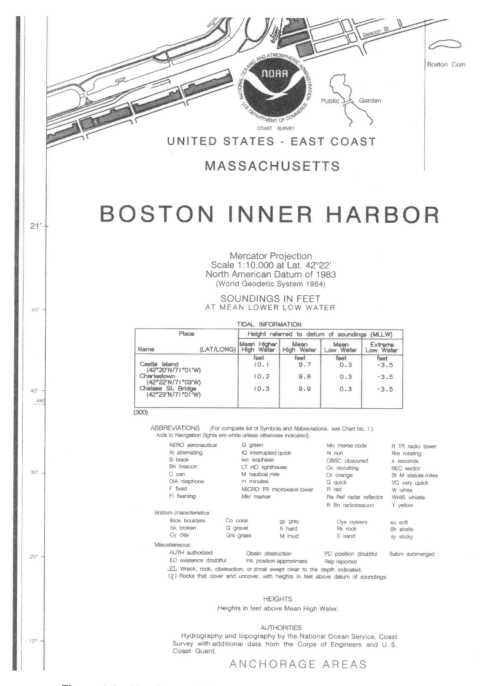

Figure 1.6   The General Information Block from a nautical chart
(Source: NOAA nautical chart).

Always allow yourself a margin for error when using water depths shown on a nautical chart. Personally, I highlight every location on my chart that indicates a water depth of six feet or lower. This gives me a quick visual alarm when I get near shoal areas. Set the "bottom alarm" feature of your depth sounder to beep when your boat transits a shoal area. Again, I set the bottom alarm on my depth sounder to six feet for this purpose.

Another safety technique that you can use is to enter any rock or shoal as a waypoint in your GPS set. Then, when you near the hazard, use the GOTO key and call up this waypoint. Your set will display the heading and DTG (Distance to Go) data so that you can keep your boat away from the danger. This is a particularly effective technique to use for unmarked and submerged navigational hazards. The use of waypoints is explained in more detail in Chapter 12.

Contour Lines

Contour lines, also called *fathom lines,* connect points of roughly equal depth to provide a linear profile of the ocean's bottom. Contour lines can be numbered or coded to show depth. Figures 1.7 and 1.19 (see the section on "Other Charted Features") show some examples of contour lines. These codes can be a series of lines, dots, or dashes. Figure 1.7 is taken from NOAA Chart No. 1 and provides information that will help you interpret the meaning of any depth contour lines you find on a nautical chart.

Shadings

Generally the shallow water on a nautical chart is tinted a darker blue, while the deeper water is tinted a lighter blue or white. The meaning of these different shades is explained in Chart No. 1 in the section called "Depth Contours" (see Figure 1.7).

Heights of Bridges

Heights are measured in feet above mean high water (MHW) datum. The clearance heights for bridges on a nautical chart are measured upward from the high water datum, which is found in the General Information Block on a nautical chart under the heading "Tidal Information." The height of a bridge is measured from the lowest projection of the bridge over the navigable channel to the high water datum. Note that in Figure 1.6 mean high water is shown as 9.7 feet at Castle Island and 9.8 feet

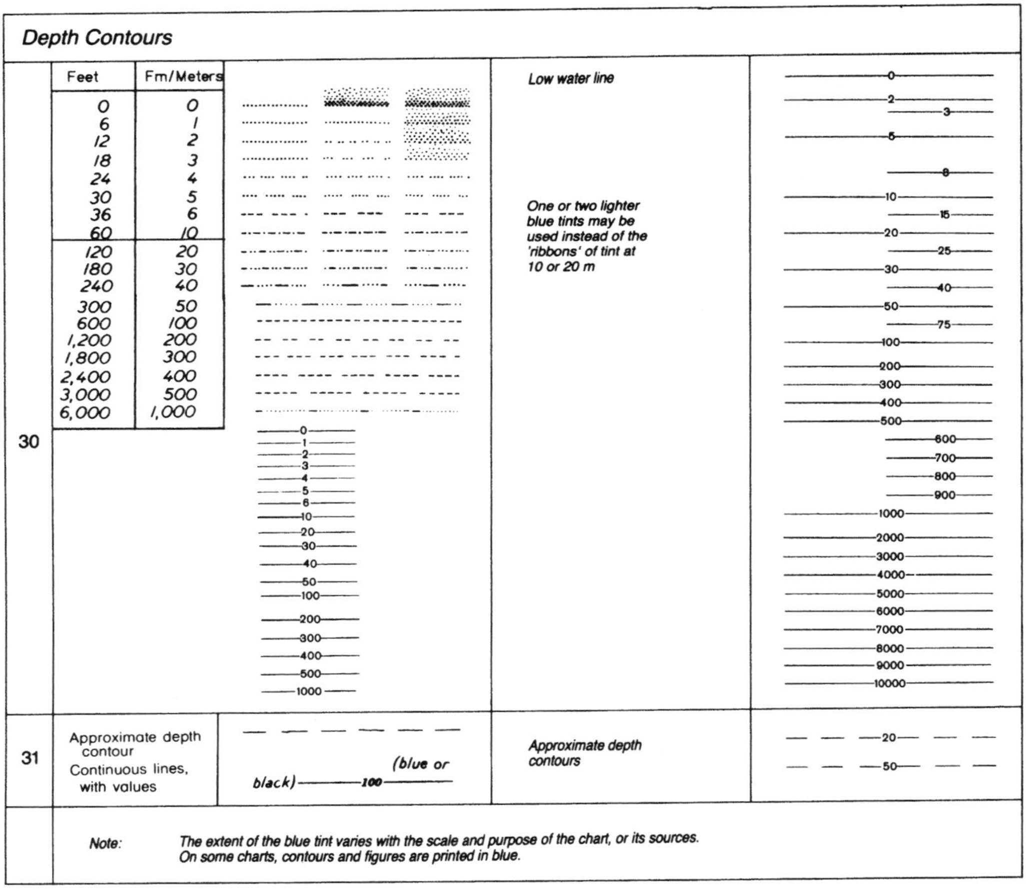

Depth Contours

Feet	Fm/Meters		Low water line	
0	0			0
6	1			2 / 3
12	2			5
18	3			
24	4			8
30	5			10
36	6		One or two lighter	15
60	10		blue tints may be	20
120	20		used instead of the	25
180	30		'ribbons' of tint at	30
240	40		10 or 20 m	40
300	50			50
600	100			75
1,200	200			100
1,800	300			200
2,400	400			300
3,000	500			400
6,000	1,000			500

30 (contour scale: 0, 1, 2, 3, 4, 5, 6, 10, 20, 30, 40, 50, 100, 200, 300, 400, 500, 1000)

(right column: 600, 700, 800, 900, 1000, 2000, 3000, 4000, 5000, 6000, 7000, 8000, 9000, 10000)

31 — Approximate depth contour / Continuous lines, with values — (blue or black) ——100——

Approximate depth contours — — — 20 — — — / — — — 50 — — —

Note: The extent of the blue tint varies with the scale and purpose of the chart, or its sources. On some charts, contours and figures are printed in blue.

Figure 1.7 Depths *(Source: Chart No. 1).*

at Charlestown. Always use the high water datum that is closest to your boat's position. Chapter 13 has a procedure for calculating the predicted height under a bridge at any time.

Heights of Objects

Heights of objects such as lighthouses are also measured upward from the high water datum. Heights of lights are measured upward from the waterline of the buoy, or, if a fixed light, from the high water mark, to the height of the focal plane of their light source—the height of the light bulb.

BASIC CHART INFORMATION

It is important to read all of the information printed on your nautical chart. Scan the complete chart for this information. You may be surprised at what you can learn about your boating area from a nautical chart. Figures 1.8 and 1.9 show, respectively, sample standard layouts for printing information on a nautical chart and an explanation of the notation.

The General Information Block

The General Information Block on a nautical chart contains very important data about your chart. Take another look at the information shown in Figure 1.6 and identify the following items:

1. The *chart title* is usually the name of the prominent navigational body of water in the area of coverage of the chart. You may use the chart title when ordering charts.

2. A statement of the *type of projection*—Mercator or polyconic.

3. A definition for the *scale of the chart* at indicated latitude, for example, 1:10,000. This means that 1 inch on the chart represents 10,000 inches on the earth's surface. The scale is precisely as stated only at the latitude quoted. Chart scale is discussed in more detail in the section on "The Scale of a Nautical Chart."

4. A statement defining the *horizontal datum* that was used to create the chart. Most new charts will reflect the World Geodetic Survey of 1984 (WGS84) as datum. Selection of the correct horizontal datum has a serious implication to the accuracy of positions provided by your GPS navigation equipment. The datum referenced on your nautical chart and the datum that is entered into your GPS must match in order to attain accurate positioning capability from your GPS. Check the operating manual for your GPS set to be sure that you are using the correct horizontal datum in your GPS.

5. *A unit of measurement* definition for depths printed on the chart. This vertical datum can be feet, meters, or fathoms, for example, "Soundings in Feet." Use this datum in your depth sounder.

6. Read all *cautionary notes* before you use a nautical chart for navigating your boat because these notes contain information that cannot be graphically presented on the chart. Look for notes that:

Schematic layout of a chart (reduced in size)

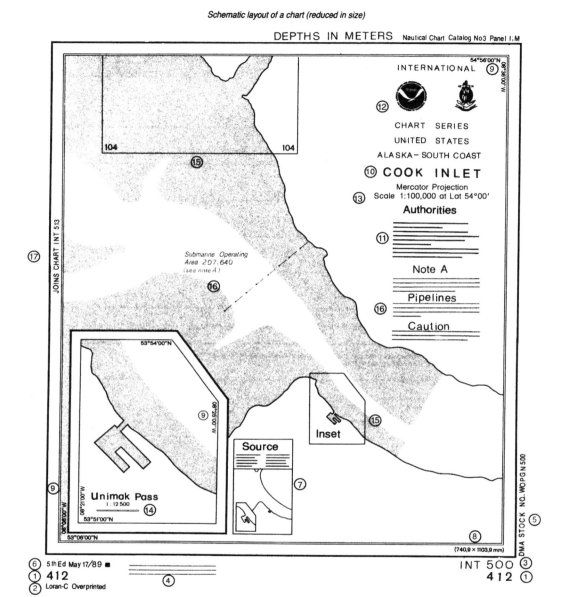

Figure 1.8 Chart number, title, and marginal notes: sample chart
(Source: Nautical Chart No. 1).

- Explain the meaning of special abbreviations used on the chart.
- Indicate the need for caution regarding dangers found on the chart.

1	Chart number in national chart series
2	Identification of a latticed chart (if any): D — Loran-C Over-printed — Omega Over-printed for Decca — for Loran-C — for Omega
3	Chart number in international chart series (if any)
4	Publication note (imprint)
5	Stock number
6	Edition note. In the example: Fifth edition published in May, 1989
7	Source data diagram (if any). For attention to navigators: use caution where surveys are inadequate.
8	Dimensions of inner borders
9	Corner co-ordinates
10	Chart title } May be quoted when ordering a chart, in addition to chart number.
11	Explanatory notes on chart construction, etc. To be read before using chart.
12	Seals: In the example, the national and International Hydrographic Organization seals show that this national chart is also an international one. Purely national charts have the national seal only. Reproductions of charts of other nations (facsimile) have the seals of the original producer (left), publisher (center), and the IHO (right).
13	Projection and scale of chart at stated latitude. The scale is precisely as stated only at the latitude quoted.
14	Linear scale on large-scale charts.
15	Reference to a larger-scale chart.
16	Cautionary notes (if any). Information on particular features, to be read before using chart.
17	Reference to an adjoining chart of similar scale.

Figure 1.9   Chart number, title, and marginal notes: explanation of chart notation
(Source: Chart No. 1).

- Show special tidal and current information for the area.
- Explain special magnetic interference information that exists in the area.
- Refer to anchorage areas and special lighting requirements in anchorage areas.

46th Ed., Apr. 15/00 ∎

13272

Figure 1.10   Number and edition of a nautical chart
(Source: NOAA nautical chart).

Number and Edition of the Chart

The chart number, edition number, and the date of the chart are located in the lower left margin of the chart. Figure 1.10 shows an example. Traditionally, this date indicated the last time when corrections had been made from the Notice to Mariners published weekly by the National Imagery and Mapping Agency (NIMA) and the Local Notice to Mariners issued periodically by each Coast Guard district. This means that all essential corrections concerning lights, buoy positions, and dangers that were known to NOAA as of this date are included on the chart. The weekly Notice to Mariners published by NIMA is available on the Internet five to eight weeks before the issue date of the chart. This causes a significant difference in the publication dates of the latest Notice to Mariners data and the Local Notice to Mariners. National Ocean Service has established a policy in which the edition date on new charts will consist of only a month and year. Separate dates will be listed nearby indicating the date of the latest NIMA weekly Notice to Mariners corrections and the date of the latest Coast Guard Local Notice to Mariners. Also explained in this area is the identification of any lattice lines, such as LORAN TD lines, overprinted on the chart. Figure 1.8 shows an example of a "LORAN-C Overprinted" note.

From time to time, the Coast Guard makes corrections to nautical charts. As mentioned above, you can correct your chart from the Local Notice to Mariners, which is available through your local Coast Guard district office or from the Internet at http://www.navcen.uscg.gov/lnm/default.htm. Appendix 8 shows a complete listing of the addresses and the telephone numbers of all of the Coast Guard district offices. Their numbers can also be obtained from the Internet address above.

Another NOAA publication, called the "Dates of Latest Editions," lists all nautical charts and their edition numbers, dates, and costs. This booklet is usually available at any authorized chart dealer. This publication is explained in Chapter 2.

The Scale of a Nautical Chart

The scale of a nautical chart is printed in the chart's General Information Block. This scale is the ratio of a unit of distance on the chart to the actual distance on the earth's surface. On a chart with a scale of 1:2,500, 1 inch equals 2,500 inches (approximately 70 yards) on the earth's surface. Please note the following information:

- Small-scale charts cover a large geographic area but show little detail. They have large-scale ratios, that is, 1:150,000.

- Large-scale charts cover smaller geographic areas and show more detail and features of the earth's surface. They have low scale ratios, that is, 1:5,000. When navigating in an area, always use the chart with the largest available scale.

- Coastal charts are produced with scales between 1:40,000 and 1:150,000. These charts are used for coastal navigation, for entering bays and harbors of considerable width, and for navigating large inland waterways.

- Harbor charts are produced with scales larger than 1:50,000 and are used in harbors, anchorage areas, and smaller waterways.

- Small craft charts are produced with scales of 1:40,000 and larger. They are special charts of inland waters, including the Intracoastal Waterway (ICW). These special editions of conventional charts are printed on lighter weight paper and are folded. The chart numbers on small craft charts will have the suffix SC, for example, 11354SC. Small craft charts contain additional information of interest to the small craft operator, such as data on facilities, tide predictions, weather broadcasts, launching ramps, marinas, repairs, and fuel. Figure 1.4 shows a section of a small-craft chart.

Chart Symbols and Abbreviations

Chart No. 1 lists all of the standard symbols and abbreviations used on a nautical chart. Often, you may find some symbols and abbreviations printed on a nautical chart in the "Notes" section. These symbols are the shorthand used to identify physical characteristics in a charted area, local aids to navigation, and the significant landmarks found on the chart. Figures 1.7, 1.8, and 1.9 are sample pages from Chart No. 1.

Use of Color on a Nautical Chart

Color is used on a nautical chart to distinguish various categories of information for the mariner, such as shoal water, deep water, and land areas. Red, green, yellow, and black are used to color aids to navigation so that they are easier to interpret.

A nautical purple or magenta-colored ink is used for some notes and to highlight lighted aids to navigation. Charted objects colored with this ink are easily recognized under a red light, which is commonly used in a navigation area on a boat at night.

> CAUTION: *Red light is commonly used on the bridge (steering) area of a vessel because it does not interfere with the night vision of the helmsperson and lookouts. A sudden burst of white light will impair night vision for approximately 30 minutes. This is why you should never show bright white lights forward at night (running lights excluded) and never shine your searchlight at another boat's bridge area.*

Lettering on a Nautical Chart

The lettering on a nautical chart provides important information about aids to navigation. All information about objects that are affected by tidal change and current—floating objects that move about in a range circle—are printed with *slanted lettering.* Bottom soundings are the exception. All script for floating aids to navigation will be slanted. Vertical lettering is used to label all information that is not affected by tidal changes or current. Lighthouses, ranges, daymarks, and small lights, which are fixed in position, are lettered vertically. Figure 1.11 illustrates this charting procedure.

The Accuracy of a Nautical Chart

A nautical chart is no more accurate than the survey on which it is based. Charting agencies make every effort to keep charts updated and accurate. However, hurricanes, earthquakes, and other major disturbances can cause sudden and extensive damage to a bottom contour or destroy floating and fixed aids to navigation. The everyday forces of

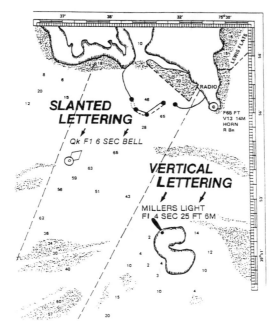

Figure 1.11 Lettering on a nautical chart
(Source: USCG Coxswain Training Manual).

wind and waves can erode or fill a channel, creating uncharted shoals. As a prudent mariner you must be alert to this potential for change and for the possible inaccuracy of charted information.

The source and date of the horizontal survey used on a nautical chart are printed under the chart title in the General Information Block. On Figure 1.6, the WGS84 is referenced. Set your GPS set to this horizontal datum. The vertical or depth datum is also listed in the General Information Block. Calibrate your depth sounder to this datum. In Figure 1.6, the vertical datum is shown as *feet*.

To judge the accuracy and completeness of a depth survey, use the following criteria:

1. The source and date of the survey are printed on your chart along with an indication of the changes that have taken place since that date. Older surveys were often made under circumstances that precluded accuracy and detail. Except in frequented waters, few surveys have been thorough enough to make certain that all dangers have been found. The QE 2 grounding is a good example. The ship struck an uncharted rock when speed was increased to make up lost time to New York. The increase in speed caused the ship to sit lower in the water. Had she traveled at a normal speed, that rock may have remained uncharted today. Until a chart, based on an old survey, is tested by you, regard it with caution.

2. Note the fullness of the detail or lack of detail of the soundings within an area. Scant soundings are an indication of the lack of detail in the survey that was used to make the chart. Use caution when transiting these areas.

3. Large or rectangular blank spaces mean that no soundings were taken. Regard these areas with suspicion and avoid them. The term "Dumping Ground" indicates that material was dumped in the area and that the soundings in this area are questionable. Use caution when transiting these areas.

NORTH AMERICAN DATUM OF 1983 AND WORLD GEODETIC SURVEY OF 1984

The horizontal datum on a nautical chart serves as the reference for the placement of lines of latitude and longitude. Recently, with the advent of the Global Positioning System (GPS), horizontal data used on nautical charts have changed. Most charts now reflect the North American Datum of 1983 (NAD83) or the WGS84 datum. If you are hanging on to old charts and want to upgrade to the new GPS navigation systems, you must acquire the latest version charts with the upgraded datum or else change the horizontal datum reference in your GPS set. See your owner's manual for instructions for selecting or changing the horizontal datum reference. The change in datum did not change the position of objects in relationship to each other. The difference is a shift in the latitude and longitude grid. The result is that the latitude and longitude position of a charted object will be different on charts referencing older datum.

In general, the range of the latitude and longitude shift varies in the United States from 15 yards in the Great Lakes, 34 yards on the Atlantic Coast and the Gulf of Mexico, 100 yards on the Pacific Coast, 500 yards in Hawaii, to 240 yards in Puerto Rico. As a precaution, always use the latest edition of a nautical chart.

When you buy a new chart, remember to check the horizontal datum on the chart and verify that the same horizontal datum is being used in your GPS set.

SYMBOLS FOR AIDS TO NAVIGATION

The basic symbol for a buoy is a diamond atop a small circle. The small circle indicates the approximate position of the buoy's mooring. The diamond symbol is used to draw your attention to the position of the circle and to describe the aid to navigation on the chart. When a buoy is lighted, this small circle will be overprinted with a magenta circle so that it will be conspicuous under red night-lights. Figure 1.12 shows some examples of buoy symbols.

Keep in mind that after the publication date of the chart, the Coast Guard may change the position of an aid to navigation—usually a buoy. The Coast Guard alerts mariners when buoys are moved, discontinued, added, or changed by publishing the change in the Local Notice to Mariners, described earlier in this chapter. First, an intention to move the aid is published. Another message appears when the aid is physically moved, deleted, or changed. The new latitude and longitude will be given so you can update your chart. Buoy symbols and markings are explained in more detail in Chapter 3.

Abbreviations that Indicate Buoy Shape

When a buoy does not have a light, its shape is indicated by letter abbreviations beside the buoy on the chart. An "N" indicates a nun or cone-shaped buoy. A "C" indicates a can-shaped buoy. Check the abbreviations used for the aids to navigation shown in Figure 1.12.

Abbreviations that Indicate Color

When a buoy is lighted (fixed with a lamp fixture), a nautical purple (magenta) disk is printed around the small circle that marks the position of these aids on a nautical chart. The color of the light is indicated by the following abbreviations:

- "R" indicates that the light is red.
- "G" indicates that the light is green.
- "Y" indicates that the light is yellow.

When no color abbreviation is used, the light is assumed to be white.

Other Features on Buoys

Buoys may be fitted with sound signals, radar reflectors, numbers and letters, or any combination of these features. The existence of bells, whistles or horns mounted on a buoy is printed near the buoy symbol on the chart. These features are also noted in the *Light List*. The abbreviation for radar reflectors (Ra Ref) will not be shown on the chart. Consult the *Light List* for this information.

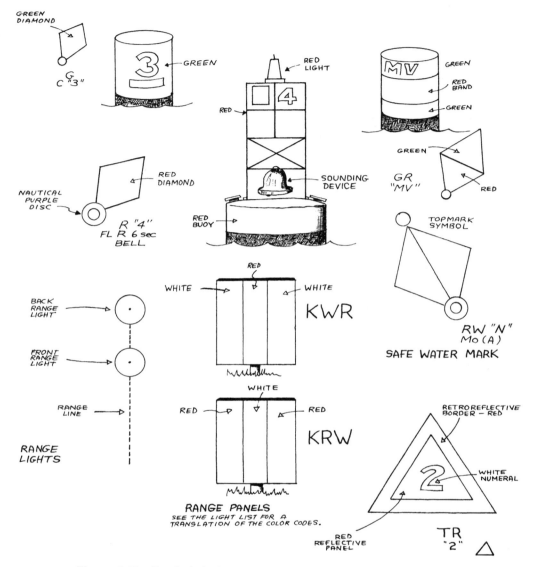

Figure 1.12   Symbols for buoys, ranges, and daymarks *(F. J. Larkin).*

Numbers and Letters

The numbers or letters that physically appear on the aid to navigation are printed on the nautical chart beside the chart symbol in quotation marks. For example, a can buoy with the number 3 on it would be identified as C "3" on the chart. Figure 1.12 shows an example of this in the upper left-hand corner.

Symbols for Lighthouses and Other Fixed Aids to Navigation

The symbol for major or minor lights is a black dot with a nautical purple flare. The flare looks like a large exclamation point. *Major lights*—lighthouses—have names that are printed on the chart. *Minor lights* show only their numbering and equipment characteristics. Figure 1.13 illustrates the symbol and description of a major light—Boston Light—as it appears on a nautical chart.

Symbols for Ranges

A *range* consists of two daymarks or beacons positioned so that they appear in a line when viewed from a predetermined line of position (LOP) or direction referred to as the *range line*, which is delineated by the position of the range markers. Ranges are not always lighted. Most ranges display rectangular daymarks with various multicolored panels. The *Light List* and Chart No. 1 contain a translation for the codes that are used to indicate the color of these panels. Lighted ranges are identified on a nautical chart with symbols for their lights, light characteristics, and with a dashed line to show the direction from which the range is viewed.

Unlighted ranges are identified on a chart with symbols for their panel color and the dashed line that shows the direction from which they are viewed.

Small triangles and squares are often used as symbols for ranges. Unlike the symbols used for marking navigable channels, these symbols are not colored. Figure 1.12 shows some typical chart symbols used for ranges on a nautical chart. In the figure, the panel colors are identified as KWR and KRW. The "K" indicates the king or full-panel color. This color code immediately follows the "K." The center stripe color appears next. Therefore, the KWR panel would show a white background colored panel with a red center stripe. The KRW panel would show a red background color with a white center stripe.

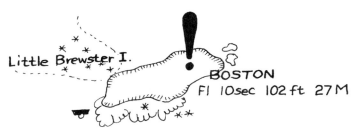

Figure 1.13 Symbol, name, and description of a major light
(F. J. Larkin).

CAUTION: *Remember that, when traveling on a range line, there is a point at which you will run aground unless you turn away on a new course. It seems stupid to have to mention this, but many novices ground their boats in this manner. Ranges are usually fixed on land or in shallow waters. Don't make this mistake.*

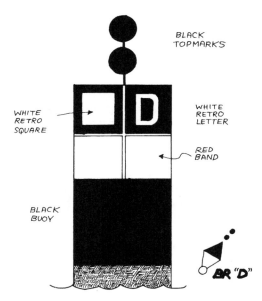

Figure 1.14 An isolated danger mark *(F. J. Larkin).*

Isolated Danger Marks

An isolated danger mark is an aid to navigation erected on, or moored above or near, an isolated danger that has navigable water around it. These aids are horizontally banded black and red, and, when lighted, exhibit a white light. A top mark consisting of two black spheres, one above the other, may be fitted on lighted or unlighted isolated danger marks. These buoys are charted with a standard symbol that represents their type but will show two dots over the diamond symbol to identify them as an isolated danger mark. Figure 1.14 shows a drawing of a lighted isolated danger mark, its chart symbol, and abbreviations.

Day Beacons

Day beacons (daymarks) are structures that are permanently fixed in the earth's surface. They are fitted with panels that should be readily visible and easily identified against background conditions. During daylight hours, the daymark conveys to the mariner the same information a light would convey at night.

CAUTION: *Boats should not pass near (close aboard) fixed aids to navigation due to the danger of colliding with the structure, its foundation, its protective riprap—rocks protecting the aid from surf—or with the obstruction marked by these aids.*

Day beacons are identified on a nautical chart with small triangles or squares. These symbols may be colored to match the color of the aid. Triangles, when colored red, have lateral significance similar to a nun buoy. Squares, when colored green, have lateral significance similar to a can buoy. Lateral buoyage systems are explained in Chapter 3.

OTHER CHARTED FEATURES

Prominent Landmarks

Water towers, smoke stacks, church spires, flagpoles, large public buildings, and so on are considered prominent landmarks and are often charted. You may find these objects marked with the chart symbol of a dot within a circle. The dot indicates that the position of the landmark is surveyed and is usable for taking an accurate position fix. A notation next to the chart symbol defines the landmark. Abbreviations such as "TWR" for tower, "STACK," and "CUPOLA" are typical.

The omission of the dot within the circle indicates that the position of the landmark is only an approximation and is subject to some error when taking a fix. Figure 1.15 shows some typical examples of symbols used for landmarks. Landmarks located on private property are usually not plotted on a nautical chart.

Wrecks, Rocks, and Reefs

These types of obstructions are shown with standardized symbols that you should learn and memorize. A sunken wreck or rock may be shown with a symbol or as an abbreviation and a number. The number indicates the depth of the obstruction at the low water datum for the nautical chart. A dashed or dotted line printed around any symbol calls special attention to its hazardous nature. NOAA Chart No. 1 contains the chart symbol for every hazard that appears on a nautical chart. Figure 1.16 shows some obstructions and dangers that you should avoid.

Bottom Characteristics

A system of abbreviations, used alone or in combination, describes the composition of the ocean bottom. Figure 1.17 lists a series of typical abbreviations that describe the seabed. Use this information for selecting the best holding ground when anchoring your boat.

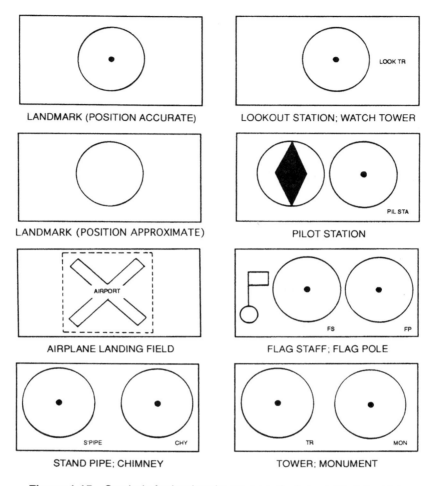

Figure 1.15 Symbols for landmarks on a nautical chart *(F. J. Larkin).*

Structures

Shorthand representations have been devised for low-lying structures such as jetties, docks, drawbridges, and waterfront ramps. These structures are drawn to scale and are viewed from overhead on a nautical chart. Some docks do not appear on a chart due to their size in relationship to the scale of the chart. Large-scale charts may show docks, while small-scale charts may not show any. Figure 1.18 illustrates some examples of these charted features.

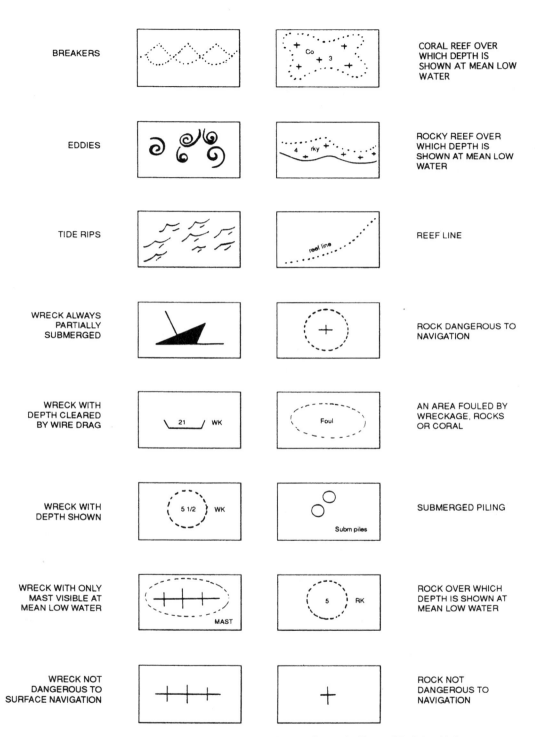

Figure 1.16 Symbols for breakers, rocks, reefs, and pilings *(F. J. Larkin).*

Types of Seabed		
Rocks → K		Supplementary national abbreviations: a–ag
1	S	Sand	S
2	M	Mud	M
3	Cy; Cl	Clay	Cy
4	Si	Silt	Si
5	St	Stones	St
6	G	Gravel	G
7	P	Pebbles	P
8	Cb	Cobbles	Cb
9	Rk; rky	Rock; Rocky	R
10	Co	Coral and Coralline algae	Co
11	Sh	Shells	Sh
12	S/M	Two layers, eg. Sand over mud	S/M
13.1	Wd	Weed (including Kelp)	Wd
13.2	Kelp	Kelp, Seaweed	
14	Sandwaves	Mobile bottom (sand waves)	
15	Spring	Freshwater springs in seabed	

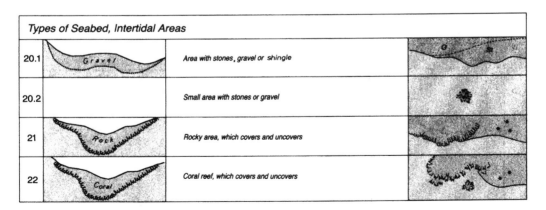

Types of Seabed, Intertidal Areas		
20.1	Gravel	Area with stones, gravel or shingle	
20.2		Small area with stones or gravel	
21	Rock	Rocky area, which covers and uncovers	
22	Coral	Coral reef, which covers and uncovers	

Figure 1.17   Nature of the seabed *(Source: Chart No. 1).*

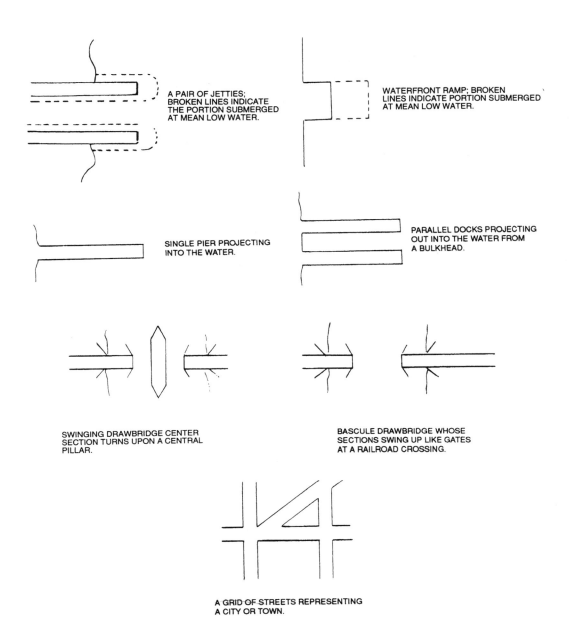

A PAIR OF JETTIES; BROKEN LINES INDICATE THE PORTION SUBMERGED AT MEAN LOW WATER.

WATERFRONT RAMP; BROKEN LINES INDICATE PORTION SUBMERGED AT MEAN LOW WATER.

SINGLE PIER PROJECTING INTO THE WATER.

PARALLEL DOCKS PROJECTING OUT INTO THE WATER FROM A BULKHEAD.

SWINGING DRAWBRIDGE CENTER SECTION TURNS UPON A CENTRAL PILLAR.

BASCULE DRAWBRIDGE WHOSE SECTIONS SWING UP LIKE GATES AT A RAILROAD CROSSING.

A GRID OF STREETS REPRESENTING A CITY OR TOWN.

Figure 1.18   Chartable structures *(F. J. Larkin).*

Coastlines

Coastlines are portrayed on nautical charts at high and low water. The land area between these points is usually colored a light green. Any prominent landmark along a coastline that can help you fix your position may be printed on a nautical chart. Details located a short distance inland from a shoreline are usually omitted. Figure 1.19 displays some typical coastline configurations that you may find on a nautical chart.

METRIFICATION OF NAUTICAL CHARTS

The Metric Conversion Act of 1975 and the Omnibus Trade and Competitiveness Act of 1988 established the metric system of weights and measures as the preferred system for the United States. These acts require that all federal agencies move as fast as practical to convert to the metric system in all activities.

As a result of these acts, and to conform to international charting practices, NOAA's Coast and Geodetic Survey (C&GS) is planning to replace existing units of measures on its nautical charts with metric equivalents. This policy will not affect the use of the international *nautical mile* used for distances at sea.

In responding to these requirements, C&GS will adhere to the following general policies:

1. Safety of navigation will continue to be of primary importance.

2. Every effort will be made to convert charts in logical groupings so that travel on the water will require minimal shifting between two measurements.

3. Conversion will be a multiyear effort with implementation expected in 10 to 15 years.

The following items on nautical charts will change as a result of the conversion:

- Depths.
- Depth curve intervals and labels.
- Depths over submerged objects such as rocks, wrecks, reefs, ledges, obstructions, etc.
- Heights of objects, such as landmarks and fixed aids to navigation.
- Bridge clearances both vertical and horizontal.
- Overhead cables and pipeline clearances.

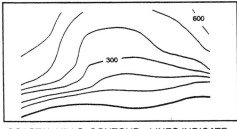

COASTAL HILLS; CONTOUR LINES INDICATE ELEVATIONS.

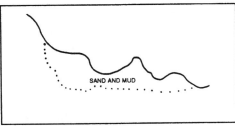

SAND AND MUD FLATS THAT ARE EXPOSED AT MEAN LOW WATER.

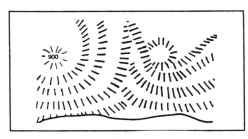

STEEP INCLINED COASTLINE; HACHURES (HATCH MARKS) ARE DRAWN IN THE DIRECTION OF THE SLOPES

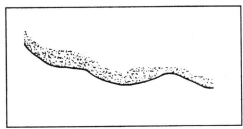

SANDY SHORE THAT IS EXPOSED AT MEAN LOW WATER.

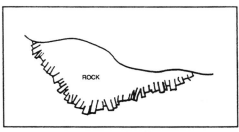

ROCK SHELF; UNCOVERS AT MEAN LOW WATER.

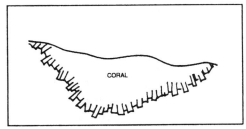

CORAL SHELF; UNCOVERS AT MEAN LOW WATER.

Figure 1.19 Symbols for coastlines and contour lines.
(Source: Chart No. 1).

- Drying height of objects, such as rocks, piles, poles, etc.
- Elevations, such as summits, contours, etc.
- Land contour intervals and labels.
- Channel legend depths.
- Channel tabulation depths.
- Tide values (given in the Tidal Information section of the General Information Block).
- Charted notes associated with depths, distances, heights, or elevations.

Your radar sets and GPS receivers will not become obsolete. Programmed waypoints will remain valid. Depth sounders will have to be calibrated in meters. Many nautical publications provide metric conversion tables.

NOAA POD—PRINT-ON-DEMAND CHARTS

NOAA, in partnership with OceanGrafix, provides up-to-date print-on-demand (POD) nautical charts. NOAA updates these charts each week for the latest NIMA, Coast Guard, and Canadian notices to mariners and for all unpublished critical safety items known to NOAA. OceanGrafix prints charts from these up-to-date digital files. New edition charts are available as POD charts 5 to 8 weeks before their release as a traditional NOAA chart. The box on the lower left corner of each POD chart states the "Additional Corrections Through . . ." to which the chart is updated beyond the corrections done at the time when a chart is released as a new edition. POD charts are available through POD chart agents at http://oceangrafix.com or call 1-877-56CHART, or contact NOAA at http://nauticalchart.gov. POD charts are available for sale one day after NOAA releases a new edition.

Reader Study Note

Spend some time reviewing what you just read and try to interpret the symbols that you find on your nautical chart. If you don't own a chart, Chapter 2 describes publications that will show you how to acquire the correct chart you need in your area. Read the General Information Block carefully as well as every note on your chart.

Check the horizontal datum on your chart. Now, read the owner's manual that came with your GPS set, and learn how to enter this datum in your GPS set. The horizontal datum for most newer charts and GPS sets will usually be WGS84. Recheck to be sure that this is true with your chart and GPS.

Check the vertical datum on your chart. Now, read the owner's manual that came with your depth sounder and learn how to enter the datum in your depth sounder.

Answer the review questions. Test your understanding and knowledge by trying to find the answer in the text before you look up the answers that are provided at the end of the chapter. If you do poorly, reread the chapter and try again.

I hope you have drawn the conclusion that you cannot properly operate your GPS without referencing the latest paper chart of the area.

Reader Progress Note

You should be familiar with the makeup of a nautical chart and some of the more important symbols and abbreviations that are used to indicate aids to navigation, depths, objects, and structures. Also, you should have a basic knowledge of where and how to find the explanations of charted symbols. You should also have an idea of the inadequacy and limitations of the small charts that may exist on your GPS. You may have also concluded that you can get away with using an inexpensive GPS set without a charted display, which is true.

REVIEW QUESTIONS

1.1 A Mercator projection is made by transferring the spherical surface of the earth onto a _____.

1.2 Parallels of latitude increase numerically northward and southward from the _____ to 90 degrees at the earth's poles.

1.3 Any position on a nautical chart can be expressed in terms of _____ and _____.

1.4 True directions are printed on the outer circle of the _____ _____.

1.5 _____ _____ is a known compass error and it is printed in the center of the compass rose.

1.6 The _____ of water can, at times, be lower than the depth printed on a nautical chart.

1.7 The NOAA publication Chart No. 1 shows all the _____ and _____ used on a nautical chart.

1.8 The chart title, the type of projection, the scale of the chart, and the unit of measurement for soundings are all information that is found in the _____ _____ _____ on a nautical chart.

1.9 The _____ and _____ of a nautical chart are printed on the lower left-hand corner of the nautical chart.

1.10 A large-scale chart covers a _____ area and shows more details and features of the earth's surface.

1.11 Nautical purple (magenta) ink is used to highlight notes and _____ aids to navigation.

1.12 The prudent mariner must be alert to the possibilities of _____ and the possible _____ of charted information.

1.13 The basic chart symbol for an aid to navigation is a _____ with a small circle.

1.14 _____ and letters appear with a chart symbol for a buoy.

1.15 The symbol for a _____ or other fixed lights is a black _____ with a nautical purple flare.

1.16 _____ are indicated on a nautical chart with small triangles and squares.

1.17 The omission of a dot within a circle for a landmark symbol indicates that the position is _____.

1.18 Coastlines are indicated on a nautical chart at both _____ and _____ water. The landmass between these points is colored _____ _____.

1.19 Boats should not pass near (close aboard) fixed aids to navigation due to the danger of _____ with the structure's foundation, or with the _____ marked by the aid.

1.20 _____ daymarks, when colored green, have lateral significance similar to can buoys.

1.21 The _____ _____ found in the General Information Block must be the same as the _____ _____ entered in a GPS set.

1.22 The vertical datum found in the _____ _____ _____ must be the same as the datum established in a _____ _____.

ANSWERS

1.1 A Mercator projection is made by transferring the spherical surface of the earth onto a CYLINDER.

1.2 Parallels of latitude increase numerically northward and southward from the EQUATOR to 90 degrees at the earth's poles.

1.3 Any position on a nautical chart can be expressed in terms of LATITUDE and LONGITUDE.

1.4 True directions are printed on the outer circle of the COMPASS ROSE.

1.5 VARIATION ERROR is a known compass error and it is printed in the center of the compass rose.

1.6 The DEPTH of water can, at times, be lower than the depth printed on a nautical chart.

1.7   The NOAA publication Chart No. 1 shows all the SYMBOLS and ABBREVIATIONS used on a nautical chart.

1.8   The chart title, the type of projection, the scale of the chart, and the unit of measurement for soundings are all information that is found in the GENERAL INFORMATION BLOCK on a nautical chart.

1.9   The NUMBER and EDITION of a nautical chart are printed on the lower left-hand corner of the nautical chart.

1.10 A large-scale chart covers a SMALL area and shows more details and features of the earth's surface.

1.11 Nautical purple (magenta) ink is used to highlight notes and LIGHTED aids to navigation.

1.12 The prudent mariner must be alert to the possibilities of CHANGE and the possible INACCURACY of charted information.

1.13 The basic chart symbol for an aid to navigation is a DIAMOND with a small circle.

1.14 NUMBERS and letters appear with a chart symbol for a buoy.

1.15 The symbol for a LIGHTHOUSE or other fixed lights is a black DOT with a nautical purple flare.

1.16 DAYBEACONS are indicated on a nautical chart with small triangles and squares.

1.17 The omission of a dot within a circle for a landmark symbol indicates that the position is APPROXIMATE.

1.18 Coastlines are indicated on a nautical chart at both HIGH and LOW water. The landmass between these points is colored LIGHT GREEN.

1.19 Boats should not pass near (close aboard) fixed aids to navigation due to the danger of COLLISION with the structure's foundation, or with the OBSTRUCTION marked by the aid.

1.20 SQUARE daymarks, when colored green, have lateral significance similar to can buoys.

1.21 The HORIZONTAL DATUM found in the General Information Block must be the same as the HORIZONTAL DATUM entered in a GPS set.

1.22 The vertical datum found in the GENERAL INFORMATION BLOCK must be the same as the datum established in a DEPTH SOUNDER.

TWO

Navigational Reference Publications and Almanacs

YOUR GPS OPERATING MANUAL

One of the most important publications that you should keep aboard your boat is the operating manual for your GPS set. This publication, although possibly very confusing and complicated, contains all of the information about how your GPS works. Sometimes it may seem as if it is written in Sanskrit and is, unfortunately, very difficult to understand. However, it is your only source of information. I have found that there are only a few key screens that you need to learn and understand in order to get the most navigational benefit from your GPS. The rest of the features in your set are really just nice to have and I find that very few people ever use them.

If you are having difficulty understanding how to work your GPS set, try writing your own procedures. Type them out and put them in a little binder stored near your helm for quick reference during critical situations or when someone else is helping you navigate your boat. Most GPS sets come with Quick Reference Cards. See Figures 12.1 and 12.2 for examples of these cards. Always keep these cards near your helm for ready reference.

On small boats, it is often difficult to plot courses while you are under way especially during stormy periods. Prudent mariners plan and plot their courses in advance so they can devote their full attention to handling the boat. This is also true when you are using GPS. Enter all the waypoints and routes into your set before you start your trip. Use a trip log, so you can verify the sanity of the readouts from your GPS. All of these tips are explained in more detail in Chapter 12 on GPS systems for small boats.

NAUTICAL CHART CATALOGS

Nautical chart catalogs provide a graphical presentation of all of the nautical charts available in U.S. waters. You will often find this publication displayed at chandleries and nautical chart stores. Its purpose is to help you select the proper chart for your cruising plans. Figure 2.1 is a small section of Nautical Chart Catalog 1 showing the Massachusetts Bay area and the charts available for that area. Nautical chart catalogs are published by the National Oceanic and Atmospheric Administration (NOAA) and are available free of charge. The following types of information are found in these publications:

- A list of nautical publications published and issued by NOS. The retail price is also shown.
- A list of authorized nautical chart agents by state who sell NOAA charts and related publications from NOS.
- A list of all nautical chart numbers, chart titles, and chart scales for all of the charts that are graphically depicted in the catalog.

Nautical chart catalogs are available in five versions:

- Nautical Chart Catalog 1 showing the Atlantic and Gulf Coasts in the United States and Puerto Rico and the Virgin Islands.
- Nautical Chart Catalog 2 showing the Pacific Coast of the United States and including Hawaii, Guam, and Samoan Islands.
- Nautical Chart Catalog 3 for Alaska.
- Nautical Chart Catalog 4 showing the Great Lakes and adjacent waterways.
- Nautical Chart Catalog 5 for bathymetric maps and special-purpose charts.

DATES OF LATEST EDITIONS

The NOAA publication *Dates of Latest Editions, Nautical Charts & Misc. Maps* contains the latest information on the edition number and date of last publication for each nautical chart. Authorized nautical chart agents receive copies of this document quarterly. Refer to this publica-

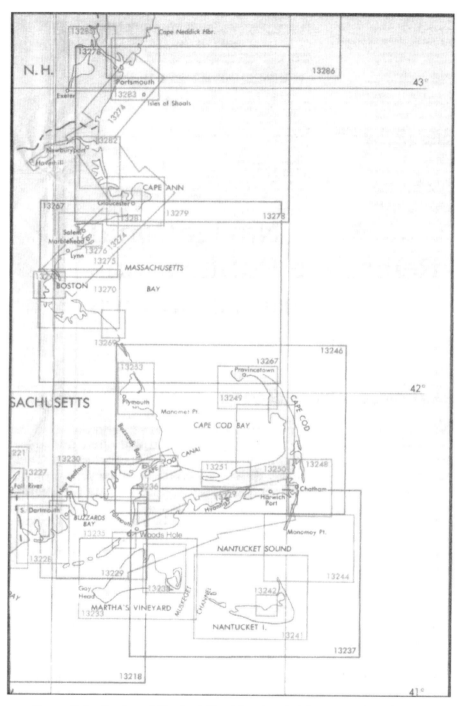

Figure 2.1   Section of Nautical Chart Catalog 1: Atlantic and Gulf Coasts
including Puerto Rico and the Virgin Islands
(Source: Nautical Chart Catalog 1).

U.S. DEPARTMENT OF COMMERCE
National Oceanic and Atmospheric Administration
National Ocean Service

DATES OF LATEST EDITIONS

NOS Nautical Charts & Misc. Maps

July 1, 2001

(Issued Quarterly)

NOTE: Charts with edition dates prior to those listed are obsolete for use in navigation.

LEGEND
(N) NEW CHART – No prior edition
(E) NEW EDITION – Prior edition is now OBSOLETE
(X) DISCONTINUED – Chart is cancelled and no longer available
(R) REVISED PRINTING – Charts with an Edition Date or a Revised Date prior to that listed are cancelled and must be removed from Agent's stock.
(C) Includes Loran-C Lines of Position
SC Small Craft Chart
(M) Metric
(F)/(M) Feet-Fathoms and Metric back to back
(O) Omega (Discontinued on next Edition)
(D) 1983 North American Datum added. See explanatory note on each chart for conversion data.

IMPORTANCE OF UP–TO–DATE CHARTS
The date of a chart is of vital importance to the navigator. When charted information becomes obsolete, further use of the chart for navigation may be dangerous. Natural and artificial changes, many of them critical, are occuring constantly; and it is important that navigators use up-to-date charts.

New NOS products are not to be used until their availability is announced in the Notice to Mariners. All products should be promptly annotated with the Notice to Mariners number that authorizes their use. This will ensure that only valid products are used.

MAIL CHART ORDERS TO:
National Aeronautical Charting Office, AVN-530
Federal Aviation Administration
Riverdale, Maryland 20737-1199
Telephone: 1-800-638-8972
Fax: 301-436-6829
E-mail: Distribution@noaa.gov
Web: http://acc.nos.noaa.gov

Enclose in U.S. FUNDS, remittance payable to FAA   Agents Stamp

THE PRICES SHOWN ARE SUBJECT TO CHANGE

Figure 2.2 *Dates of Latest Editions,* cover *(Source: Dates of Latest Editions).*

tion to ensure that you are buying the latest edition chart. The following information is given for each chart:

- Chart number.
- Scale of the chart.
- Price.
- Edition number.
- Edition date.
- Printing revision date.

Figures 2.2 and 2.3 show examples of the *Dates of Latest Edition.*

NOAA updates the *Dates of Latest Editions* on the internet daily at http://chartmaker.ncd.noaa.gov.

3

CHART NUMBER	SCALE	PRICE	EDITION NUMBER	EDITION DATE	LATEST REVISED DATE
(D) 11554	40,000	17.00	15	Oct 24 1992	
(D) 11555 (C)	80,000	17.00	36	Jan 11 1997	
(D) 12200 (C)	419,706	17.00	46	Nov 4 2000	
(D)(E) 12204 (C)	80,000	17.00	34	Apr 21 2001	
(D) 12205 SC	40,000; 80,000	17.00	26	Dec 16 2000	
(D) 12206 SC	40,000	17.00	28	Jun 3 1995	
(D) 12207 (C)	80,000	17.00	20	Apr 4 1998	
(D) 12208	50,000	17.00	7	Dec 5 1998	
(D) 12210 (C)	80,000	17.00	34	Dec 28 1996	
(D) 12211 (C)	80,000	17.00	39	Apr 29 2000	
(D) 12214 (C)	80,000	17.00	43	Dec 16 2000	
(D)(E) 12216	40,000	17.00	26	May 12 2001	
(D) 12221 (C)	80,000	17.00	71	Aug 5 2000	
(D) 12222	40,000	17.00	41	Dec 16 2000	
(D) 12224	40,000	17.00	22	Dec 9 2000	
(D) 12225 (C)	80,000	17.00	52	May 13 2000	
(D) 12226	40,000	17.00	15	Jul 8 1995	
(D) 12228	40,000	17.00	25	Dec 9 2000	
(D) 12230 (C)	80,000	17.00	57	Apr 29 2000	
(D) 12231	40,000	17.00	24	Sep 25 1993	
(D) 12233	40,000	17.00	33	May 2 1998	
(D) 12235	40,000	17.00	28	Dec 5 1998	
(D)(E) 12237 SC	40,000	17.00	26	Mar 31 2001	
(D)(E) 12238	40,000	17.00	36	Mar 3 2001	
(D) 12241	20,000	17.00	20	Jul 13 1996	
(D)(E) 12243	40,000	17.00	13	Feb 24 2001	
(D)(E) 12244	40,000	17.00	13	Feb 24 2001	
(D)(E) 12245	20,000	17.00	59	Apr 28 2001	
(D)(E) 12248	40,000	17.00	58	May 19 2001	
(D)(E) 12251	20,000; 40,000	17.00	23	May 12 2001	
(D)(E) 12252	20,000	17.00	23	May 12 2001	
(D) 12253	20,000	17.00	43	Mar 25 2000	
(D) 12254	20,000	17.00	42	Dec 9 2000	
(D) 12255	5,000	17.00	14	Jan 18 1997	
(D) 12256	20,000	17.00	12	Sep 7 1996	
(D) 12261	40,000	17.00	27	Jan 13 2001	
(D) 12263 (C)	80,000	17.00	49	May 9 1998	
(D) 12264	40,000	17.00	27	Oct 18 1997	
(D) 12266	40,000	17.00	27	Dec 23 2000	
(D) 12268	40,000	17.00	9	Apr 20 1996	
(D) 12270	40,000	17.00	30	Oct 16 1999	
(D) 12272	40,000	17.00	27	Jun 7 1997	
(D) 12273 (C)	80,000	17.00	51	Jun 3 2000	
(D) 12274	40,000	17.00	32	Jul 1 2000	
(D) 12277	20,000	17.00	30	Apr 29 2000	
(D)(E) 12278	40,000	17.00	71	Apr 28 2001	
(D) 12280 (C)	200,000	17.00	1	May 25 1996	
(D) 12281	15,000	17.00	49	May 13 2000	
(D) 12282	25,000	17.00	32	Apr 25 1998	
(D) 12283	10,000	17.00	24	Jan 6 2001	
(D) 12284	10,000	17.00	15	Mar 15 1997	
(D) 12285 SC	80,000	17.00	33	Mar 2 1996	
(D) 12286	40,000	17.00	28	Jun 13 1998	
(D) 12287	20,000	17.00	17	Feb 3 1996	
(D) 12288	40,000	17.00	19	May 23 1998	
(D) 12289	40,000	17.00	47	Mar 14 1998	
(D)(D) 12290 (C)	400,000	17.00	42	Feb 17 2001	
(D) 12304 (C)	80,000	17.00	41	Apr 22 2000	
(D) 12311	40,000	17.00	40	May 6 2000	
(D) 12312	40,000	17.00	50	Jun 10 2000	
(D) 12313	15,000	17.00	47	Oct 7 2000	
(D) 12314	20,000	17.00	29	Apr 4 1998	
(D) 12316 SC	40,000	17.00	27	Jul 26 1997	
(D) 12317	10,000	17.00	30	Feb 3 1996	
(D)(E) 12318 (C)	80,000	17.00	40	Feb 17 2001	
(D) 12323 (C)	80,000	17.00	23	Mar 11 2000	
(D)(E) 12324 SC	40,000	17.00	29	Apr 7 2001	
(D)(E) 12325	15,000	17.00	2	Apr 28 2001	
(D)(E) 12326 (C)	80,000	17.00	48	Apr 21 2001	
(D) 12327	40,000	17.00	94	Jan 13 2001	
(D) 12331	15,000	17.00	29	Jun 26 1999	
(D)(E) 12332	20,000	17.00	21	Jan 20 2001	
(D) 12333	15,000	17.00	31	Jun 17 2000	
(D) 12334	10,000	17.00	64	Aug 12 2000	
(D) 12335	10,000	17.00	38	Apr 1 2000	
(D) 12337	20,000	17.00	22	Nov 15 1997	
(D) 12338	5,000	17.00	8	Jun 2 1990	
(D) 12339	10,000	17.00	43	Jul 15 2000	
(D) 12341	10,000	17.00	24	Apr 1 2000	
(D) 12342	10,000	17.00	22	Nov 8 1997	
(D) 12343	40,000	17.00	17	Jun 1 1996	
(D) 12345	10,000	17.00	9	Jul 7 1990	
(D) 12346	10,000	17.00	10	May 19 1990	
(D) 12347	40,000	17.00	29	Dec 9 2000	
(D) 12348	40,000	17.00	33	Dec 23 2000	
(D) 12350	20,000	17.00	56	Jan 6 2001	
(D) 12352 SC	20,000; 40,000	17.00	28	May 6 2000	
(D) 12353 (C)	80,000	17.00	17	Jun 13 1992	
(D) 12354 (C)	80,000	17.00	38	May 13 2000	
(D) 12358	40,000	17.00	18	Apr 2 1994	
(D) 12362	10,000	17.00	16	Jul 7 1990	

Figure 2.3 Half of a sample page from *Dates of Latest Editions* *(Source: Dates of Latest Editions).*

CHART NO. 1

Serious navigators own a copy of *Chart No. 1, USA: Nautical Chart Symbols, Abbreviations, and Terms.* This publication is one of the best bargains for the amount of information provided, containing all of the symbols and abbreviations that have been approved for use on nautical charts published in the United States. A glossary of terminology used on the charts of other nations is also included. Every good nautical chart store stocks this publication. Figure 2.4 is a reprint of the cover of Chart No. 1 and Figure 2.5 shows a sample page. You have already seen many samples from this publication used in Chapter 1.

NOAA and the Department of Defense's Defense Mapping Agency (DMA) produce Chart No. 1 and it is now being published by private parties. Corrections for this publication appear in the Local Notice to Mariners (LNM).

LIGHT LIST

The *Light List* provides mariners with more complete details about aids to navigation (ATONs) than can be printed on the nautical chart. It is a catalog of all aids to navigation, their lights, sound signals, color, type, radio beacons, and LORAN stations. The *Light List* is published periodically by the U.S. Coast Guard in seven volumes:

- *Volume I:*   St. Croix River, ME, to Toms River, NJ.
- *Volume II:*   Toms River, NJ, to Little River, SC.
- *Volume III:*   Little River, SC, to Econfina River, FL.
- *Volume IV:*   Econfina River, FL, to Rio Grande, TX.
- *Volume V:*   Mississippi River System.
- *Volume VI:*   Pacific Coast and Pacific Islands; also includes some lighted aids to navigation on the coast of British Columbia, which are maintained by Canada.
- *Volume VII:* Describes the aids to navigation in U.S. waters of the Great Lakes. Also includes some lighted ATONs on the Great Lakes and the St. Lawrence River above the St. Regis River, which are maintained by Canada.

Figure 2.6 shows the cover of Volume I of the *Light List* and Figure 2.7 shows a typical page. Note the following information listed about the aids printed on the sample page:

1. *A Light List number:* Each aid to navigation is assigned a special number. The abbreviation for this number is "LLNR." The Coast Guard changes the LLNR for an aid from time to time.

Chart No. 1

United States of America

Nautical Chart Symbols
Abbreviations and Terms

TENTH EDITION

UpDated through AUGUST, 2000

Corrections and additions which have appeared in the Department of Defense
Automated Notice to Mariners System have been posted through NM 36/2000

Prepared Jointly by

DEPARTMENT OF COMMERCE
National Oceanic and Atmospheric Administration
National Ocean Service

DEPARTMENT OF DEFENSE
National Imagery and Mapping Agency

Published by
WATERPROOF CHARTS, Inc.
320 Cross Street
Punta Gorda, FL 33950
 1-800-423-9026
© 2000, Waterproof Charts, Inc.

Figure 2.4 Cover of Chart No. 1
(Source: Chart No. 1).

2. *Name of the aid to navigation:* Each ATON has a unique name. The name for the section under which the aid is listed is included as part of the name of the aid. For example, Buoy SC is listed in the section labeled Squantum Channel. The proper name of this aid is Squantum Channel Buoy SC.

3. *Geographic position of the aid:* The latitude and longitude are shown for most aids in the *Light List.* You can use the provided positions as waypoints for your GPS. However, be sure you have made all of the updates published in the LNM.

4. *Light characteristics for all lighted aids.*

5. *Height above water:* For all floating aids, the height of a light is measured from the water line of the buoy to the level of the light bulb—called the *focal plane.* On fixed aids, the height of the light is measured from the high tide mark to the focal plane of the light. Check the General Information Block on a chart for this information.

6. *Nominal range of lights aids:* The nominal range is defined as the maximum distance in nautical miles at which a light can

16	⊠	Buddhist temple	✈ 卍	
17	Ö ŏ Λ	Mosque, Minaret	ŏ	Λ ŏ
18	▣ ŏ	Marabout	● Marabout	
19	┌─────┐ │ Cem │ └─────┘	Cemetery (for all religious denominations)	┌─────┐ │ └ └ └ │ │ └ └ │ └─────┘	┌─────┐ │ ∪ ∪ │ └─────┘
20	⊙TOWER ○ Tr	Tower	⬚	Tr
21	STANDPIPE ⊙ ○S'pipe	Water tower, Water tank on a tower Standpipe	⬚	
22	⊙CHIMNEY ○ Chy	Chimney	⬚	◀Chy	⬚
23	⊙FLARE ● Flare	Flare stack (on land)	⬚	
24	MONUMENT ⊙ ○ Mon	Monument	⬚	Mon	⬚ ☙
25.1	⊙WINDMILL ⊙WINDMILL ○ Windmill ⊗	Windmill	✗	⬚ ✗
25.2		Windmill (wingless)	✗ Ru	
26	⊙ WINDMOTOR ○ Windmotor	Windmotor	⬚	⊗ ✗
27	⊙F S ⊙F P ○ F S ○F P	Flagstaff, Flagpole	⬚	FS
28	⊙ R MAST ⊙ MAST ○ R Mast ○ TV Mast	Radio mast, Television mast	⬚	
29	⊙ R TR ⊙ TV TR ○ R Tr ○ TV Tr	Radio tower, Television tower	⬚	
30.1		Radar mast	● Radar Mast	

Figure 2.5 Typical page from Chart No. 1, landmarks
(Source: Chart No. 1).

be seen in clear weather. Nominal range is not stated for range and directional lights.

7. *Structural characteristics of the aid:* Special construction characteristics or construction materials are indicated.

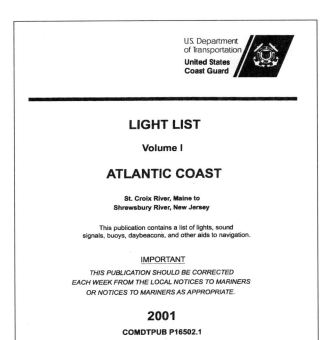

Figure 2.6 Cover of Volume I of the *Light List*
(*Source: Light List*).

8.   *General remarks:* This section may include information on radio beacon signals and characteristics, a light sector arc of visibility, radar reflectors, emergency backup lights, seasonal aid deployment schedules, and information about private aids to navigation.

The *Light List* is sold by the Government Printing Office bookstores located in many cities, by Government Printing Office agents located in principal ports, by local chandleries, or you can purchase it directly from:

U.S. Government Printing Office
Superintendent of Documents
Washington, DC 20402

The stock number for the *Light List* is 050-012-00303-3. Corrections to the *Light List* appear in the Local Notice to Mariners published by the USCG District Office in your area. The *Light List* is also available for download from the Internet at http://www.navcen.uscg.gov/pubs/lightlist/.

(1) No.	(2) Name and location	(3) Position	(4) Characteristic	(5) Height	(6) Range	(7) Structure	(8) Remarks
			MASSACHUSETTS – First District				
	BOSTON INNER HARBOR (Chart 13272)	N/W					
	Bird Island Flats						
10720	– Buoy 1	42 21.5 71 01.9				Green can.	
10725	– Buoy 2					Red nun.	
10730	– Buoy					Red and green bands; nun.	
10735	Jeffries Point Wreck Buoy WR	42 21.7 71 01.9				Red and green bands; nun.	
10736	EAST BOSTON DOCK LIGHT SE	42 21.6 71 02.0	F Y			On pile.	Private aid.
10737	EAST BOSTON DOCK LIGHT NW		F Y			On pile.	Private aid.
	BOSTON HARBOR (Chart 13270)						
	Dorchester Bay						
10740	– Buoy 2	42 19.6 71 00.1				Red nun.	
10745	– Buoy 3					Green can.	
10750	– Buoy 4	42 19.3 71 00.8				Red nun.	
10755	– Lighted Buoy 5	42 19.0 71 01.3	Fl G 4s		4	Green.	Replaced by can from Dec. 1 to Mar. 15.
10760	– Buoy 6					Red nun.	
10765	– Buoy 8	42 18.8 71 01.6				Red nun.	
10770	– Buoy 10	42 18.6 71 01.8				Red nun.	
10775	– Lighted Buoy 12	42 18.5 71 02.0	Fl R 4s		3	Red.	Replaced by nun from Nov. 15 to Mar. 15.
10780	PLEASURE BAY JETTY LIGHT	42 19.8 71 00.9	Fl W 2.5s	25	6	NR on skeleton tower.	
10781	COLUMBIA POINT LIGHT	42 18.9 71 02.0	Fl W 5s			On post at northeast corner of dike.	Private aid.
	Squantum Channel						
10785	– Buoy SC	42 18.5 71 01.9				Green and red bands; can.	
10790	– Buoy 2					Red nun.	
	Dorchester Bay Basin						
10795	– Channel Buoy 1	42 18.3 71 03.0				Green barrel.	Maintained from May 1 to Dec. 1. Private aid.
10796	– Channel Buoy 2					Red barrel.	Maintained from May 1 to Dec. 1. Private aid.
10797	– Channel Buoy 3					Green barrel.	Maintained from May 1 to Dec. 1. Private aid.

Figure 2.7 Sample page from the *Light List (Source: Light List).*

COAST PILOT

NOAA publishes the *U.S. Coast Pilot* annually. This document supplements the information shown on nautical charts that cannot be coded or abbreviated on a nautical chart. The *Coast Pilot* is updated by field inspectors from information published in the LNM, from reports from hydrographic vessels and field parties, and from information provided by other governments, maritime and pilotage associations, port authorities, and boaters like you. Figure 2.8 is a reprint of the cover of Volume 1 of the *Coast Pilot*. The *Coast Pilot* is published in nine volumes:

- *Coast Pilot 1—Eastport to Cape Cod:* This edition covers the Massachusetts Bay side of Cape Cod.
- *Coast Pilot 2—Cape Cod to Sandy Hook, NJ:* This edition covers the Nantucket Sound side of Cape Cod.
- *Coast Pilot 3—Sandy Hook to Cape Henry.*
- *Coast Pilot 4—Cape Henry to Key West.*
- *Coast Pilot 5—Gulf of Mexico, Puerto Rico, and the Virgin Islands.*
- *Coast Pilot 6—Great Lakes and connecting waterways.*
- *Coast Pilot 7—California, Oregon, Washington, and Hawaii.*
- *Coast Pilot 8—Alaska, Dixon Entrance to Cape Spenser.*
- *Coast Pilot 9—Alaska, Cape Spenser to the Beaufort Sea.*

Most of the information in the *Coast Pilot* cannot be shown graphically on a standard nautical chart and it is not readily available on other publications and documents. The following typical subject matter is provided in the *Coast Pilot*:

- Channel descriptions.
- Anchorages.
- Bridge and cable clearances, and bridge regulations and opening signals and communications.
- Currents.
- Tide and water levels.
- Prominent features in each area.
- Pilotage information.
- Towage information.
- Weather.
- Ice conditions.
- Wharf descriptions and usage.

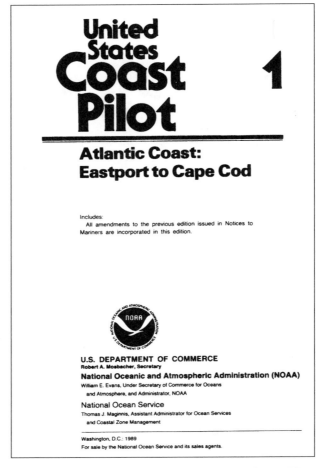

Figure 2.8 Cover of Volume 1 of the *U.S. Coast Pilot*
(*Source: U.S. Coast Pilot*).

- Dangers.
- Routes.
- Traffic separation schemes.
- Small craft facilities.
- Federal regulations applicable to the mariners in the area.
- Locks and dam regulations and signals.

The *Coast Pilot* has several major sections:

- General information.
- Navigation regulations—excerpts from the *Code of Federal Regulations* applicable to the area.

- Local information about the area covered by the edition.
  - Special anchorage areas.
  - Drawbridge operation regulations.
  - Vessel Traffic Services (VTS).
  - Restricted areas, safety zones, and limited access areas.
- Appendix.
- Sales information.
- Climatological tables.
- Meteorological tables.
- Mean surface water temperatures and densities.
- Atmospheric pressure conversion table.
- Determination of wind speed by sea conditions.
- National Weather Service coastal warning displays.
- Nautical miles between points.
- Radio bearing conversion table.
- Distance of visibility of objects at various elevations at sea.
- Conversion table—degrees to points and vice versa.
- Table for estimating time of transit.
- Index.
- Standard abbreviations for broadcasts.
- Measurement and conversion factors.
- Metric style guide.
- *Coast Pilot* reports—for use to report discrepancies found in the *Coast Pilot*. Send your reports to:

  National Ocean Service, NOAA (N/CS261)
  1315 East-West Highway, Station 7317
  Silver Springs, MD 20910-3282
  FAX: 301-713-4516

The *Coast Pilot* is now available for download from the Internet at http://chartmaker.ncd.noaa.gov/nsd/coastpilot.htm. This site also includes critical correction updates to the *Coast Pilot*. Corrections to the *Coast Pilot* appear in the Local Notice to Mariners.

LOCAL NOTICE TO MARINERS

The Local Notice to Mariners is the Coast Guard's method for communicating to you any information concerning the establishment, the changing, and the discontinuance of aids to navigation. Also reported are channel conditions and depths, obstructions, hazards to navigation, danger areas, special events related to marine safety, and other important information. These notices are essential to mariners because they are used to update nautical charts, *Light Lists, Coast Pilots,* and other nautical catalogs and publications. Figure 2.9 shows a sample cover from a Local Notice to Mariners.

The Local Notice to Mariners is published weekly and summarized monthly by the Coast Guard District Office in your area and is available on the Internet at http://www.navcen.uscg.gov. Chart corrections and *Light List* changes appear only once. A complete listing of current discrepancies and temporary changes appear monthly. Subscription to this weekly publication is free. The LNM is arranged in sections as discussed next.

Section I: Special Notices

Special notices include information that affects a wide segment of the maritime public or is otherwise noteworthy with regard to particular events and general development in navigation.

Section II: Discrepancies—Discrepancies Corrected

This is a list of all aids to navigation in the *Light List* that are not currently operating. Discrepancies that are expected to be fixed before printing or release time are not shown. Discrepancies that have been corrected since the publication of the last edition of the LNM are listed as corrected. Discrepancies to private aids to navigation are also reported.

Section III: Temporary Changes—Temporary Changes Corrected

Aids that have been changed on a temporary basis are listed in this section. Temporary changes that have been corrected since the publication of the last edition of the LNM are listed as corrected. Once listed as corrected, the entry for the aid does not appear in a subsequent LNM unless a problem reoccurs. When aids are temporarily relocated for dredging, a temporary correction will appear in Section V that also gives the aid's new latitude and longitude.

Section IV: Index of Waterways

This section provides an index of the waterways and chart numbers that are affected by chart corrections (coded C), advance notice of changes (coded A), and proposed notice of change (coded P).

U.S. Department
of Transportation

United States
Coast Guard

LOCAL NOTICE TO MARINERS
COASTAL WATERS FROM EASTPORT, MAINE TO SHREWSBURY, NEW JERSEY

WEEKLY SUPPLEMENT

INTERNET ADDRESS
HTTP://www.navcen.uscg.gov

Weekly supplemental editions contain new information only available following the monthly edition. NOTE: Chart corrections and Light List changes appear only once each. A complete listing of current discrepancies and temporary changes appear in the monthly issue, LNM 32/02. Subscription to this weekly publication is free. If you have questions about the LNM or wish to be on the mailing list, contact:

COMMANDER, FIRST COAST GUARD DISTRICT (oan)
408 Atlantic Avenue, Boston, Massachusetts 02110-3350
Telephone (Day): 1-800-848-3942. To order LNM: Ext. 8222 or 8351
24 Hour FAX: (617) 223-8073
Coast Guard's Customer Infoline (8:00 a.m. - 4:00 p.m.): 1-800-368-5647
Hearing impaired (TDD) 1-800-689-0816

All bearings are in degrees TRUE - All times are in Local Time unless otherwise noted.
NOTE: A vertical line in the RIGHT MARGIN of sections I, V, VI, VII indicates new information.
BROADCAST NOTICE TO MARINERS
The following Broadcast Notice to Mariners (BNM's) have been issued since last week:

First District	CG1- 0327	to	0340
Group Boston	BOS- 0055	to	0060
Group Long Island Sound	LIS- 0139	to	0144
Group Moriches	MOR- 0034	to	0035
Group New York	NEW- 0143	to	0144
Group Portland	POR- 0061	to	0062
Group Southwest Harbor	SWH- 0034	to	0034
Group Woods Hole	WHO- 0096	to	0096

Light List Reference: ATLANTIC COAST, VOLUME 1, COMDTPUB P16502.1, 2002 Edition

Figure 2.9   Cover of a sample Local Notice to Mariners
(Source: Local Notice to Mariners).

Section V: Chart Corrections

Chart corrections include information about actual work performed, whether temporary or permanent, on federal or private aids that should be reflected on a nautical chart. New editions of nautical charts are listed in this section as well as NOS chart corrections. Special codes are used in this section as follows:

- The letters "TEMP" below the chart number indicate that the chart correction is only temporary in nature.

- The letter "M" immediately following the chart number indicates that the correction should be applied to the metric side of the chart only.

- Courses and bearings are given in degrees clockwise from 000 True.

- Bearings of light sectors are toward the light from the sea.

- The nominal range of lights is expressed in statute miles (St M).

Section VI: Advance Notice of Scheduled Changes in Aids to Navigation

The advance notices of approved projects that are scheduled to be completed on a certain date are printed in this section. Also, there may be notices of future temporary changes, such as dredging. The notice is written in a manner similar to a regular notice except for a statement indicating that the change will take place in the future.

Advance notice must be given for significant changes to aids used by mariners engaged in the transportation trade. The timing of these notices is prescribed by law. Major changes to major seacoast aids require four months' notice with the information repeated monthly until the change is completed. Other major changes require two months with the change notice appearing every two weeks until the change is completed. If a change cannot be completed within a week of its announced date, a postponement notice is issued. For important aids, the postponement notice will be broadcast by the Coast Guard twice daily on VHF Channel 22A.

Section VII: Proposed Changes in Aids to Navigation

Periodically the Coast Guard evaluates its system of aids to navigation within an area to determine whether the conditions for which the aids were established have changed. When changes are contemplated, the feasibility of improving, relocating, replacing, or discontinuing the aid(s) is considered. This section contains notices of projects conceived and in the planning stage, but that have not been approved or scheduled. Comments are always requested from mariners regarding the proposed changes.

Section VIII: General

This general section contains information about navigational publications, channel conditions, obstructions, hazards to navigation, regattas, and other matters of marine information that do not fit into any of the other sections of the LNM. Each entry is first entered in paragraph form showing all of the pertinent information. If the discrepancy lasts for more than one week, it is placed on a summary list until the approximate completion or repair date. You must retain copies of the Local Notice to Mariners for reference in case you need to refer back to them for the details of a prior entry.

Section IX: *Light List* Corrections

All current *Light List* discrepancies and those corrected since the publication date of the last LNM are tabulated in this section. Discrepancies that have occurred and have been corrected during this period are not listed. These corrections include:

- Proposed changes.
- General information of concern to the mariner.
- Summary of dredgings still in effect.
- Applications received for permits for bridge reconstruction.
- Discrepancies in LORAN chains.
- *Light List* corrections.
- Approved marine events and regattas, including information and restrictions on local regattas, marine parades, races, and other marine events in your area.

TIDE TABLES

The *Tide Tables* contain predictions for the times and heights of high and low water for every day of the year for many of the important major harbors, which are called *reference stations*. Also provided are the time and height differences for numerous other locations called *substations*. Chapter 15 explains the use of the *Tide Tables* for calculating the depth of the water at any time and for determining the height available under a bridge at any time. Under license from NOAA, International Marine publishes four versions of the *Tide Tables*:

- East Coast of North and South America, including Greenland.
- West Coast of North and South America, including the Hawaiian Islands and the Alaskan Supplement.
- Central and Western Pacific Ocean and Indian Ocean.
- Europe and West Coast of Africa, including the Mediterranean Sea.

Figure 2.10 shows the inside cover of the *Tide Tables*. The *Tide Tables* have a wealth of additional information including:

- Astronomical data showing both lunar and solar information. This chart is printed on the inside of the back cover.
- An important notice that advises mariners about the importance of outside forces on the predictions found in the *Tide*

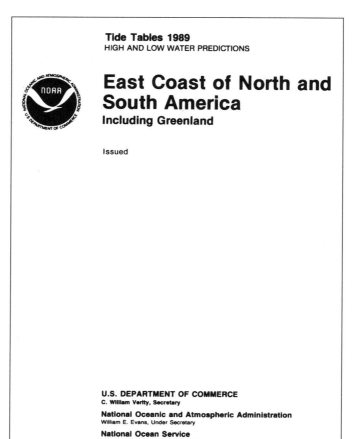

Figure 2.10   Cover of the *Tide Tables*
(Source: Tide Tables).

Tables. Mariners are cautioned about using only a single source of information for their piloting decisions.

The tables included in this publication are:

Table 1— *Daily Tide Predictions for Reference Stations.* Figure 2.11 shows a sample page from this table. The heights and times for high and low water at reference stations are provided in Table 1. Data in this table change from year to year. Many different almanacs provide data extracted from Table 1—often at no charge. Pick them up at bait shops, marine stores, and at boat shows.

Table 2— *Time Differences for Substations.* A sample of this table is provided in Chapter 13. This table shows the height and time differences from a reference station to a series

BOSTON, MASS.

Times and Heights of High and Low Waters

JANUARY

Day	Time h m	Height ft	m	Day	Time h m	Height ft	m
1 Su	0537	8.9	2.7	16 M	0556	10.3	3.1
	1154	1.7	0.5		1223	0.2	0.1
	1805	8.0	2.4		1838	8.7	2.7
2 M	0006	1.9	0.6	17 Tu	0035	0.9	0.3
	0627	9.0	2.7		0657	10.3	3.1
	1249	1.5	0.5		1328	0.2	0.1
	1902	7.9	2.4		1942	8.6	2.6
3 Tu	0057	1.9	0.6	18 W	0135	1.1	0.3
	0716	9.2	2.8		0758	10.3	3.1
	1344	1.2	0.4		1430	0.0	0.0
	1954	8.0	2.4		2045	8.6	2.6
4 W	0148	1.8	0.5	19 Th	0235	1.1	0.3
	0805	9.5	2.9'		0856	10.4	3.2
	1435	0.8	0.2		1528	-0.1	0.0
	2045	8.2	2.5		2142	8.7	2.7
5 Th	0237	1.5	0.5	20 F	0328	1.0	0.3
	0853	9.9	3.0		0949	10.4	3.2
	1522	0.3	0.1		1617	-0.2	-0.1
	2135	8.5	2.6		2231	8.9	2.7
6 F	0325	1.2	0.4	21 Sa	0417	0.9	0.3
	0939	10.4	3.2		1036	10.5	3.2
	1609	-0.2	-0.1		1703	-0.3	-0.1
	2221	8.9	2.7		2317	9.0	2.7
7 Sa	0413	0.8	0.2	22 Su	0503	0.8	0.2
	1026	10.8	3.3		1121	10.5	3.2
	1654	-0.6	-0.2		1744	-0.3	-0.1
	2307	9.2	2.8		2358	9.1	2.8
8 Su	0500	0.4	0.1	23 M	0549	0.7	0.2
	1112	11.1	3.4		1203	10.3	3.1
	1740	-1.0	-0.3		1822	-0.2	-0.1
	2353	9.6	2.9				
9 M	0549	0.1	0.0	24 Tu	0036	9.2	2.8
	1200	11.3	3.4		0631	0.7	0.2
	1826	-1.2	-0.4		1242	10.1	3.1
					1901	0.0	0.0
10 Tu	0039	9.9	3.0	25 W	0113	9.2	2.8
	0637	-0.2	-0.1		0712	0.8	0.2
	1249	11.3	3.4		1324	9.8	3.0
	1912	-1.3	-0.4		1938	0.3	0.1
11 W	0126	10.2	3.1	26 Th	0151	9.2	2.8
	0727	-0.3	-0.1		0754	0.9	0.3
	1338	11.1	3.4		1404	9.4	2.9
	1958	-1.2	-0.4		2018	0.6	0.2
12 Th	0215	10.4	3.2	27 F	0231	9.2	2.8
	0822	-0.3	-0.1		0839	1.1	0.3
	1431	10.7	3.3		1448	9.0	2.7
	2049	-0.9	-0.3		2057	1.0	0.3
13 F	0307	10.5	3.2	28 Sa	0313	9.1	2.8
	0918	-0.2	-0.1		0924	1.3	0.4
	1527	10.2	3.1		1534	8.5	2.6
	2141	-0.4	-0.1		2140	1.3	0.4
14 Sa	0401	10.5	3.2	29 Su	0356	9.0	2.7
	1017	0.0	0.0		1014	1.4	0.4
	1628	9.6	2.9		1625	8.1	2.5
	2237	0.1	0.0		2227	1.7	0.5
15 Su	0457	10.4	3.2	30 M	0445	8.9	2.7
	1119	0.1	0.0		1143	1.6	0.5
	1730	9.1	2.8		1718	7.8	2.4
	2335	0.6	0.2		2318	2.0	0.6
				31 Tu	0537	8.9	2.7
					1205	1.5	0.5
					1816	7.7	2.3

FEBRUARY

Day	Time h m	Height ft	m	Day	Time h m	Height ft	m
1 W	0014	2.0	0.6	16 Th	0118	1.5	0.5
	0630	9.1	2.8		0745	9.7	3.0
	1302	1.3	0.4		1419	0.5	0.2
	1915	7.7	2.3		2037	8.3	2.5
2 Th	0109	1.9	0.6	17 F	0221	1.4	0.4
	0726	9.4	2.9		0846	9.8	3.0
	1358	0.9	0.3		1515	0.4	0.1
	2011	8.0	2.4		2131	8.6	2.6
3 F	0205	1.6	0.5	18 Sa	0317	1.2	0.4
	0821	9.9	3.0		0938	10.0	3.0
	1451	0.3	0.1		1603	0.2	0.1
	2106	8.5	2.6		2219	8.8	2.7
4 Sa	0258	1.1	0.3	19 Su	0405	1.0	0.3
	0914	10.4	3.2		1024	10.1	3.1
	1542	-0.3	-0.1		1643	0.1	0.0
	2154	9.0	2.7		2257	9.1	2.8
5 Su	0351	0.4	0.1	20 M	0448	0.7	0.2
	1005	11.0	3.4		1106	10.1	3.1
	1630	-0.9	-0.3		1720	0.1	0.0
	2242	9.7	3.0		2334	9.3	2.8
6 M	0440	-0.2	-0.1	21 Tu	0529	0.5	0.2
	1052	11.4	3.5		1143	10.1	3.1
	1716	-1.4	-0.4		1756	0.1	0.0
	2329	10.3	3.1				
7 Tu	0529	-0.7	-0.2	22 W	0008	9.5	2.9
	1142	11.6	3.5		0608	0.4	0.1
	1802	-1.6	-0.5		1220	9.9	3.0
					1829	0.2	0.1
8 W	0015	10.8	3.3	23 Th	0042	9.6	2.9
	0619	-1.1	-0.3		0645	0.4	0.1
	1231	11.6	3.5		1257	9.7	3.0
	1848	-1.7	-0.5		1904	0.4	0.1
9 Th	0101	11.1	3.4	24 F	0117	9.6	2.9
	0710	-1.2	-0.4		0725	0.5	0.2
	1322	11.3	3.4		1335	9.4	2.9
	1935	-1.4	-0.4		1941	0.7	0.2
10 F	0149	11.2	3.4	25 Sa	0153	9.5	2.9
	0802	-1.1	-0.3		0806	0.7	0.2
	1415	10.8	3.3		1415	9.0	2.7
	2023	-0.9	-0.3		2018	1.0	0.3
11 Sa	0239	11.1	3.4	26 Su	0231	9.4	2.9
	0857	-0.8	-0.2		0848	0.9	0.3
	1510	10.1	3.1		1458	8.6	2.6
	2116	-0.3	-0.1		2100	1.4	0.4
12 Su	0332	10.8	3.3	27 M	0311	9.2	2.8
	0956	-0.4	-0.1		0935	1.1	0.3
	1608	9.4	2.9		1545	8.1	2.5
	2211	0.4	0.1		2145	1.7	0.5
13 M	0430	10.4	3.2	28 Tu	0358	9.1	2.8
	1057	0.2	0.1		1027	1.4	0.4
	1712	8.7	2.7		1639	7.8	2.4
	2310	1.0	0.3		2237	2.0	0.6
14 Tu	0533	10.0	3.0				
	1204	0.4	0.1				
	1821	8.3	2.5				
15 W	0014	1.4	0.4				
	0638	9.8	3.0				
	1313	0.6	0.2				
	1932	8.2	2.5				

MARCH

Day	Time h m	Height ft	m	Day	Time h m	Height ft	m
1 W	0453	9.0	2.7	16 Th	0619	9.4	2.9
	1123	1.4	0.4		1253	1.0	0.3
	2335	2.1	0.6		1913	8.2	2.5
2 Th	0549	9.1	2.8	17 F	0102	1.8	0.5
	1223	1.3	0.4		0728	9.3	2.8
	1838	7.8	2.4		1400	0.9	0.3
					2017	8.4	2.6
3 F	0035	1.9	0.6	18 Sa	0206	1.6	0.5
	0651	9.4	2.9		0827	9.4	2.9
	1323	0.9	0.3		1453	0.8	0.2
	1938	8.2	2.5		2109	8.7	2.7
4 Sa	0135	1.5	0.5	19 Su	0259	1.3	0.4
	0750	9.9	3.0		0920	9.6	2.9
	1421	0.3	0.1		1538	0.7	0.2
	2035	8.8	2.7		2153	9.0	2.7
5 Su	0233	0.8	0.2	20 M	0346	1.0	0.3
	0849	10.5	3.2		1003	9.7	3.0
	1512	-0.4	-0.1		1615	0.5	0.2
	2126	9.6	2.9		2231	9.3	2.8
6 M	0328	0.0	0.0	21 Tu	0427	0.7	0.2
	0941	11.0	3.4		1044	9.8	3.0
	1603	-1.0	-0.3		1650	0.5	0.2
	2215	10.4	3.2		2303	9.6	2.9
7 Tu	0420	-0.8	-0.2	22 W	0506	0.4	0.1
	1033	11.5	3.5		1120	9.8	3.0
	1649	-1.4	-0.4		1724	0.5	0.2
	2303	11.1	3.4		2335	9.8	3.0
8 W	0510	-1.4	-0.4	23 Th	0543	0.3	0.1
	1122	11.7	3.6		1155	9.7	3.0
	1736	-1.7	-0.5		1757	0.6	0.2
	2348	11.6	3.5				
9 Th	0600	-1.8	-0.5	24 F	0009	9.9	3.0
	1213	11.6	3.5		0620	0.2	0.1
	1823	-1.6	-0.5		1231	9.5	2.9
					1832	0.7	0.2
10 F	0034	11.8	3.6	25 Sa	0042	9.9	3.0
	0650	-1.9	-0.6		0658	0.3	0.1
	1304	11.2	3.4		1309	9.2	2.8
	1909	-1.2	-0.4		1909	1.0	0.3
11 Sa	0123	11.8	3.6	26 Su	0117	9.8	3.0
	0742	-1.6	-0.5		0737	0.4	0.1
	1356	10.6	3.2		1346	8.9	2.7
	1959	-0.7	-0.2		1946	1.2	0.4
12 Su	0212	11.5	3.5	27 M	0155	9.7	3.0
	0836	-1.1	-0.3		0819	0.6	0.2
	1451	9.9	3.0		1428	8.6	2.6
	2051	0.0	0.0		2028	1.5	0.5
13 M	0308	10.9	3.3	28 Tu	0237	9.5	2.9
	0934	-0.4	-0.1		0903	0.9	0.3
	1549	9.2	2.8		1516	8.3	2.5
	2147	0.8	0.2		2114	1.8	0.5
14 Tu	0406	10.3	3.1	29 W	0324	9.3	2.8
	1035	0.2	0.1		0956	1.1	0.3
	1654	8.6	2.6		1608	8.0	2.4
	2249	1.4	0.4		2206	2.0	0.6
15 W	0512	9.8	3.0	30 Th	0419	9.3	2.8
	1051	0.7	0.2		1051	1.2	0.4
	1804	8.2	2.5		1706	8.0	2.4
	2354	1.7	0.5		2305	2.0	0.6
				31 F	0519	9.3	2.8
					1152	1.0	0.3
					1806	8.2	2.5

Time meridian 75° W. 0000 is midnight. 1200 is noon.
Heights are referred to mean lower low water which is the chart datum of soundings.

Figure 2.11 Sample page showing Table 1 of the *Tide Tables* (Source: Tide Tables).

of substations. The data in this table remain relatively constant so save it for future use.

Table 3— *Height of Tide at Any Time*. This table never changes and a sample is available in Chapter 13. Table 3 provides a means to calculate a correction factor for predicting the height of tide at any time. Keep in mind that nothing is perfect in navigation and that the government height and time predictions can be changed by storms and high winds. Always leave yourself a margin for error.

Table 4— *Local Mean Time of Sunrise and Sunset.*

Table 5— *Reduction of Local Mean Time to Standard Time.*

Table 6— *Moonrise and Moonset* for eight locations.

Table 7— *Conversions of Feet to Meters.*

The *Tide Tables* also contain a glossary of terms and an index of stations that gives you the page number for each reference station.

Corrections to *Tide Tables*

Like every dynamic publication, changes and errors may occur from time to time. Corrections are summarized in the national weekly Notice to Mariners each quarter. The numbers of these quarterly LNM summations are 13, 26, 39, and 52. These corrections may also appear in the Local Notice to Mariners published weekly by the local Coast Guard District.

Most new GPS sets provide a screen that displays the daily tide predictions and shows the predicted height of tide on a continuous basis.

TIDAL CURRENT TABLES

The annual *Tidal Current Tables*, published by International Marine under license from NOAA, provide advance information relative to currents. These data include daily predictions of the times of slack water and the times and velocities (*speed*) of maximum flood and ebb currents for a number of major waterways (*reference stations*). Tables are also provided for obtaining current predictions for numerous other locations (*substations*). There are two versions of the *Tidal Current Tables:* (1) Atlantic and (2) Pacific Coast of North America and Asia.

The *Tidal Current Tables* also have a wealth of nautical information including:

- An informative introduction on currents.
- A list of reference stations.
- Information on rotary currents.
- Information on the Gulf Stream.
- Information on wind-driven currents.

- A section on how to use current diagrams.
- A glossary of terms.

The current tables included in the publication are:

Table 1— *Daily Current Predictions.* The times of maximum and slack water are furnished in Table 1. This table changes from year to year.

Table 2— *Current Difference and Other Constants and Rotary Tidal Currents.* Table 2 lists a series of substations associated with the reference stations and shows the time differences for maximum and slack current from the reference station. Data in this table are constant, so save the table for use in the future.

Table 3— *Speed of Current at Any Time.* This table provides a correction factor for determining the speed (drift) of the current at any time.

Table 4— *Duration of Slack.*

Table 5— *Rotary Tidal Currents.*

TIDAL CURRENT CHARTS

The *Tidal Current Charts*, published by NOS, is a set of 11 charts that depict, by means of arrows and figures, the direction (set) and velocity (drift) of tidal currents for each hour of the tidal cycle. These charts, which can be used from year to year, present a comprehensive view of the tidal current movements within the waterway covered by the chart(s). Tidal current charts are produced for:

- Boston Harbor.
- Narragansett Bay to Nantucket Sound.
- Narragansett Bay.
- Long Island Sound and Block Island Sound.
- New York Harbor.
- Delaware Bay.
- Upper Chesapeake Bay.
- Charleston Harbor.
- Tampa Bay.
- San Francisco Bay.
- Puget Sound—Northern Part.
- Puget Sound—Southern Part.

TIDAL CURRENT DIAGRAMS

The *Tidal Current Diagrams,* published by NOS, are a series of 12 monthly diagrams that are used in conjunction with the *Tidal Current Charts* to provide a convenient method for determining the flow of the current on a particular day. *Tidal Current Diagrams* are produced for the following locations:

- Long Island Sound and Block Island Sound.
- Boston Harbor.
- Upper Chesapeake Bay.
- New York Harbor.

The *Tidal Current Diagrams* may be ordered from the NOS Distribution Division.

RULES OF THE ROAD

Officially named *Navigation Rules: International—Inland,* this publication contains all of the inland and international rules for the prevention of collisions at sea (see Figure 2.12). These rules apply to all vessels regardless of size, method of propulsion, whether private or commercial in ownership, or national origin of registry. Owners of vessels of 40 feet or larger are required to have a copy of the Navigation Rules aboard their boats when they are under way. Every small boat operator should familiarize themselves with the Navigation Rules, which are divided into several sections:

U.S. Department of Transportation
United States Coast Guard

NAVIGATION RULES
INTERNATIONAL—INLAND

Figure 2.12 Cover from the "Rules of the Road" *(Source: Navigation Rules: International—Inland).*

I. Introduction.

II. Navigation Rules and Regulations.

    A. General Rules.

    B. Steering and Sailing Rules.

    C. Lights and Shapes.

    D. Sound Signals.

    E. Exemptions.

III. Interpretive Rules.

IV. Lines of Demarcation.

V. Penalty Provisions.

VI. Alternative Compliance.

VII. Vessel Bridge-to-Bridge Radiotelephone Regulations.

VIII. Legal Citations.

IX. Conversion Tables—Feet to Metric.

Requests to change the navigational rules are published in the *Federal Register* with requests for comments from the boating industry and the general public. Actual changes to these rules are published in the Local Notice to Mariners.

The Rules of the Road are available for download from the Internet at http://www.navcen.uscg.gov/mwv/navrules.htm. This publication is available in marine book stores or can be ordered from the Government Printing Office under number NSN 7642-01-436-9514.

Readers Study Note

The purpose of this chapter was to familiarize you with some of the nautical publications that are available and to briefly explain the types of navigational and safety information that they provide. You are not expected to become an expert from reading this chapter. You may want to acquire some of these publications for your personal reference library. You will find that each publication provides decent instruction on how to use the information contained within them.

Reader Progress Note

You should be familiar with the nautical chart and most of the navigational publications that support and enhance the data provided on nautical charts. You are at least a mile ahead of the average boat owner. However, you still have a lot to learn, so don't give up just yet.

REVIEW QUESTIONS

2.1 Nautical chart catalogs show all of the _____ _____ for a given geographical area.

2.2 The list of charts for the Great Lakes and adjacent waters is found in Nautical Chart Catalog _____.

2.3 The latest edition number, edition date, and printing revision date for a nautical chart for a nautical chart are found in the publication _____ _____ _____ _____.

2.4 A glossary of terminology used on a nautical chart of various nations is found in the publication _____.

2.5 The _____ and _____ that have been approved for use on nautical charts published in the United States are found in the publication _____.

2.6 The nautical publication that contains a catalog of aids to navigation is called the _____ _____.

2.7 The aids to navigation for the Great Lakes are found in Volume _____ of the *Light List*.

2.8 Data that cannot be coded or abbreviated on a nautical chart are found in the _____ _____.

2.9 The publication used by the Coast Guard to communicate with mariners concerning the establishment, changing, and the discontinuance of aids to navigation is called the _____ _____ _____ _____.

2.10 The publication that contains predictions of the times and heights of high and low water for every day in the year is called the _____ _____.

2.11 The local mean time of sunrise and sunset is found in the _____ _____.

2.12 A listing of approved marine events and regattas is found in the _____ _____ ____ _____.

2.13 A table showing the distance of visibility of objects at sea is found in the _____ _____.

2.14 Federal regulations applicable to the mariner in a particular area are found in the _____ _____.

2.15 Corrections to the *Tide Tables* are published in _____ summaries of the Local Notice to Mariners.

ANSWERS

2.1   Nautical chart catalogs show all of the NAUTICAL CHARTS for a given geographical area.

2.2   The list of charts for the Great Lakes and adjacent waters is found in Nautical Chart Catalog FOUR (4).

2.3   The latest edition number, edition date, and printing revision date for a nautical chart for a nautical chart are found in the publication DATES OF LATEST EDITIONS.

2.4   A glossary of terminology used on a nautical chart of various nations is found in the publication CHART No. 1.

2.5   The SYMBOLS and ABBREVIATIONS that have been approved for use on nautical charts published in the United States are found in the publication CHART NO. 1.

2.6   The nautical publication that contains a catalog of aids to navigation is called the LIGHT LIST.

2.7   The aids to navigation for the Great Lakes are found in Volume VII of the *Light List*.

2.8   Data that cannot be coded or abbreviated on a nautical chart are found in the COAST PILOT.

2.9   The publication used by the Coast Guard to communicate with mariners concerning the establishment, changing, and the discontinuance of aids to navigation is called the LOCAL NOTICE TO MARINERS.

2.10 The publication that contains predictions of the times and heights of high and low water for every day in the year is called the TIDE TABLES.

2.11 The local mean time of sunrise and sunset is found in the TIDE TABLES.

2.12 A listing of approved marine events and regattas is found in the LOCAL NOTICE TO MARINERS.

2.13 A table showing the distance of visibility of objects at sea is found in the COAST PILOT.

2.14 Federal regulations applicable to the mariner in a particular area are found in the COAST PILOT.

2.15 Corrections to the *Tide Tables* are published in QUARTERLY summaries of the Local Notice to Mariners.

THREE

The IALA-B Aids to Navigation System

The term *aid to navigation* refers to a device outside of a vessel used to assist the mariner in determining his or her position or course, or to warn of dangers and obstructions. Several aids to navigation (ATONs) are used together to form a local ATON system that helps the mariner follow natural or improved channels. These aids provide a continuous system of charted marks for coastal piloting.

In April 1982, the United States agreed to conform to the International Association of Lighthouse Authorities System B (IALA-B). This system applies to buoys and beacons that indicate the lateral limits (edges) of navigable channels, obstructions, dangers, and other areas of importance to the mariner.

Aids are numbered according to a prescribed method. The lowest numbered aids are farthest out to sea. The numbers on aids increase as you approach the shore. The channels around islands are numbered in a clockwise direction. Aids on rivers are numbered from the mouth of the river upward. Even-numbered aids mark the right side of a channel as you progress from seaward. The memory aid "Red on Right, Returning from the Sea" is something you should memorize. The right side of a channel on a river is the bank that is on your right-hand side as you drift with the flow of the river current.

PORT SIDE MARKS OR LATERAL MARKS

When returning from seaward, the aids to navigation that mark the port (left) side of the navigable channel will have the following characteristics:

1. **Green** in color.
2. **Odd** numbered. Numbers increase from the farthest point at sea toward the land.
3. **Can** or pillar-shaped or **square** day marks.
4. Lighted with **green** lights.
5. **Green** retroreflective panels.
6. Light characteristics can be:
   - *Flashing:* The total duration of light is shorter than the total duration of darkness.
   - *Occulting:* The total duration of light is longer than the total duration of darkness.
   - *Quick flashing:* Light flashes are emitted at a rate of 60 flashes per minute.
   - *Isophase (ISO):* Duration of light and darkness are equal.

See Figure 3.1 for an illustration of a port side mark.

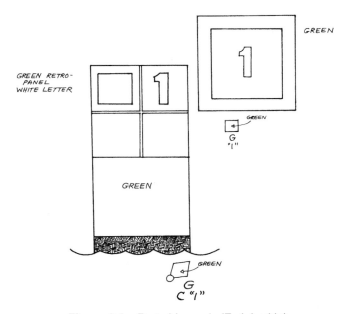

Figure 3.1 Port side mark *(F. J. Larkin).*

STARBOARD SIDE MARKS OR LATERAL MARKS

When returning from seaward, the aids to navigation that mark the starboard (right) side of the channel will have the following characteristics:

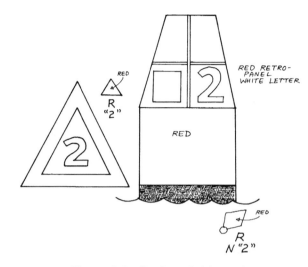

Figure 3.2 Starboard side mark
(F. J. Larkin).

1. **Red** in color.

2. **Even** numbered. Numbers increase from seaward.

3. **Nun** or conical-shape or **triangular** day marks.

4. Lighted with **red** lights.

5. **Red** retroreflective panels.

6. Light characteristics may be flashing, occulting, quick flashing, or isophase (ISO), as explained earlier.

See Figure 3.2 for an illustration of a starboard side mark.

MEMORY AID: *"Red on Right, Returning."*

SAFE WATER MARKS

Safe water marks are used to mark fairways, midchannels, and offshore approach points. They will have unobstructed water on all sides. They are also known as *midchannel marks* or *fairway marks.* Pass these aids to starboard. The aid will be off your port, or left side, to help separate incoming traffic from outgoing traffic and avoid collisions. Always enter on the red side of the channel and depart on the green side. Safe water marks have the following characteristics:

1. **Red and white** vertical stripes.

2. No numbers but may be **lettered.**

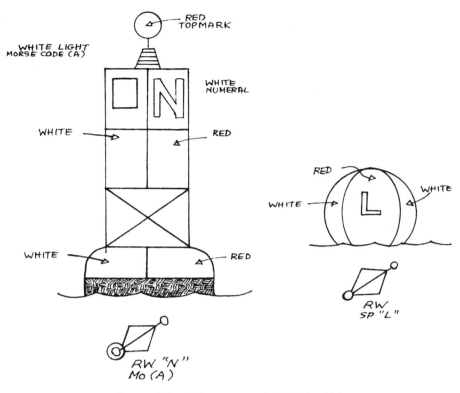

Figure 3.3 Safe water mark *(F. J. Larkin).*

3. **Spherical** in shape when not lighted. When lighted, buoys will be fitted with a round red ball topmark.

4. Lighted with **white** lights only.

5. **White and red** retroreflective panels.

6. Light characteristic will be **Morse Code A** (short-long flash). If the aid is fitted with a radio beacon, it will transmit a Morse Code A (dot-dash).

Figure 3.3 illustrates a safe water mark.

PREFERRED CHANNEL MARKS

At a point where a main channel divides or a side channel meets a main channel, when you are proceeding in the conventional (lateral) direction of buoyage, a preferred or main channel may be marked with a modified port or starboard lateral mark. Figure 3.4 illustrates this special marking scheme.

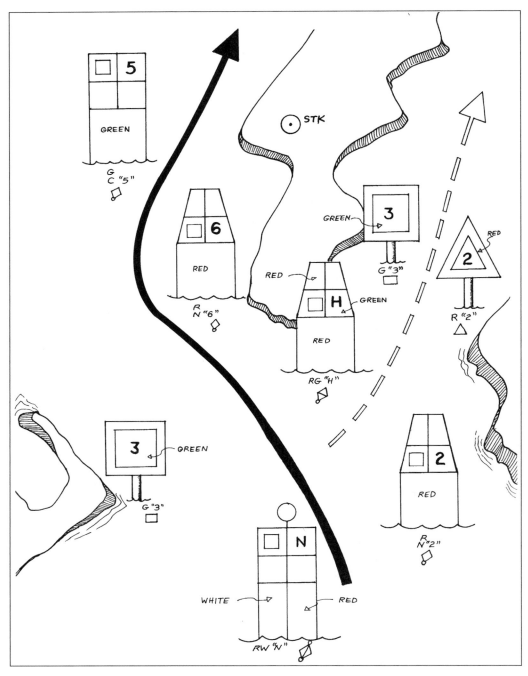

Figure 3.4　Preferred channel scheme *(F. J. Larkin).*

Preferred Channel to Starboard (Right)

Remember "red on right, returning," so green goes on your left.

1. *Color:* Green with one broad red horizontal band. The green band will be at the top.
2. *Shape:* Can or pillar shaped.
3. *Day mark:* Green square, lower half is red.
4. *Light color:* Green.
5. *Light characteristic:* Composite group flashing (2 + 1).
6. *Markings:* Preferred channel aids are never numbered, but may be lettered.
7. *Retroreflective panel color:* Green.

Figure 3.5 shows an illustration of this aid.

> CAUTION: *When proceeding toward the sea, it may not always be possible to pass on either side of a preferred channel aid to navigation. Always check the appropriate nautical chart for the area.*

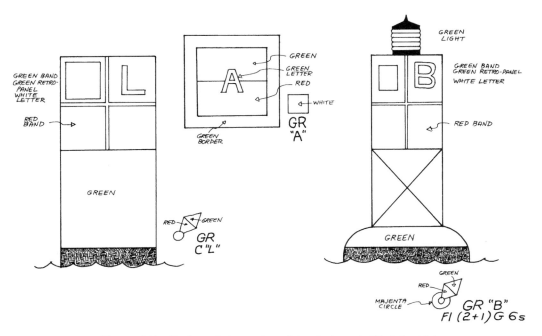

Figure 3.5   Preferred channel mark to starboard   *(F. J. Larkin).*

Preferred Channel to Port (Left)

Again, "red on right, returning."

1. *Color:* Red band on top with one broad green horizontal band below. The top color indicates the preferred or main channel.
2. *Shape:* Conical or nun-shaped.
3. *Day mark:* Red triangle, lower half is green.
4. *Light color:* Red.
5. *Light characteristic:* Composite group flashing (2 + 1).
6. *Markings:* Preferred channel buoys are never numbered but may be lettered.
7. *Retroreflective panel color:* Red.

Figure 3.6 shows an illustration of this aid.

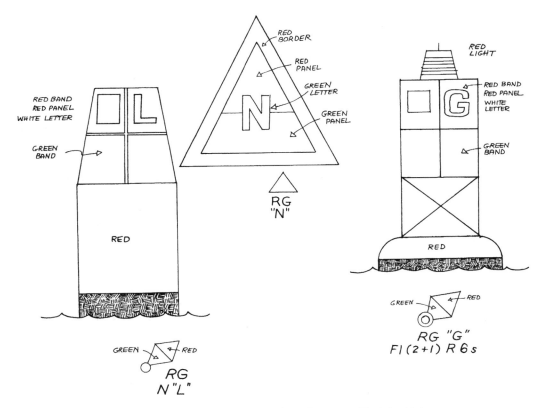

Figure 3.6 Preferred channel mark to port *(F. J. Larkin).*

> CAUTION: *When proceeding toward the sea, it may not always be possible to pass on either side of a preferred channel aid to navigation. Always check the appropriate nautical chart for the area.*

Figure 3.7 shows more examples of the IALA-B system of buoyage.

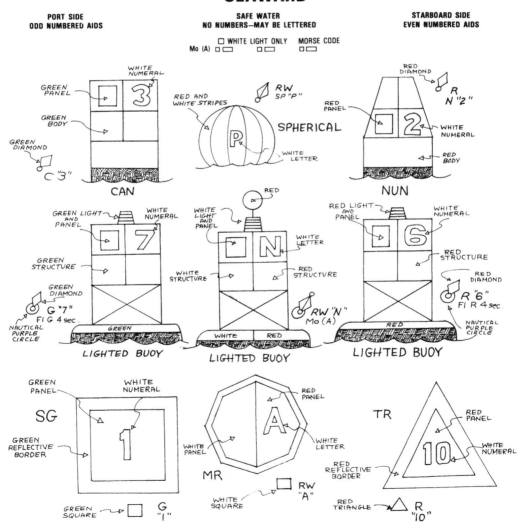

Figure 3.7 IALA-B buoyage system *(F. J. Larkin).*

SPECIAL MARKS

These marks are not intended to assist in navigation but rather to alert the mariner to a special feature or area. The feature will be described in a nautical document such as a nautical chart, the *Light List,* the *Coast Pilot,* or the Local Notice to Mariners.

Some items marked by special marks are spoil areas, pipelines, traffic separation schemes, jetties, or military exercise areas.

Special marks are yellow in color and, if lighted, will show a yellow light.

INTRACOASTAL WATERWAY AIDS TO NAVIGATION SYSTEM

The Intracoastal Waterway runs parallel to the Atlantic and Gulf coasts from Manasquan Inlet, New Jersey, to the Mexican border. Aids marking these waters have some portion marked with a small yellow panel. Otherwise, the coloring and numbering of buoys and day marks follow the IALA-B System.

While the lateral buoyage system is numbered from seaward toward the shore ("red on right, returning"), the direction of buoyage in the Intracoastal Waterway system is generally south along the Atlantic Coast and generally west along the Gulf Coast.

When an intracoastal route joins another marked waterway, special yellow markings are applied to the ATONs that already mark this waterway for another purpose or direction, for example, a channel returning from the sea. These special marked aids are referred to as *dual-purpose* aids to navigation.

An example of this situation would be a channel with standard lateral buoys numbered low to high from seaward ("red on right, returning") where an intracoastal route uses a section of this channel. The intracoastal route enters at an inland point and heads toward the sea for a distance and then turns off out of the channel. Figure 3.8 illustrates the special yellow marking.

Dual-purpose aids that should be kept or passed on your port (left) side (heading generally southward on the Atlantic Coast) are marked with small yellow squares. The yellow squares indicate that you are to pass the aid as if it were a can buoy while you are operating on this section of the Intracoastal Waterway.

Dual-purpose aids that should be kept or passed on your starboard (right) side (heading generally southward on the Atlantic Coast) are marked with small yellow triangles. The yellow triangles indicate that you are to pass the aid as if it were a nun buoy while you are operating on this section of the Intracoastal Waterway. Again, see Figure 3.8 for an example of this type of dual-purpose aid.

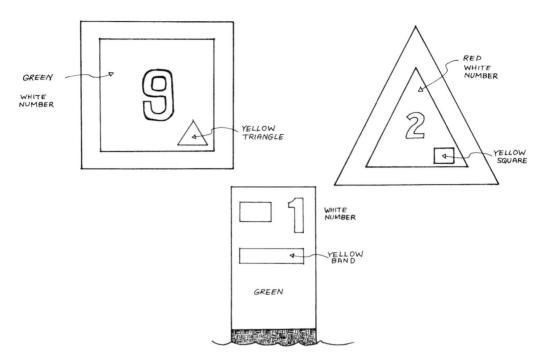

Figure 3.8   Intracoastal Waterway aids to navigation *(F. J. Larkin).*

When operating on the Intracoastal Waterway (ICW) where dual-purpose aids are used, the mariner must disregard the lateral significance of the color, number, and shape of the aid and be guided solely by the shape of the yellow square or triangle. This can become a problem during nighttime operations since the lighting for dual-purpose ICW aids reflects the channel direction as if you were returning from seaward. Use extra caution and follow your chart carefully in this situation.

THE UNIFORM STATE WATERWAY MARKING SYSTEM

The Uniform State Waterway Marking System (USWMS) was developed in 1966 to provide an easy-to-understand navigational system for small boats on state waterways. The port and starboard markings for USWMS aids to navigation are similar to the federal system except that the lateral colors are red and black. The regulatory buoys in the USWMS are colored white with orange stripes. The standard regulatory markings are outlined in the following subsections.

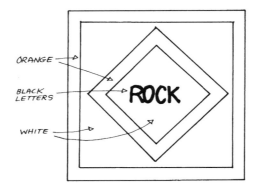

Figure 3.9   USWMS diamond shape *(F. J. Larkin).*

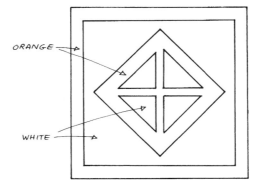

Figure 3.10   USWMS diamond shape with cross inside *(F. J. Larkin).*

Diamond Shape

A diamond-shaped display on a buoy is an indication of a dangerous area. The nature of the danger may be indicated inside the diamond shape. Messages such as *Rock, Wreck, Shoal,* or *Dam* are typical (see Figure 3.9). You should be alerted by the diamond shape that there is a danger nearby.

Diamond Shape with Cross Inside

A diamond-shaped display with a cross inside is an indication of a prohibited or boat exclusion area (see Figure 3.10). The explanation for the exclusion may be shown outside of the crossed diamond. Messages such as *Dam, Rapids,* and *Swimming Area* are typical. The diamond shape and the cross should alert you that you should not operate your boat in this area.

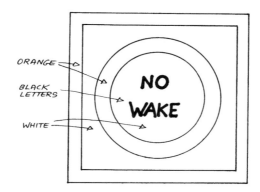

Figure 3.11   USWMS circle shape *(F. J. Larkin).*

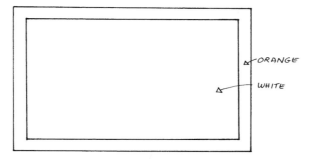

Figure 3.12   USWMS rectangle shape *(F. J. Larkin).*

Circle Shape

A circular-shaped display indicates a controlled area (see Figure 3.11). This means that a vessel operated in this marked area is subject to certain restrictions or rules. The classification of the regulation is indicated within the circle. *No Wake, Slow,* and *No Anchoring* are typical messages found within a circular-shaped display on a buoy.

Rectangular or Square Shape

General information is shown within rectangular displays. This could include directions, distances, and locations (see Figure 3.12).

All of these regulatory buoys may be lighted with white lights and may be lettered.

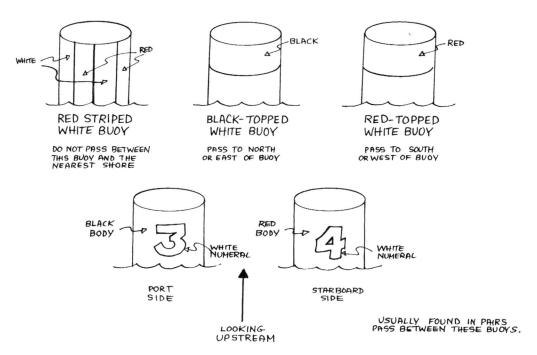

Figure 3.13 USWMS buoyage system *(F. J. Larkin).*

Other USWMS Variations

The rules for passing buoys is different with the USWMS. The buoys are said to have cardinal significance. That is, they are passed from specific directions of north, south, east, or west. These variations are illustrated in Figure 3.13.

A **white** buoy with a **red** top indicates an obstruction. Pass the buoy to the south or west.

> MEMORY AID: *Think of the red top as warm and that warmth comes from the south and west.*

A **white** buoy with a **black** top also indicates an obstruction. Pass this buoy to the north or east.

> MEMORY AID: *Think of the black top as a storm such as a Nor'easter.*

A **red and white** vertically striped buoy indicates that an obstruction exists between the buoy and the nearest shore, so do not pass between them.

CAUTION: *Sometimes it's hard to distinguish which shore is indicated when this type of buoy is placed near the center of a channel. Use local knowledge to find out the correct side before you put your boat and passengers in jeopardy by passing it on the wrong side. Report all position problems to the local harbormaster or to the officials of the town or county where the waterway is located.*

EXTRA CAUTION: *Don't confuse this state waterway buoy with the center channel buoy used in the IALA-B buoyage system. I have seen this vertically red and white buoy incorrectly deployed in inland waterways. If you become confused, use local knowledge. Ask around before you transit such an area.*

ANOTHER CAUTION: *The Coast Guard is formulating a plan to change the USWMS so that it conforms more closely to the IALA-B system. Keep an eye on the Local Notice to Mariners for the announcement and publication of these changes.*

Mooring Buoys

A standard color scheme for mooring buoys was also established in 1966. Mooring buoys should be white with a horizontal blue band. Mooring buoys have no lateral significance in navigation. I suggest that you stay out of mooring areas because you can catch a painter (a pick-up line for, say, a dinghy) in your props. Some inexperienced boat owners use polypropylene line for this purpose and polypro floats.

Lobster Trap Buoys

Lobster trap buoys are painted in the various colors authorized by the license of the lobster fisherman. Lobster trap buoys have no lateral significance in navigation except that they should be avoided.

Sailboats seem to have the worst problem with lobster buoys. They usually snag the buoy's line between their keel and their rudder. Prudent mariners keep a constant lookout for lobster buoys especially when backing their boats.

Bridges

Bridges that open usually have a clearance gauge installed to minimize the number of times they are opened. These gauges should be located at the right side of the channel facing an approaching vessel. Clearance gauges indicate the lowest vertical clearance under the draw over the navigable channel.

Certain bridges may be equipped with sound signals, racons, and radar reflectors where unusual geographic or weather conditions exist. Check your *Coast Pilot* for information about bridges and the federal regulations concerning the bridge openings. Your nautical chart will show horizontal and vertical clearances for each charted bridge.

Private Aids to Navigation

Some aids to navigation are maintained by local municipal organizations or private citizens and are termed *private aids*. As of December 31, 1995, private aids are required by federal law to conform to the standard U.S. system for federal aids to navigation. Private aids may only be established, changed, or discontinued with the permission of the local Coast Guard district commander.

CAUTION: *While federal aids are serviced by the Coast Guard and are usually kept in fine repair, private aids are serviced by their owner. Use caution when operating your boat in areas marked by private aids. Private aids can be off station, missing, or worse, misleading, that is, the wrong shape, color, or number.*

The Coast Guard provides information regarding the authorization process for private aids to navigation on a link on their Local Notice to Mariners website at http://www.navcen.uscg.gov.

REPORTING DEFECTS AND DISCREPANCIES TO AIDS TO NAVIGATION

As a boater, you should be aware that the Coast Guard cannot keep the thousands of aids to navigation that comprise the federal ATON system under continuous surveillance. Add to this total the thousands of private aids and the lighting on all the bridges. It is virtually impossible for the Coast Guard to guarantee that every aid is operating properly, or is on its assigned position at all times. This situation worsens after any large storm in your area.

Therefore, for the general safety of all mariners, any person who recognizes that an aid to navigation is not on its assigned position or is not exhibiting its advertised light characteristic should promptly notify the nearest Coast Guard station about the problem.

Reader Study Note

Using red, green, and yellow pencils, color all the figures that have drawings of aids to navigation in this chapter. This will help you become familiar with the color and shape of these aids.

Reader Progress Note

Add the aids to navigation system to your basic navigation knowledge. You should be able to recognize these aids on nautical charts as well as on the water.

REVIEW QUESTIONS

3.1 Returning from seaward, a starboard side mark is _____ in color, has _____ numbers, and is _____ in shape.

3.2 Returning from seaward, a port side mark is _____ in color, has _____ numbers, and is _____ shaped.

3.3 Returning from seaward, port side marks have _____ lights, while starboard side marks have _____ lights.

3.4 In the IALA-B system, midchannel marks are also known as _____ or _____.

3.5 Returning from seaward, the starboard preferred channel mark is _____ with one broad _____ horizontal stripe.

3.6 The light characteristic of a preferred channel mark is _____.

3.7 When proceeding toward the sea, it may not always be prudent to _____ on _____ side of a preferred channel aid to navigation.

3.8 In the ICW, dual-purpose marks that should be kept on your port side consist of a yellow _____.

3.9 In the USWMS, diamond shapes are an indication of _____.

3.10　In the IALA-B system, a red and white vertically striped aid is called a ＿＿＿＿＿＿ and can be ＿＿＿＿＿ close aboard on either side.

3.11　In the USWMS, a red and white vertically striped buoy indicates that an ＿＿＿＿＿＿ exists between the buoy and the nearest ＿＿＿＿＿.

3.12　When returning from the sea, toward the shore, the numbers on the buoys will ＿＿＿＿＿＿ and the red-colored buoys are kept on the ＿＿＿＿＿ side of your boat.

ANSWERS

3.1　Returning from seaward, a starboard side mark is RED in color, has EVEN numbers, and is TRIANGULAR in shape.

3.2　Returning from seaward, a port side mark is GREEN in color, has ODD numbers, and is CAN shaped.

3.3　Returning from seaward, port side marks have GREEN lights, while starboard side marks have RED lights.

3.4　In the IALA-B system, midchannel marks are also known as SAFE WATER MARKS or FAIRWAY MARKS.

3.5　Returning from seaward, the starboard preferred channel mark is RED with one broad GREEN horizontal stripe.

3.6　The light characteristic of a preferred channel mark is COMPOSITE GROUP FLASHING (2 + 1).

3.7　When proceeding toward the sea, it may not always be prudent to PASS on EITHER side of a Preferred channel aid to navigation.

3.8　In the ICW, dual-purpose marks that should be kept on your port side consist of a yellow SQUARE.

3.9　In the USWMS, diamond shapes are an indication of A DANGEROUS AREA.

3.10　In the IALA-B system, a red and white vertically striped aid is called a SAFE WATER MARK and can be PASSED close aboard on either side.

3.11　In the USWMS, a red and white vertically striped buoy indicates that an OBSTRUCTION exists between the buoy and the nearest SHORE.

3.12　When returning from the sea, toward the shore, the numbers on the buoys will INCREASE and the red-colored buoys are kept on the STARBOARD (RIGHT-HAND) side of your boat.

FOUR

How to Use the Basic Navigational Instruments

THE MAGNETIC COMPASS

The *magnetic compass* is one of the most important tools that you can use for controlling the heading of a small boat (see Figure 4.1). Prudent navigators check the accuracy of their compasses frequently because they know that the magnetic compass is not only influenced by the earth's magnetic field, but also by magnetic fields radiating from metallic and electronic material aboard their boats. Magnetic compasses, barring any other magnetic problems aboard your boat, will point to magnetic north, which is different from true north—the usual orientation of a nautical chart.

The accuracy of your compass's alignment to the keel of your boat and any improper steering habits affect your steering accuracy. Take the time to review the appendices at the end of this book relating to the installation and use of your compass for many practical tips that will help you steer with greater accuracy.

Stray magnetic fields caused by electronic equipment, electric wires, small motors with magnetic cores, large masses of metal, radio speakers, etc., will cause your compass to deviate from pointing directly toward magnetic north. This discrepancy is called *deviation error.* It has been my experience that deviation error is almost impossible to eliminate on a small boat. To resolve the deviation error problem on my small boat, I have resorted to using an electronic or digital compass that

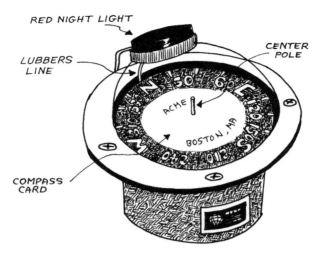

Figure 4.1   A typical small boat compass *(F. J. Larkin).*

has a built-in compensating feature for eliminating deviation error. It also provides a full 360-degree compass card incremented in single degrees. Most analog or mechanical compasses found on small boats have compass cards that are incremented in only 5- or 10-degree segments and, therefore, are only able to hold a course on a small boat within 5 or 10 degrees. Another benefit of the electronic compass is an offset-installation feature that can be used to remove variation error to make the compass read true north. I use this technique to eliminate the need to make any compass course corrections. My courses are plotted to true north, my compass reads true north, and I have set my GPS to read out true north headings.

If you have an analog or mechanical compass, set your GPS to read out magnetic north headings. You must correct for deviation error with a deviation table. See Appendices 3, 4, and 5 for information on generating a deviation table for your boat.

There is a popular misconception that a GPS set is a nautical compass. A GPS set only reports directional information when your boat is moving. In effect, your GPS set is simply calculating the direction from one position to another as your boat moves along on a course track line. Older LORAN and GPS sets that recalculate positions at slow rates—say, every 20 or 30 seconds—often display inaccurate headings especially when the boat is making wide turns. The newer and faster GPS sets that recalculate every second are much more accurate but still are reporting averages. Regardless, the practice of steering a boat from a compass is the only proper steering method.

Calibrate your GPS to read either true or magnetic headings—whichever type of heading matches the way your compass is set. Review the instructions in your GPS operating manual for setting your GPS set readout capability.

The Compass Card

The compass card is the round disk on your compass that looks like a compass rose. The arc of the compass card is divided into 360 degrees. Most compass cards are only marked in 5- or 10-degree increments, which limits small boat owners in their ability to steer a course. The compass card is aligned to magnetic north by a magnet that is usually attached to the underside of the compass card. When the boat turns, the compass card swings on a pivot point and continues to align itself with the earth's magnetic field.

Because of the limitations of the analog compasses that are normally installed on small boats, it is virtually impossible to develop an accurate deviation table. The use of an electronic compass, as mentioned earlier, solves this problem. Figure 4.2 shows a picture of an electronic compass.

The Lubber's Line on a Compass

The lubber line is a mark scribed into a compass housing to indicate the direction in which the boat's bow is heading. When installing a compass, align the lubber line and the center pole of the compass card with the keel line of the boat and the steering post that you must install on your boat. Appendix 1 describes and illustrates this procedure. Failure to achieve this alignment will result in a permanent steering error problem on your boat.

Deck Mount

FEATURES
- Advanced Magnetic Sensor
- Weather Proof Construction
- Accuracy to 0.5 degrees.
- Easy-to-read Course Digits
- Transflective Polarizer LCD Display for Clarity Day or Night
- 26 Segment Off Course Indicator
- Compensation for Deviation Error
- Dampening for Heavy Sea Conditions
- Simple 3-Button Operation
- Easy to Install on Any Boat

Figure 4.2 An electronic compass.

Direction

Direction is measured clockwise from 000 degrees around the compass card to 360 degrees. Always use three digits when writing or expressing direction in degrees. Direction can be stated in true degrees, magnetic degrees, or compass degrees. Note that each is a different point of the compass:

1. *True directions* or headings use the North Pole (top of a nautical chart) as their reference.

2. *Magnetic directions* use magnetic north as their reference. Magnetic north is located at a different point on the earth than the true North Pole. While true north is fixed, magnetic north moves around and this movement is predictable. The movement is very small and negligible to the small boater.

3. *Compass direction* is the point of the compass in which your boat is heading or should be heading. A compass heading is a calculated direction that is found by correcting a magnetic direction for all magnetic influences that are unique to your boat, the *deviation error* mentioned earlier. Chapter 9 explains the procedure for correcting a true course to a compass course.

THE STEERING POST

Unless a boat's helm—steering wheel—is centered over the boat's keel, you cannot steer your boat from the burgee staff, which is usually located in the center of your boat's bow rail. When the helm is offset from the keel line of your boat, you must install a steering (or aiming) post aligned with your keel and positioned immediately in front of your compass. In effect, you need to align the helm seat, the compass, and your steering post in a line parallel to your boat's keel. When your helm is off-center and you steer by aligning your bow rail with your intended direction, you cause your boat to track along a curved rather than a straight-line course, which introduces error to your speed and time predictions. Check out Appendix 1 for a procedure for rigging a steering post on your boat. Using a proper aiming post is a very important part of navigation accuracy.

DIVIDERS

A set of *dividers* is a two-armed pointed instrument that is used to measure distance on a nautical chart. Distance is measured from the "Nautical Mile Scale" or from the latitude scales which are located at the

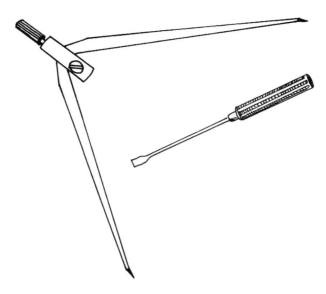

Figure 4.3 Dividers and small screwdriver *(F. J. Larkin).*

left- and right-hand margins on a nautical chart. As explained in previous chapters, never use longitude scales for measuring distance.

A good set of dividers will have an adjusting screw to tighten the tension of the divider's arms (see Figure 4.3). You will also want to add a small screwdriver to your navigation kit. Any good chart store sells dividers. You can get a suitable screwdriver at an electronics store. I use dividers that have a worm drive to control the opening of the arms. I find dividers of this type to be more accurate and dependable.

PENCILS

Fine-pointed automatic pencils using 2H or 3H 0.5 leads are the best for plotting courses. Add a pack of extra leads and erasers to your navigation kit (see Figure 4.4). If you use wooden pencils, add a pencil sharpener to your navigation kit.

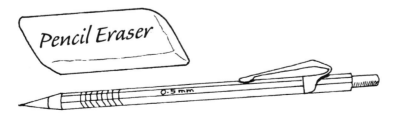

Figure 4.4 Automatic pencil and eraser *(F. J. Larkin).*

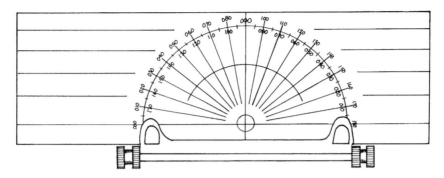

Figure 4.5   Paraglide plotter *(F. J. Larkin).*

PARAGLIDE PLOTTERS

Figure 4.5 shows an example of a paraglide plotter. I have found this type of plotter to be the most convenient and accurate instrument for measuring courses (directions) on a small boat. The paraglide plotter rolls easily across a nautical chart without losing the course angle. The proper technique for reading a course with a paraglide plotter is explained in detail in Chapter 6.

PARALLEL RULES

Parallel rules can also be used to measure course headings (directions), but I do not recommend their use on a small boat since they can easily slip and give an erroneous heading. If you insist on using this instrument, measure your course with a parallel rules as follows:

Step 1.   Place the edge of the parallel rules along your course line.

Step 2.   Carefully walk the parallel rules to the nearest compass rose until the edge of the parallel rules intersects the center of the compass rose.

Step 3.   Read the true course from the outer scale of the compass rose. You can read your magnetic heading from the inner scale. Keep your intended direction in mind so that you will avoid reading a reciprocal course heading.

A STOPWATCH

A good stopwatch (see Figure 4.5) is an integral part of a navigator's tool kit. Often, you will need to time the various legs of your trips to develop

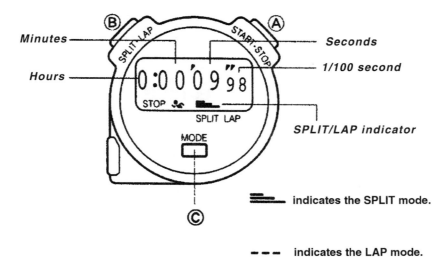

Figure 4.6   Stopwatch.

and check a speed curve. Your GPS set provides a TTG—Time to Go—feature and calculates the speed of your boat as it tracks over the bottom (earth's surface) and a DTG—Distance to Go—feature, which gives you the distance to the next waypoint. This speed data takes into account all of the elements that are affecting your boat at the time. Unfortunately, this speed cannot be used to predict the future unless all of those current elements remain the same in the future. Environmental phenomena that could be contained in GPS speed projections are currents, wind, weight, attitude of the boat, your steering ability, etc. You will learn more about these effects as you read the later chapters of this book.

Reader Study Note

Try to become familiar with navigational instruments while reading this chapter. It is not necessary to master them at this time. Extensive coverage about the use of these instruments is provided throughout the book along with many practical exercises to develop your skill and confidence with navigational instruments. Start reading the operating manuals for all of your navigational instruments. Keep these manuals aboard your boat for quick reference.

Reader Progress Note

In addition to becoming familiar with the nautical chart, nautical publications, and the different aids to navigation that are found on your chart and those that will be used when you are under way, you are now aware of the various navigational tools and are ready to start using them for plotting courses.

REVIEW QUESTIONS

4.1   A GPS set is ____ a compass.

4.2   The _____ _____ is a mark scribed into a compass housing to indicate the direction in which the boat is headed.

4.3   GPS only shows a _____ when the boat on which it is used is _____.

4.4   The _____ _____ should be aligned with the boat's _____ and the boat's _____ _____ in order to track accurately.

4.5   Distance on a nautical chart is measured with _____.

4.6   Direction on a nautical chart is measured _____ from 000 to 360 degrees.

4.7   The _____ _____ or the _____ _____ are used to measure course angles on a nautical chart.

ANSWERS

4.1   A GPS is NOT a compass.

4.2   The LUBBER LINE is a mark scribed into a compass housing to indicate the direction in which the boat is headed.

4.3   GPS only shows a HEADING when the boat on which it is used is UNDER WAY.

4.4   The LUBBER LINE should be aligned with the boat's KEEL and the boat's STEERING POST in order to track accurately.

4.5   Distance on a nautical chart is measured with DIVIDERS.

4.6   Direction on a nautical chart is measured CLOCKWISE from 000 to 360 degrees.

4.7   The PARAGLIDE PLOTTER or the PARALLEL RULES are used to measure course angles on a nautical chart.

FIVE

Reading, Measuring, and Plotting Latitude and Longitude and Converting for GPS Use

In Chapter 1 you learned that your position or location on the earth's surface is measured in terms of latitude and longitude—those crossing lines that appear on nautical charts. On GPS sets, almost every screen will have a latitude and longitude readout. Therefore, it is critical that you learn how to plot latitude and longitude on a nautical chart and how to enter latitude and longitude correctly into your GPS set.

The newer and larger GPS sets have chart plotters and provide chart cursor features that simplify the latitude and longitude entry process. I find that it is more difficult to enter data on the smaller portable GPS sets that have only a few entry keys. Because waypoints are the key to effective GPS use and every waypoint must be identified with a LAT/LON expression, study this chapter very carefully.

Always use your GPS with a paper nautical chart with an identical horizontal datum. I have found that the chart screens on smaller GPS sets are often either too tiny or too clogged with data to be clearly read while under way on a small boat. These screens are especially difficult to read and harder to enter data into during stormy conditions. Think of worst case scenarios. For my money, it is too easy to not notice a rock or a shoal on these small screens, so I always supplement my GPS navigation with reference to a paper nautical chart. As a result, I can use a smaller, less expensive GPS set without a chart plotter feature very effectively on my 25-foot boat. It also means that I have to plan my trips and preset the waypoints and routes in advance. I use simple waypoint designations—1, 2, 3, 4, etc.—and label the waypoints on my charts for quick reference. These procedures eliminate much of the confusion that clutter causes on a GPS chart plotter screen. Chapter 12 explains these techniques in more detail.

The latitude and longitude expression is often different when plotted on a nautical chart than when used in a GPS set. On a nautical chart, the LAT/LON expression is written and plotted using degrees, minutes, and seconds, that is 042 deg. 15 min. 25 sec N / 070 deg. 56 min. 35 sec. W. Most government publications, such as the *Light List,* present LAT/LON in this manner. The LAT/LON expression, usually found on a GPS, uses degrees, minutes, and decimal minutes. The charted LAT/ LON example shown above would appear as 42 15.417 N / 070 56.583 W in a GPS set. Most GPS sets allow you to change the LAT/LON expression. Check your GPS operating manual for this feature.

The purpose of this chapter is to show you how to measure and plot your position on a nautical chart and to enter your position in a GPS set using the correct latitude and longitude expression and understanding the difference.

LATITUDE

MEMORY AID: *"Lat is Flat."*

The horizontal or flat lines on a nautical chart are called *parallels of latitude.* The equator is a parallel of latitude and is numbered as zero (000) degrees. All parallels of latitude are the angular measurement of positions north and south of the equator. Latitude values increase from 0 degrees at the equator to 90 degrees at the north and south poles. Boston Light in Boston Harbor, Massachusetts, is positioned at 042 deg. 19 min 42 sec. N or 2,639.7 nautical miles north of the equator. Because Boston Light is north of the equator, the suffix "N" for north is used after its latitude expression. Positions south of the equator would use the suffix "S" for south latitude.

Latitude is read from the latitude scales found on the left- and right-hand margins of a regular nautical chart. Study Figure 5.1, which is an illustration of latitude (longitude is illustrated in Figure 5.2 and discussed later). Latitude is expressed in degrees, minutes, and seconds on a nautical chart.

- One degree of latitude equals 60 minutes of latitude.
- One minute of latitude equals 60 seconds of latitude.

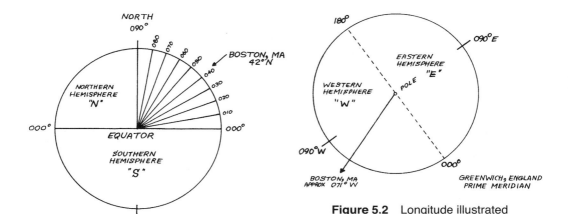

Figure 5.1 Latitude illustrated
(F. J. Larkin).

Figure 5.2 Longitude illustrated
(F. J. Larkin).

- One minute of latitude also equals one nautical mile or 6,071.1 feet. This means that the latitude scales on a nautical chart can be used to measure distance on that chart.

Understanding How the Latitude Seconds Scale Works

The only element of latitude that you physically have to measure is the seconds. Check out the latitude seconds scale on Figure 5.3, which is located in the left margin between the 20 and 21 minutes of latitude lines. Note that the seconds scale is divided into 10-second segments—10, 20, 30, 40, 50, with the 21 minutes of latitude line representing 60 seconds. Just below the 20 minutes of latitude line is a 10-second scale that is incremented in single seconds.

As an example, the latitude of the rock just north of the "SH" Fl R 6s GONG buoy on the Navigation Practice Chart of Figure 5.3 is determined as follows. The degrees and minutes are simply read from the latitude scales. The degrees are 042. Since the rock is north of the 20 minutes of latitude line and south of the 21 minutes of latitude line, the minutes are 20. To find the seconds of latitude for the rock, follow these simple steps:

1. Measure the seconds using dividers. Measure up or down from your position target (the rock) to the nearest minute of latitude line. In this example, measure down from the rock to the 20 minutes of latitude line.

Navigation Practice Chart

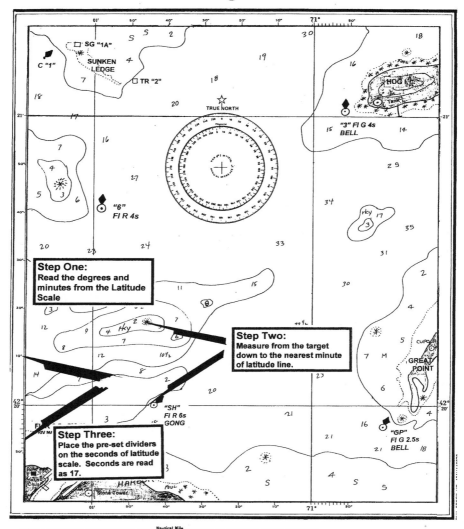

Figure 5.3   The measurement of seconds on the latitude scale
(F. J. Larkin).

SOUNDINGS IN FEET

2. Without disturbing the opening of the dividers, move the dividers to the latitude scale in the left margin of the Navigation Practice Chart (Figure 5.3).

3. Place one arm point of the preset dividers on the appropriate 10-second position, and let the other arm point fall downward along the seconds scale and, if necessary, below the full 60-seconds scale to the 10-second scale that is divided into

individual seconds. In this example, one arm of the dividers would be placed on the 10-second point and the other arm would fall down the scale to the 7-second point on the single-second-incremented scale. The seconds of latitude are read as 17.

Since you measured down to a minute of latitude line from a position target, the rock, the seconds are 17. This is the normal direction of latitude on a chart. If you measured up to a minute of latitude line, the seconds would be 43. This is not the normal direction of latitude on a chart so you must subtract the measured seconds from 60: 60 – 43 = 17.

GPS sets often express latitude differently—degrees, minutes, and a fraction of minutes or decimal minutes. Failure to convert seconds to decimal minutes before entering LAT/LON in a GPS set is a common mistake that is the cause of most errors in GPS navigation.

- *To convert seconds into decimal minutes,* divide the seconds by 60. By doing this, 42 deg. 20 min. 17 sec. N converts to a GPS expression of 42 20.283 N (17 seconds divided by 60 equals 0.283 minute). Note that for most GPS sets, degrees of latitude are expressed by only two digits since the highest latitude that you can have is 90 degrees.

- *To revert decimal minutes into seconds,* multiply the fraction of minutes by 60. By doing this, 71 23.450 W converts to a chart expression of 071 deg. 23 min. 27 sec. W (0.450 minute times 60 equals 27 seconds).

- Most newer GPS sets offer optional LAT/LON expressions. Check your GPS operating manual for this capability.

Exercise: Pause for a minute and look at a nautical chart or the Navigation Practice Chart of Figure 5.3. Note that (in the Northern Hemisphere) the latitude scales in the left and right margins increase as you move from the bottom of the chart to the top. Remember that one minute of latitude is equal to one nautical mile.

Latitude on Small-Scale Charts

On small-scale charts that cover large geographic areas, the minutes of latitude scale may be simply divided into tenths. The same principles for determining latitude are used with the exception that the seconds are read as tenths of minutes directly from the latitude scale. It may not be necessary to convert the fractional minutes to seconds for plotting them on a nautical chart or entering them in a GPS set. Always check the latitude scale carefully. Never assume!

LONGITUDE

The vertical lines on a nautical chart are called *meridians of longitude.* Meridians of longitude represent the angular measurement of positions east or west of the prime meridian. The *prime meridian* is located in Greenwich, England, and is assigned the value of zero (000) degrees of longitude. Longitude values increase east and west from Greenwich, England, to meet at 180 degrees in the Pacific Ocean. As an example, Boston Light is positioned at 070 deg. 53 min. 24 sec. W—west of the prime meridian. Because Boston Light is west of the prime meridian, the suffix "W" for west is used after its longitude expression. Positions east of the prime meridian would use the letter "E" for east as a suffix.

Longitude is read from the longitude scales found in the top and bottom margins of a standard nautical chart. Review Figure 5.2, which is a graphic illustration of longitude. Longitude is expressed in degrees, minutes, and seconds on a nautical chart.

- One degree of longitude has 60 minutes of longitude.

- One minute of longitude has 60 seconds of longitude.

- Note that one minute of longitude *does not equal* a nautical mile and can **never** *be used for measuring distance.*

Understanding How the Longitude Seconds Scale Works

As with latitude, the only element of longitude that you physically have to measure is the seconds. The longitude seconds scale on the Navigation Practice Chart (see Figure 5.4) is divided into 10-second segments—10, 20, 30, 40, 50, with the 01 minutes of longitude line representing 60 seconds. Just to the right of the 71 degrees, 00 minutes, of longitude line is a 10-second scale that is divided into single seconds. Stop for a minute and find the longitude seconds scale on Figure 5.4.

For example, the longitude of the rock just south of the "SH" Fl R 6s GONG buoy on the Navigation Practice Chart is determined as follows. The degrees and minutes are simply read from the longitude scales at the top or bottom of the chart. The degrees are 071. Because the rock is west of the 00 minute of longitude line and east of the 01 minute of longitude line, the minutes are 00. To measure the seconds of longitude for the rock, follow these simple steps:

1. Measure the seconds using dividers. Measure to the right or east from the position target (the rock) to the nearest minute of longitude line.

Navigation Practice Chart

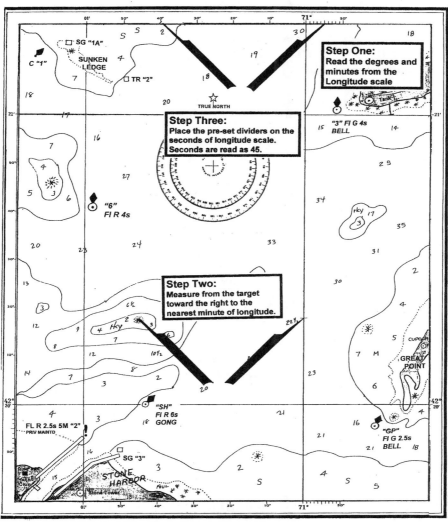

SOUNDINGS IN FEET

Figure 5.4   The measurement of seconds on the longitude scale
(F. J. Larkin).

2. Without disturbing the opening of the dividers, move the dividers to the longitude scale at the top or bottom of the chart.

3. Place one arm point of the dividers on the appropriate 10-second scale increment and place the other arm point to the right or east so that it falls along the seconds scale and, if

necessary, into the 10-second scale that is divided into individual seconds. Read the seconds from the longitude seconds scale. In our example, one arm of the dividers is placed on the 40-second point and the other arm points to 5 in the 10-second scale to the right of the 71 degrees, 00 minute, longitude line. The seconds are read as 45.

Since you measured to the right to a minute of longitude line from a position target, the seconds are 45. This is the normal direction of longitude on a chart. If you had measured to the left of the 01 minute of longitude line, the measurement would be 15 seconds. This is not the normal direction of longitude on a chart, so you must subtract the measured seconds from 60: 60 − 15 = 45.

GPS sets express longitude differently—degrees, minutes, and a fraction of minutes or decimal minutes. Failure to convert seconds to decimal minutes before entering LAT/LON in a GPS set is the most common mistake and the cause of most errors in GPS navigation.

- *To convert seconds into decimal minutes,* divide the seconds by 60. By doing this, 071 deg. 00 min. 45 sec. W converts to the GPS expression of 071 00.750 W. (45 seconds divided by 60 equals 0.750 minute). Note that in most GPS sets, the degrees of longitude are expressed with three digits since they can be as high as 180 degrees.

- *To revert decimal minutes to seconds,* multiply the fraction of minutes by 60. By doing this, the GPS expression of 070 59.650 W converts to a chart expression of 070 deg. 59 min. 39 sec. W (0.65 minute times 60 equals 39 seconds).

EXERCISE: Pause for a minute and look at a nautical chart or a Navigation Practice Chart. Note that (in the Western Hemisphere) the longitude designations on the top and bottom margin scales increase from the right-hand side of the chart toward the left-hand side.

PROCEDURE FOR MEASURING LATITUDE ON A NAUTICAL CHART

Use an enlarged copy of Form 1, the Navigation Practice Chart, found in Appendix 7 to perform this exercise. Enlarge the chart copy to 11 × 17. Follow this step-by-step procedure to measure the latitude for the "6" Fl R 4s lighted buoy due south of Sunken Ledge on the Navigation Practice Chart.

Step 1. Start by reading the degrees and minutes of latitude from the latitude scale found in the left margin. The degrees are 042 and, since this buoy is above the 20 minutes of latitude line and below the 21 minutes of latitude line, the minutes are 20.

Step 2. To measure the seconds of latitude, align the edge of your paraglide plotter along a parallel of latitude or at the top or bottom margin lines of the chart—the horizontal or flat lines. Note that the margin lines will not work for a small craft chart and try not to be confused by any LORAN lattice lines on your chart.

Step 3. Roll the paraglide plotter to the object so that the object ("6" Fl R 4s lighted buoy) falls along the edge of the plotter. Using the same edge as a guide, draw a light pencil line on the nearest meridian of longitude—the vertical lines— or at a margin line at the left- or right-hand sides of the chart. In this example, your mark would be placed on the 01 minute of longitude line or on the left-hand margin line on the chart. Also note that at this point in the procedure, when you use a margin line, you are just using the margin edge as a reference point for measuring and not as the latitude or longitude scale.

Step 4. Using your dividers, measure the distance from the pencil mark that you made on the 01 minute of longitude line to the nearest parallel of latitude below the object's position—the 20 minutes of latitude line in this exercise. Place one arm point of the dividers on the pencil mark and the other arm point on the 20 minutes of latitude line.

NOTE: *Sometimes it is appropriate to measure up to the next parallel of latitude line because it is much closer. Remember that since the object will be below the object's position, your position will be one minute of latitude less than that minute of latitude line. Also, you must correct the answer that you determine in Step 5 by subtracting it from 60.*

Step 5. Being careful not to disturb the opening, move the dividers to the latitude scale at the left margin of the Navigation Practice Chart. Because the opening will be slightly larger than the 40-second indicator, place the first arm point of the dividers on the 40-second segment of the seconds scale and the other arm point of the dividers downward along the seconds scale. The second point should be at the 01-second point within the 10-second scale located below the 20 minutes of latitude line. The total seconds are read as 41.

Step 6.   Compose your latitude expression for this position.
- In Step 1, we read the degrees and minutes as 042 deg 20 min.
- In Step 5, the seconds were read as 41.
- The full latitude reading is 42 deg. 20 min. 41 sec. North.
- The full latitude reading converted for GPS input is 042 deg. 20.683 min. N because 41 sec. divided by 60 equals 0.683 min.

Often the entry format for latitude on a GPS set is as follows:

- Two-digit degree entry,
- Two-digit minute entry,
- Three-digit (after the decimal point) decimal minute entry.

The correct latitude entry format is: 42 20.683 N.

> *Check your GPS operating manual to validate the input format before entering latitude in your GPS set.*

PROCEDURE FOR MEASURING LONGITUDE ON A NAUTICAL CHART

Use the same Navigation Practice Chart (Form 1, Appendix 7) you used in the preceding section to perform this exercise. Follow this step-by-step procedure to measure the longitude for the "6" Fl R 4s lighted buoy due south of Sunken Ledge.

Step 1.   Start by reading degrees and minutes of longitude from the longitude scale found in the top margin. The degrees are 071 and, since this buoy is located to the right of the 01 minutes of latitude line and left of the 00 minutes of latitude line (which is located at the 71 degrees mark), the minutes are 00. Always read longitude from right to left in the Western Hemisphere.

Step 2.   To measure the seconds of longitude, align the edge of your paraglide plotter along a meridian of longitude or at the left- or right-hand margin lines of the chart—the vertical lines. Note that the margin lines will not work for a small craft chart and try not to be confused by any LORAN lattice lines on your chart.

Step 3. Roll the paraglide plotter to the object so that the object ("6" Fl R 4s lighted buoy) falls along the edge of the plotter. Using the same edge as a guide, draw a light pencil line on the nearest parallel of latitude—the horizontal or flat lines—or at a margin line at the top or bottom sides of the chart. In this example, your mark would be placed on the 21 minutes of latitude line or on the top margin line on the chart. Note that at this point in the procedure, when you use a margin line, you are just using the margin edge as a reference point for measuring and not as the latitude or longitude scale.

Step 4. Using your dividers, measure the distance from the pencil mark that you made on the 21 minutes of latitude line or the top margin to the nearest meridian of longitude at the right of the object's position, which will be the 00 minute of longitude line in this exercise. Place one arm point of the dividers on the pencil mark and the other point on the 00 minute of longitude line.

NOTE: *Sometimes it is appropriate to measure to the left meridian of longitude line because it is much closer. Remember that since the object will be positioned to the right of this minute of longitude's meridian, your position will be one minute of longitude less than that minute of latitude. Also, you must correct the answer that you determine in Step 5 by subtracting it from 60.*

Step 5. Being careful not to disturb the opening, move the dividers to the longitude scale at the top or bottom margin of the Navigation Practice Chart. Because the opening will be larger than the 50-second increment, place the first arm point of the dividers on the 50-second segment of the seconds scale and the other arm point of the dividers toward the right along the seconds scale. The second arm point should be at the 8-second position within the 10-second scale, which is to the right of the 00 minute of longitude line. The seconds are read as 58.

Step 6. Compose your longitude expression for this position.

- In Step 1, we read the degrees and minutes as 071 deg 00 min.
- In Step 5, the seconds were read as 58.
- The full longitude reading is 071 deg. 00 min. 58 sec. West.
- The full longitude reading converted for GPS input is 071 00.967 West (58 seconds/60 = 0.967).

Often the entry format for longitude on a GPS set is:

- Three-digit degree entry,
- Two-digit minute entry,
- Three-digit (after the decimal point) fractional-minute entry.

The correct longitude entry format is 071 00.967 W.

> *Check your GPS operating manual to validate the input format*
> *before entering longitude in your GPS set.*

THE SAFETY ASPECTS OF KNOWING LATITUDE AND LONGITUDE

Whether you are north or south of the equator or east or west of the prime meridian, knowing latitude and longitude allows you to fix your position to one location on the earth's surface. Knowing how to express it correctly makes you stand out among a few knowledgeable mariners on the water today as well as preparing you for the wonderful world of GPS navigation systems.

In an emergency, the more accurately you can report your position in a language that is readily understood by skilled mariners, the quicker you will receive assistance. You will be able to speak to the Coast Guard in their language. In an emergency, a few minutes often may mean the difference between life and death. In a Mayday message, send your position first just in case you lose power during the broadcast.

NAVIGATION EXERCISE ONE: LAT/LON

Use an 11 × 17 copy of Form 1, Navigation Practice Chart, from Appendix 7 to perform these measurements.

1. What is the LAT/LON for the tank on Hog Island?

2. Convert the LAT/LON for Hog Island into an acceptable format for a waypoint entry to a GPS set using decimal seconds.

3. What is the LAT/LON for Can "1" near Sunken Ledge?

4. Convert the LAT/LON for Can "1" into an acceptable format for a waypoint entry to a GPS set using decimal seconds.

ANSWERS

1. 042 deg. 21 min. 03 sec. N / 070 deg. 59 min. 43 sec. W

2. 42 21.050 N / 070 59.717 W

3. 042 deg. 21 min. 12 sec. N / 071 deg. 01 min. 14 sec. W

4. 42 21.200 N / 071 01.233 W

Reader Study Note

If you did not complete Navigation Exercise One for measuring latitude and longitude correctly, there's a strong chance that you still don't understand latitude and longitude. This is such a very important part of your basic navigation and GPS education—please don't skip it. LAT/LON is an integral part of using and understanding GPS. Put yourself in a quiet situation away from the pressure of everyday events and reread this chapter until you fully understand the concepts and the simple calculations and measurements involved. From a boating safety aspect, LAT/LON is critical today. We are living in a GPS navigation world and LAT/LON skill and knowledge is essential for survival.

Reader Progress Note

Add to your navigating skills the ability to find, express, and convert your LAT/LON position on a nautical chart and update a LAT/LON position to a GPS set. Congratulations! You have just increased your chance for survival in an emergency at sea by a huge margin.

REVIEW QUESTIONS

5.1 The horizontal lines normally found on a nautical chart are called _____ ___ _____.

5.2 Latitude is read from the margin scales found on the _____ and _____ sides of a nautical chart.

5.3 The _____ lines found on a nautical chart are named meridians of longitude.

5.4 _____ is measured east and west of the prime meridian located in _____, _____.

5.5   One _____ of _____ equals one nautical mile.

5.6   Since the United States is located _____ of the prime meridian, write the suffix "___" after an expression of longitude.

5.7   A _____ and _____ expression or position pinpoints your location on the earth's surface.

5.8   The LAT/LON expression used for GPS sets contains degrees, minutes, and _____ _____.

5.9   The _____ margin scale can be used to measure _____.

5.10 Only _____ must be measured when determining a LAT/LON position.

5.11 _____ and _____ are simply read from a latitude or a longitude scale.

ANSWERS

5.1   The horizontal lines normally found on a nautical chart is called PARALLELS OF LATITUDE.

5.2   Latitude is read from the margin scales found on the LEFT and RIGHT sides of a nautical chart.

5.3   The VERTICAL lines found on a nautical chart are named meridians of longitude.

5.4   LONGITUDE is measured east and west of the prime meridian located in GREENWICH, ENGLAND.

5.5   One MINUTE of LATITUDE equals one nautical mile.

5.6   Since the United States is located WEST of the prime meridian, write the suffix "W" after an expression of longitude.

5.7   A LATITUDE and LONGITUDE expression or position pinpoints your location on the earth's surface.

5.8   The LAT/LON expression used for GPS sets contains degrees, minutes, and DECIMAL MINUTES.

5.9   The LATITUDE margin scale can be used to measure DISTANCE.

5.10 Only SECONDS must be measured when determining a LAT/LON position.

5.11 DEGREES and MINUTES are simply read from a latitude or a longitude scale.

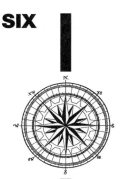

SIX

How to Plot
a True Course on a
Nautical Chart

SELECTING THE PROPER COURSE LINE

Learning to plot a course on a nautical chart is as simple as learning to draw a line between two points and measuring its course angle with a paraglide plotter. But there are a few safety points you should consider before you draw a course line. These points are important for the safe use of your GPS set as a navigation tool.

Before you plot a course, you must understand that all dead reckoning plotting starts from a fixed position. A *fix* can be many things to the experienced navigator. You can use two intersecting bearings to surveyed objects that appear on a nautical chart as a fix. You can take a LAT/LON position from a GPS set. GPS positions are considered a fix. Aids to navigation (ATONs) are also used to get a fix. ATONs are the most common objects used for fixes and are also the best choice for waypoints in your GPS set. Review the following three safety criteria before plotting a course.

FIRST: Are there any obstructions, shoaling, or rapid currents along or near your intended course line?

Check the water depths along your course line against the draft of your boat. *Draft* is the measurement from the waterline down to the lowest part of your boat under the water. Generally, for a powerboat, the lowest point will be the propeller on the engine; for a sailboat, the keel is usually the lowest part. My boat draws about two feet. I use a margin of error of six feet and I highlight all the areas on my chart that show depths below this level. I also set the bottom alarm on my depth sounder to alert me when the water depth drops below six feet. In my area, water depths can drop up to two feet below charted depth on certain days of the year. Keep in mind that water depth projections are averages or means and are subject to variance. These depth variances are published in your local newspaper as feet above or below normal—normal being the charted depth printed on your chart. GPS sets can also provide this data.

Also check for rocks, shoals, and any other obstructions near your course line. Never plot a course near an obstruction. If there is an underwater obstruction near your planned track line, enter it as a waypoint in your GPS. When you are near it, you can call up the obstruction as a waypoint allowing your GPS to provide headings and distance to the obstruction. This will give you peace of mind and help you to stay clear of the problem as you transit the area.

When your intended course fails this criteria, plot a different course around the problem.

> **SECOND:** Have you selected the best aids to navigation as waypoints in anticipation of potential bad weather or night running?

Lighted aids are best for running at night. Sounding aids are best for reduced visibility situations. Plotting directly to the fixed aids themselves can become a problem because passing too close to these aids may cause damage to your boat. Prudent mariners avoid operating their boats during periods of reduced visibility or heavy seas. However, for safety's sake, always be prepared for the worst by practicing navigation during daylight hours. Assume that your GPS will fail and you will have to resort to dead-reckoning navigation techniques to get back home.

> **THIRD:** Plot to aids to navigation at reasonable distances. The larger the interval traveled between aids or waypoints, the greater the chance for error. Current and wind will have a longer time to affect your boat. Short trip legs are like quality control position checks along your track line.

HOW TO MEASURE A COURSE LINE ANGLE USING A PARAGLIDE PLOTTER

The paraglide plotter is the best instrument to use on a small boat because it rolls easily on a chart without losing the course angle. The safest navigation practice is to always preplot your courses on a large flat table before you leave the dock. Plotting courses on a bouncing boat, especially when your attention is diverted by lookout duties and other boat operation tasks, can easily lead to serious navigation errors. I have all of the regular routes that I use plotted on my charts and have all the waypoints labeled for quick reference with small round labels.

Paraglide plotters are used in conjunction with meridians of longitude on a nautical chart. Don't get confused by LORAN TD lines that may be overprinted on your

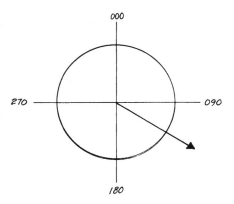

Figure 6.1 A quadrant *(F. J. Larkin).*

chart. Be sure you have selected a proper meridian. Use this simple procedure for plotting a course with a paraglide plotter. Figures 6.1 and 6.2 graphically depict this procedure.

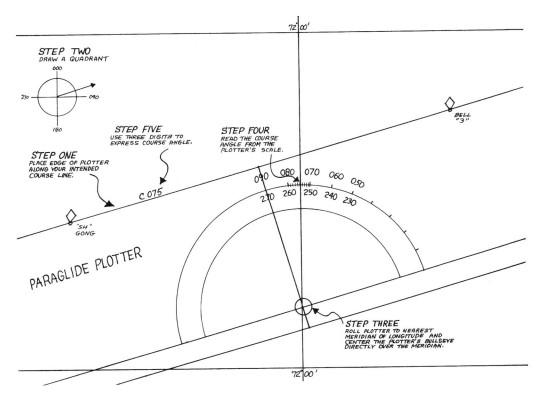

Figure 6.2 Measuring a true course line with a paraglide plotter *(F. J. Larkin).*

Step 1. Establish a course line.

- Place the edge of the paraglide plotter along your intended course line.

- Check the course line using the three safety criteria.

- If all three criteria are met, draw a light pencil course line on the chart using a sharp pencil.

Step 2. Establish your general direction.

- Draw a small quadrant (see Figure 6.1) on a copy of Form 2, the Navigation Worksheet, available in Appendix 7.

- Place an arrow on the quadrant in the general direction in which you plan to head, say, between 090 and 180 degrees. Note that the course scales on the plotter provide reciprocal (opposite) readings. This quadrant technique minimizes the possibility of selecting the wrong heading direction. Make it a standard practice to double-check each plotter reading before accepting it.

Step 3. Measure the course angle.

- Roll the paraglide plotter to the nearest meridian of longitude (vertical lines) and center the plotter's bull's eye directly over the meridian. Keep a steady downward pressure on your plotter during this procedure to keep it from slipping and losing the course angle.

- Use one eye when setting the bull's-eye. You will get a more accurate position reading.

NAVIGATION NOTE: *It is also proper to roll your plotter to the nearest compass rose and center the edge of the plotter directly over the cross in the center of the nearest compass rose in order to measure a course angle.*

Step 4. Read the course angle from the plotter scales.

- To read the course angle, let your eye follow along the meridian of longitude from the bull's-eye to where it intersects the course scales on the plotter.

- Again, closing one eye and, positioning yourself directly above the plotter, read the course angle from the plotter scale.

NAVIGATION NOTE: *If you are using the compass rose for measuring the course angle, let your eye follow along the edge of the plotter to where it intersects the course scales on the compass rose. Here, as you should know from Chapter 1, you have the option of reading a true (outer scale) or a magnetic (inner scale) course from a compass rose.*

- Double-check your quadrant to validate that you have selected the correct course heading and that it is not the reciprocal direction.

Step 5.   Record your course.

- Course headings are always written using three digits. That is, a course angle of nine degrees is written as C 009.

- In Figure 6.2, the course angle or heading would be written as C 075.

- Courses are recorded in three possible locations depending on the sophistication of your navigation:

  - On the course line on the nautical chart.

  - As a reference on a Navigation Worksheet. (See Form 2 in Appendix 7.)

  - On a Trip Log. (See Form 3 in Appendix 7.)

GPS NOTE: *Once you have plotted and labeled a course on your chart and actually run the course with your boat so that you know that everything from a navigational point of view is correct, you never have to plot it again. This is also true for waypoints used in your GPS. When a course line is validated, I use permanent ink to record it on my charts. When a GPS waypoint is validated, I attach a small blue circle label showing the waypoint number to its location on my charts. (See Figure 12.20 in Chapter 12 for an example of this technique.) I validate waypoints by actually visiting the waypoint's position on my boat to ensure that it was entered in my GPS set correctly. Validation is an important method of ensuring safe navigation with GPS.*

Figure 6.3   Labeling a course line with a true course *(F. J. Larkin).*

Figure 6.4   Labeling a course line with a magnetic course *(F. J. Larkin).*

LABELING YOUR COURSE ON A NAUTICAL CHART

In general, only true courses are plotted on nautical charts. The prefix "C" is used to identify the entry as a course designation. Course headings without any suffix are assumed to be true courses. The course angle is always expressed using three digits. Write your course above the course line near the point of departure on the leg's course line. Figure 6.3 shows the proper technique for labeling a true course on a nautical chart.

Some navigators use magnetic headings to label their course lines. It is customary to use the suffix "M" to identify a magnetic course. This differentiates it from true courses to other navigators. Figure 6.4 shows a course labeled with a magnetic course.

NAVIGATION EXERCISE TWO: PLOTTING TRUE COURSES

This exercise helps you develop your skill for measuring course angles. Use a copy of Form 1, the Navigation Practice Chart, from Appendix 7 for the plotting. Enlarge it to 11 × 17 inches at a copy center. This exercise introduces a six-leg trip that will take you around the Navigation Practice Chart. The following chapters revisit this six-leg trip and ask you to do more calculations. Be neat and you will be able to use the same chart for all of the exercises. I recommend that you use Form 2, Navigation Worksheet, from Appendix 7 to record the calculations that you make for each leg of the trip. This Navigation Worksheet makes it easy to retrace your mathematical steps if you ever need to correct an error. Also use a Form 3, Trip Log. In the real world, a trip log is a great tool for quick reference and progress checks along your course line on your boating trips.

LEG 1: Plot a true course from Fl R 6s "SH" GONG buoy off Stone Harbor to the Fl G 2.5s "GP" BELL buoy southwest of Great Point.

- Measure, plot, and label your course line on the Navigation Practice Chart.

- Update your Navigation Worksheet and Trip Log.

LEG 2: Continuing your trip, plot a course from Fl G 2.5s "GP" Bell to Fl R 4s "6" buoy, south of Sunken Ledge.

- Measure, plot, and label your course line on the Navigation Practice Chart.

- Update your Navigation Worksheet and Trip Log.

LEG 3: Continuing your trip, plot a true course from the Fl R 4s "6" buoy to the Fl G 4s "3" BELL buoy southwest of Hog Island.

- Measure, plot, and label your course line on the Navigation Practice Chart.

- Update your Navigation Worksheet and Trip Log.

LEG 4: After fishing for a few hours near Hog Island, the weather looks threatening and you decide to go back to the Stone Harbor Yacht Club. Checking your boat's position with your GPS set, the following electronic position readout was displayed at 1215:

42 21.120 N / 071 00.250 W

Since it is getting a little hazy, you decide to start your return trip by first heading for the Fl R 4s "6" buoy, south of Sunken Ledge.

- Convert the electronic fix to degrees, minutes, and seconds and plot this LAT/LON position on the Navigation Practice Chart as a fix. Record this information on your Navigation Worksheet.

NAVIGATION NOTE: *A fix is designated on a nautical chart by a dot surrounded by a small circle. The dot indicates the LAT/LON position of the fix. Label the time when the fix was taken horizontally beside the fix symbol.*

- Measure, plot, and label your course line on the Navigation Practice Chart from the fix to the Fl R 4s "6" buoy.

- Update your Navigation Worksheet and Trip Log.

LEG 5: You reach the FI R 4s "6" buoy just as the fog rolls in and the visibility drops to just under 100 yards. If you plot a course directly to Stone Harbor, you may run aground on a dangerous shoal. At 1235, you decide to set up Waypoint #12 at 042 deg. 20 min. 05 sec. N / 071 deg. 00 min. 12 sec. W, so you can use your GPS to guide your boat around the shoal.

- Plot the 1235 fix on the Navigation Practice Chart.

- Convert the LAT/LON of Waypoint #12 to GPS format so you can enter it into your GPS set.

- Measure, plot, and label your course line on the Navigation Practice Chart from the FI R 4s "6" buoy to Waypoint #12.

- Update your Navigation Worksheet and Trip Log.

LEG 6: You also decide to establish the FI R 6s "SH" GONG buoy as Waypoint #13.

- Measure the LAT/LON of FI R 6s "SH" GONG buoy.

- Convert the Waypoint #13 LAT/LON expression so you can enter it into your GPS.

- Measure, plot, and label your course line on the Navigation Practice Chart from Waypoint #12 to Waypoint #13.

- Update your Navigation Worksheet and Trip Log.

The answers are shown on the Navigation Practice Chart in Figure 6.5, on the Navigation Worksheet shown in Figure 6.6, and on the Trip Log provided in Figure 6.7. Do the plotting on your own Navigation Practice Chart and record the course on your Navigation Worksheet and Trip Log using pencil before looking up the answers. Navigation is a practiced art and you always need all the practice that you can get. The answers are only provided to give you quick reinforcement that you are performing the exercises correctly.

Navigation Note: *Remember, you can't use a true course for your boat's compass heading. We discussed variation error and deviation error in previous chapters. The procedure for converting a true course to a compass course, which deals with these errors, is covered in Chapter 9. True courses are only plotted on nautical charts. Therefore, all compass courses must be converted to true courses before they can be plotted on a nautical chart.*

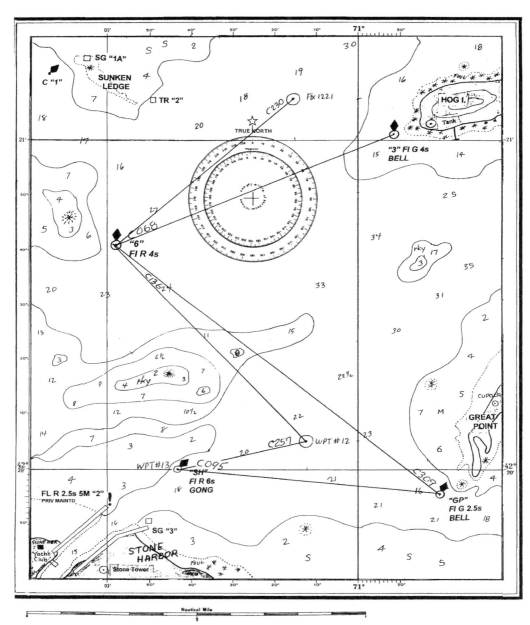

Figure 6.5 Completed Navigation Practice Chart for Navigation Exercise Two
(F. J. Larkin).

SOUNDINGS IN FEET

Navigation Worksheet | 60D=ST | TVMDC Add West Down |

Date:	Trip Name: *NAVIGATION EXERCISE TWO – HEADING*

Leg 1

Dist: _____ nm   Speed _____ kts.

60 x D = S x T

T _095_   DEP ___:___:___
V _____   TURN ___:___:___
M _____   TOT ___:___:___
D _____   ___ ___:___:___
C _____   ETA ___:___:___

Leg 2

Dist: _____ nm   Speed _____ kts.

60 x D = S x T

T _309_   DEP ___:___:___
V _____   TURN ___:___:___
M _____   TOT ___:___:___
D _____   ___ ___:___:___
C _____   ETA ___:___:___

Leg 3

Dist: _____ nm   Speed _____ kts.

60 x D = S x T

T _068_   DEP ___:___:___
V _____   TURN ___:___:___
M _____   TOT ___:___:___
D _____   ___ ___:___:___
C _____   ETA ___:___:___

Leg 4   *42-21.120 N = 042° 21'07"N*
             071-00.250W = 071°00'15"W

Dist: _____ nm   Speed _____ kts.

60 x D = S x T

T _230_   DEP ___:___:___
V _____   TURN ___:___:___
M _____   TOT ___:___:___
D _____   ___ ___:___:___
C _____   ETA ___:___:___

Leg 5   *WPT #12   042°20'05"N / 071°00'12"W*

Dist: _____ nm   Speed _____ kts.

60 x D = S x T

T _136_   DEP ___:___:___
V _____   TURN ___:___:___
M _____   TOT ___:___:___
D _____   ___ ___:___:___
C _____   ETA ___:___:___

Leg 6   *WPT #13   042° 20'00"N / 071°00'43"W*

Dist: _____ nm   Speed _____ kts.

60 x D = S x T

T _257_   DEP ___:___:___
V _____   TURN ___:___:___
M _____   TOT ___:___:___
D _____   ___ ___:___:___
C _____   ETA ___:___:___

Figure 6.6   Completed Navigation Worksheet for Navigation Exercise Two
(F. J. Larkin).

TRIP LOG		Date					Page	Boat Name:			
Leg/ WPT	To	Waypoint	TRUE Heading	DIST nm	SPEED KTS RPM	TOT hr:min:sec	DEP hr:min:sec	Turn Time hr:min:sec	ETA hr:min:sec	COMP Heading	DEP	ETA
Start Point	Fl R 6s "SH" Gong											
LEG 1	Fl G 2.5s "GP" Bell		095									
Notes												
LEG 2	Fl R 4s "6" Buoy / S. of Sunken Ledge		309									
Notes												
LEG 3	Fl G 4s "3" Bell / SW of Hog Island		068									
Notes												
LEG 4	Fl R 4s "6" Buoy / 42 21.120N / 071 00.250 W		230									
Notes												
LEG 5	Waypoint 12 / 042-20-05 N / 071-00-12 W	WP 12	136									
Notes												
LEG 6	FL R 6s "SH" Gong	WP 13	257									
Notes												

Figure 6.7   Completed Trip Log for Navigation Exercise Two *(F. J. Larkin).*

Reader Study Note

Read this chapter very carefully and do all the plotting and computations. These exercises portray a common navigation situation and each additional navigation exercise in the following chapters will build on this data. Buy yourself a paraglide plotter. If you own a small boat, this is the navigation tool to own. Also get yourself a good pair of dividers—preferably a device with a worm drive to control the opening of the arms. Get yourself a quality mechanical pencil and a plastic eraser. Use the figures that show the answers to check your work after your have done the plotting. If you are making errors, reread the chapter until you are clear about the process.

Reader Progress Note

If you have completed Navigation Exercise Two, you should know how to plot a true course and measure a course angle on a nautical chart. You also should have some ideas about correctly setting up waypoints in your GPS. Hopefully, you have started to have an appreciation for validating your courses on a nautical chart before you run them using your GPS set.

You should be getting tired of seeing the term *validation* over and over again. Unfortunately, good navigation practice requires that you validate your position continuously, so get accustomed to validating.

REVIEW QUESTIONS

6.1 Vessel draft is defined as the measurement from the waterline to the _____ part of your boat under the water.

6.2 Before drawing your course line, check for _____ _____ along your intended course line.

6.3 Lighted aids are best for running at _____.

6.4 _____ aids are best for running during periods of reduced visibility.

6.5 _____ aids to navigation are often structures built on rocks or shoal areas.

6.6 Traveling long distances between waypoints can lead to a greater chance for _____ _____.

6.7 Use of the quadrant technique helps avoid a _____ or _____ course reading error.

6.8 Course angles or headings are always expressed with _____ _____ and are written with the prefix "____" for _____ at a point nearest your starting on the top of the course line.

6.9 Courses written on a course line without a suffix are considered to be _____ courses.

6.10 _____ courses cannot be used as your boat's _____ heading.

ANSWERS

6.1 Vessel draft is defined as the measurement from the waterline to the LOWEST part of your boat under the water.

6.2 Before drawing your course line, check for OBSTRUCTIONS along your intended course line.

6.3 Lighted aids are best for running at NIGHT.

6.4 SOUNDING aids are best for running during periods of reduced visibility.

6.5 FIXED aids to navigation are often structures built on rocks or shoal areas.

6.6 Traveling long distances between waypoints can lead to a greater chance for NAVIGATION ERRORS.

6.7 Use of the quadrant technique helps avoid a RECIPROCAL or OPPOSITE course reading error.

6.8 Course angles or headings are always expressed with THREE DIGITS and are written with the prefix "C" for COURSE at a point nearest your starting on the top of the course line.

6.9 Courses written on a course line without a suffix are considered to be TRUE courses.

6.10 TRUE courses cannot be used as your boat's COMPASS heading.

SEVEN

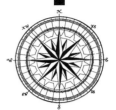

How to Measure Distance on a Nautical Chart

In review, you should already know that the latitude scale is located on the left- and right-hand margins of a regular nautical chart, and that one minute of latitude is equal to one nautical mile. Therefore, you can use the latitude scale for measuring distance. *Never use the longitude scale for this purpose.* A minute of longitude is *not* equal to a minute of latitude. Nautical charts also provide a "Nautical Mile Scale" that can be used to measure distance on a nautical chart.

DIVIDERS: YOUR MEASURING TOOL

A good set of dividers is an essential tool for measuring distance. If you are not using the worm-screw version, your dividers should have an adjusting screw or two. Loose divider arms can slip and cause measurement errors. Add a small screwdriver to your navigation kit to use for adjusting the tension on the arms of your dividers. When measuring, never open the arms of your dividers more than 60 degrees. Angle openings wider than 60 degrees cause distortion, which will result in measuring errors.

MEASURING SHORT DISTANCES ON A NAUTICAL CHART

A short distance is one that is less than the width of the opening of the dividers when they are expanded to not more than 60 degrees. If you have to open your dividers more than 60 degrees to measure a trip leg, follow the procedure for measuring long distances as explained later. To measure a short distance on a nautical chart, follow these simple steps:

Step 1. Set one point of the dividers at the starting point on your course line and the second point on the destination point without opening the dividers more than 60 degrees.

Step 2. Being careful not to disturb the opening of the dividers, move them to either the seconds scale on the latitude scale at the left and right margins of a standard nautical chart or to the nautical mile scale.

HOW TO USE THE LATITUDE SCALE TO MEASURE DISTANCE: *Use the seconds scale (printed on the latitude scale) just as if you were measuring seconds in a LAT/LON exercise. The procedure is very similar. For our example here, we use the distance for Leg 1 from Navigation Exercise Three below. After you physically measure the distance of Leg 1, follow these simple steps:*

1. Put one point of the dividers at a 00-, 10-, 20-, 30-, 40-, or 50-second segment line that is printed within the minute of latitude scale. For this example, the 40-second segment would be used.

2. Place the second point of the dividers down along the second scale. This point generally falls at or below the 00 line into the 10-second area that is incremented into single seconds. For this example, the arm would point at 6.

3. Read the number of seconds as 46.

4. Because one minute of latitude is equal to one nautical mile, convert the seconds reading to minutes or nautical miles by simply dividing the seconds by 60 (46 / 60 = 0.767). The distance in nautical miles is 0.767.

HOW TO USE THE NAUTICAL MILE SCALE TO MEASURE DISTANCE: *Again using Leg 1 of Navigation Exercise Three below, after you physically measure the distance of Leg 1, follow these simple steps:*

1. Place one point of the dividers at the 0-mile position of the nautical mile scale printed on the chart.

2. Place the second point along the scale toward the right. Mile scales usually read from left to right.

3. Read the mileage as nautical miles (nm). Estimate the fractions of nautical miles by eye. Most navigators would read the mileage as 0.770 or 0.780. As you can see, the latitude scale is a more precise method for measuring distance because you don't have to make any estimates.

Step 3. Read the distance in nautical miles from the scale that you select to use.

Step 4. Label the distance on your nautical chart, record the distance on your Navigation Worksheet, and update your Trip Log.

MEASURING LONG DISTANCES ON A NAUTICAL CHART

A long distance is defined as a distance that cannot be measured within the width of a pair of dividers opened no more than 60 degrees. Follow these simple rules when measuring long distances on a nautical chart:

Step 1. Preset your dividers to a whole mile, a multiple-mile, or a partial-mile increment without opening your dividers more than 60 degrees. The preset distance will depend on the scale of the chart that you are using. Double-check the width of the opening in order to avoid generating multiple errors as you swing the dividers along a long course line. Record the length of the opening on a Navigation Worksheet as a reminder.

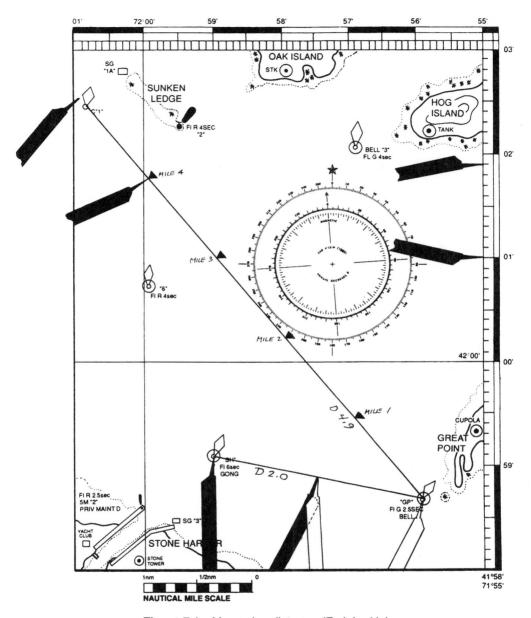

Figure 7.1   Measuring distance *(F. J. Larkin).*

Figure 7.1 provides a good example of how to measure long distances. Note that this sample chart is not the same as the Navigation Practice Chart used throughout this book. The mileage scale and LAT/LON scales are different in this figure.

Step 2. Place one point of your dividers on the starting point of your course line and carefully lay the second point along the course line toward your destination so that it touches the course line and the opening width of the dividers is not disturbed.

Step 3. Leaving the second point in place, swing or walk the first point of your preset dividers down your course line toward your destination. Continue the swings until you can't make a final swing without passing your destination point. Write the number of swings that you made on your Navigation Worksheet. It is so easy to forget the number.

Step 4. Without removing the point of your dividers from the last full-swing position on your course line, compress the other arm carefully and place it on your destination point. Note that the opening of the dividers will now be less than the original preset width.

Step 5. Being careful not to disturb the opening, move your dividers to the seconds scale within the latitude scale in the left or right margins or to the nautical mile scale. Use the procedures explained in the box above for reading distance using these scales.

Step 6. Add up all of the swing lengths. For example:

• Divider opening width: 0.5 nm.

• Number of swings: 3.

• Measured distance for last swing: 0.25 nm.

• 0.5 nm times 3 swings = 1.5 nm plus 0.25 = 1.75 nm.

Step 7. Label the distance on your course line and record the distance on your Navigation Worksheet and Trip Log.

LABELING DISTANCE ON A NAUTICAL CHART

Distance is written under the course line. It is not necessary to add a suffix since distance is always assumed to be nautical miles unless labeled differently. The letter "D" is written before the numbers to indicate that the entry is a distance label.

NAVIGATION NOTE: *Since distances do not change, I always use permanent ink to record distances on my charts but only after I verify them using GPS.*

GPS NOTE: *The DTG—Distance to Go—readout displays the distances from your boat's position to the next waypoint. When you use routes with your GPS, always check the distance from your Trip Log with the DTG readout shown on your GPS set as you pass each waypoint. I also check the heading to the next waypoint at the same time. This practice helps you pick up any data entry errors that may have been made when you entered the waypoints into your GPS set.*

Note that on some of the more sophisticated GPS sets, the distance is computed for you when you enter waypoints and routes. Check your operating manual for this feature on your GPS set and use it.

NAVIGATION EXERCISE THREE: MEASURING DISTANCE

1. Measure the distances for the six legs of the trip that were defined in Navigation Exercise Two in Chapter 6.

2. Label your Navigation Practice Chart and record the distance on your Navigation Worksheet and Trip Log that you started working on in Chapter 6.

Figures 7.2, 7.3, and 7.4 show the answers and proper labeling for Navigation Exercise Three. Note that these forms also show the answers for Navigation Exercise Two from the previous chapter.

Reader Study Note

Completing the Navigation Exercises is part of your learning process. Navigation is only mastered by actually doing the measuring work. While navigation is a relatively simple process, it is still very easy to make errors when measuring distance. Check your distance measurements for Navigation Exercise Three against Figures 7.2, 7.3, and 7.4.

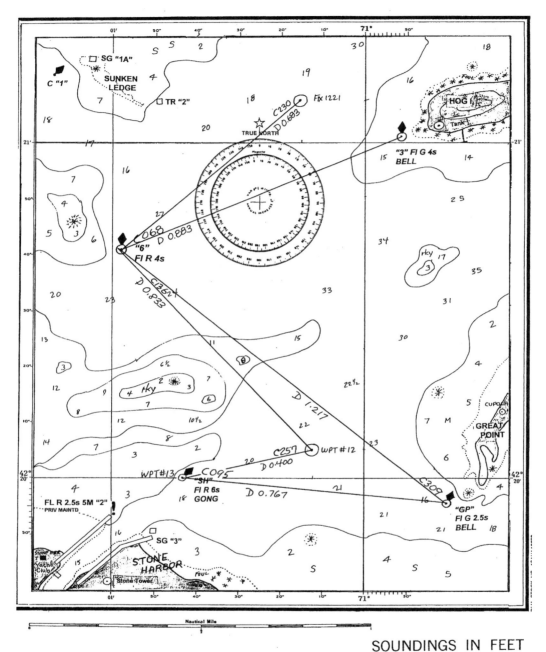

Figure 7.2 Completed Navigation Practice Chart for Navigation Exercise Three
(F. J. Larkin).

Navigation Worksheet | **60D=ST** | **TVMDC** Add West Down

| Date: | Trip Name: | *NAVIGATION EXERCISE THREE – DISTANCE* |

Leg _1_

Dist: _0.767_ nm   Speed _____ kts.

60 x D = S x T

T _095_   DEP ___:___:___
V _____   TURN ___:___:___
M _____   TOT ___:___:___
D _____   ___ ___:___:___
C _____   ETA ___:___:___

Leg _2_

Dist: _1.217_ nm   Speed _____ kts.

60 x D = S x T

T _309_   DEP ___:___:___
V _____   TURN ___:___:___
M _____   TOT ___:___:___
D _____   ___ ___:___:___
C _____   ETA ___:___:___

Leg _3_

Dist: _0.883_ nm   Speed _____ kts.

60 x D = S x T

T _068_   DEP ___:___:___
V _____   TURN ___:___:___
M _____   TOT ___:___:___
D _____   ___ ___:___:___
C _____   ETA ___:___:___

Leg _4_   42-21.120 N = 042° 21′ 07″ N
          071 - 00.250 W = 071° 00′ 15″ W

Dist: _0.683_ nm   Speed _____ kts.

60 x D = S x T

T _230_   DEP ___:___:___
V _____   TURN ___:___:___
M _____   TOT ___:___:___
D _____   ___ ___:___:___
C _____   ETA ___:___:___

Leg _5_ WPT 042° 20′05″N / 071°00′12″W
         #12

Dist: _0.833_ nm   Speed _____ kts.

60 x D = S x T

T _136_   DEP ___:___:___
V _____   TURN ___:___:___
M _____   TOT ___:___:___
D _____   ___ ___:___:___
C _____   ETA ___:___:___

Leg _6_ WPT 042° 20′06″N / 071°00′43″W
         #13

Dist: _0.400_ nm   Speed _____ kts.

60 x D = S x T

T _257_   DEP ___:___:___
V _____   TURN ___:___:___
M _____   TOT ___:___:___
D _____   ___ ___:___:___
C _____   ETA ___:___:___

Figure 7.3 Completed Navigation Worksheet for Navigation Exercise Three
(F. J. Larkin).

TRIP LOG				Date:				Page	1	Boat:	IDYLL TIME	
Leg/ WPT	To	Waypoint	TRUE Heading	DIST nm	SPEED KTS RPM	TOT hr:min:sec	DEP hr:min:sec	Turn Time hr:min:sec	ETA hr:min:sec	COMP Heading	Actual DEP	ETA
Start Point	Fl R 6s "SH" Gong											
LEG 1	Fl G 2.5s "GP" Bell		095	0.767								
	Off Great Point.											
Notes												
LEG 2	Fl R 4s "6" Buoy		339	1.217								
Notes												
LEG 3	Fl G 4s Bell		068	0.883								
	Near Hog Island											
Notes	Fishing for 2 hours.											
LEG 4	Fl R 4s "6"		230	0.683								
Notes												
LEG 5	42 20.08N / 071 00.20W	WPT 12	136	0.833								
Notes												
LEG 6	42 20.00N / 071 00.72W	WPT 13	257	0.400								
Notes												

Figure 7.4   Completed Trip Log for Navigation Exercise Three
(F. J. Larkin).

Reader Progress Note

In addition to plotting and measuring true courses on a nautical chart, you now should be able to measure and label distance on a course line and are now ready to use distances for computing other navigational data.

REVIEW QUESTIONS

7.1   A good set of dividers has an _____ screw to tighten the tension of the divider's arms.

7.2   Dividers opened more that 60 degrees can decrease your _____ when measuring distance.

7.3   If the number of swings or walks with your dividers is 20, and the width of the opening of your dividers is 2.0 nm, and the last swing of the dividers was equal to 26 seconds on the latitude scale, what is the total distance?

7.4 What measuring technique would you use to measure the distance of 1.3 nm on the Navigation Practice Chart?

7.5 Distance is written _____ the course line.

ANSWERS

7.1 A good set of dividers has an ADJUSTING screw to tighten the tension of the divider's arms.

7.2 Dividers opened more that 60 degrees can decrease your ACCURACY when measuring distance.

7.3 (20 times 2.0 = 40 nm) + (26 / 60 = 0.433) = 40 + 0.433 = 40.433 nm.

7.4 Use the technique for measuring a long distance because your dividers would have to be open more than 60 degrees.

7.5 Distance is written UNDER the course line.

EIGHT

Calculating Your Dead Reckoning Position

Many navigation students panic at this point because of their fear of math. Let me relieve your fears. You need only know how to add, subtract, multiply, and divide while following a few simple rules. Every navigation computation is explained for you in an easy-to-follow, step-by-step sequence.

NAVIGATION WORKSHEET

The Navigation Worksheet, Form 2, can be found in Appendix 7. It is good navigating practice to use this worksheet to record all of your navigation computations and to continue using this worksheet when plotting all of your boat trips in the future. I still use it after more than 35 years of boating.

NAVIGATION TERMINOLOGY

Before you get to the formula for calculating a *dead reckoning* (DR) position, familiarize yourself with a few new navigation terms and definitions.

DR Course Line

The *DR course line* is the line that you draw on a nautical chart that your boat is expected to follow. You learned to properly draw this line back in Chapter 6. Your DR course line will always have a course heading, a distance, a speed, and a time.

> CAUTION: *A DR course line makes no allowances for steering errors or for the effects of wind and current.*

Course Heading

Course heading refers to the direction in which your boat is supposed to be pointed or your boat's planned movement through the water. It is also referred to as a *heading* or the *boat's heading.* The course that you steer by the compass on your boat is different than the true course that is plotted on a nautical chart.

Distance

Distance can be either the entire length of your trip or the length of a single leg of a trip. Distance is always expressed in nautical miles on nautical charts and in the DR formula. *Trip leg* is a term that defines one leg of a trip—that is, the distance from one buoy to another could be a trip leg or the distance between one waypoint to another on your GPS.

Speed

Speed, expressed in knots or nautical miles per hour in the DR formula, is the rate at which your boat travels over a fixed geographic distance. It does not take into account the effect of currents or other weather elements. This concept of speed is often termed *speed through the water.* Note that speed through the water is entirely different from speed over the ground (SOG), which is the speed that is calculated by your GPS set. SOG is contaminated by all of the physical and weather-related elements that are affecting your boat at the time, such as wind, current, waves, weight, and boat attitude. Basically, SOG cannot be reliably used to predict future events. On the other hand, speed through the water is a more pristine number without any elemental effects. Theoretically, the physical elements, such as current, boat weight, and boat attitude, are screened out when you prepare a *speed curve*. Appendix 6 explains how to develop a speed curve for your boat.

Current

Current is defined as the flow of water. Current direction is called *set*. Current speed is called *drift*. Current hitting your boat's bow decreases the speed of your boat. Current striking the stern of your boat increases your boat's speed. These are easy corrections to compute. In both instances, the direction of your boat is not affected. Current striking the beam or side of your boat affects both the speed and direction of your boat. Chapter 14 explains how to compensate for the effects of currents.

Time

Time is defined as the hours, minutes, and seconds that it takes to travel along a leg of your trip or for the entire trip. The 24-hour clock is normally used for expressing time in navigation. The computation rules for time are explained in Chapter 10. Usually, time is computed on a Navigation Worksheet and recorded on a Trip Log rather than written on a nautical chart. The DR formula uses time expressed in minutes.

THE DEAD RECKONING FORMULA: 60D = ST

60 times DISTANCE equals SPEED times TIME" or "60D = ST."

In the dead reckoning formula, $60D = ST$, *distance* is expressed in nautical miles (nm), *speed* is expressed in knots (nautical miles per hour, abbreviated kt), and *time* is expressed in minutes.

If you can multiply and divide, you should not have any trouble with this formula. Include a small calculator with your navigation kit to help you with these calculations. Don't forget some spare batteries. Solar calculators don't work very well at night and you should not use white light in the helm area at night.

The basic principles for using the DR formula ($60D = ST$) are as follows:

1.   Whatever you do to one side of the DR formula, you must do to the other side of the formula.

2.   When you know two of the factors in the formula, you can always calculate the value of the third factor.

3. Solve for distance, speed, or time by isolating them to one side of the formula by using rule 1.

Think about how these rules work as you read the explanations that follow.

How to Calculate Distance

Distance is expressed in nautical miles. You can solve for distance (D) by isolating (D) to one side of the 60D = ST formula. Accomplish this by dividing both sides of the formula by 60:

$$60 \times D = S \times T$$

$$\frac{\cancel{60} \times D}{\cancel{60}} = \frac{S \times T}{60} \quad \text{or} \quad D = \frac{S \times T}{60}$$

or Distance equals Speed × Time divided by 60.

For example, if your speed is 12.5 kt and you have been traveling for 30 minutes, how far have you gone?

$$60 \times D = S \times T$$

$$\frac{\cancel{60} \times D}{\cancel{60}} = \frac{12.5 \times 30}{60} = \text{or D} = 6.25 \text{ minutes or 6 min 15 sec.}$$

Labeling Distance on Your Course Line. You learned how to label distance on a course line in Chapter 7. Remember that it is written *under* the course line, is given in tenths of nautical miles, and uses the prefix "D." A suffix is not needed because it is assumed to be nautical miles unless labeled differently.

How to Calculate Speed

Speed is expressed in knots (or nautical miles per hour, abbreviated kt). Solve for speed (S) by dividing both sides of the DR formula by the time (T). This isolates speed to one side of the formula:

$$60 \times D = S \times T$$

$$\frac{60 \times D}{T} = \frac{S \times \cancel{T}}{\cancel{T}} \quad \text{or S} = \frac{60 \times D}{T}$$

Or, Speed equals 60 times Distance divided by Time. For example, if your distance is 15 nm and you have traveled for 90 minutes, what is your speed?

$$60 \times D \ = \ S \times T$$

$$\frac{60 \times 15}{90} = \frac{S \times \cancel{90}}{\cancel{90}} \quad \text{or } S = \frac{60 \times 15}{90} \quad \text{or } S = 10 \text{ kt}$$

Labeling Speed on Your Course Line. Since your speed may vary on each course line or leg of your trip, it is usually not written on the chart. However, speed can be written under your course line toward the starting point of the line if you desire. Define the entry as speed by using the prefix "S." There is no need for a suffix with a speed entry because speed is assumed to be knots unless otherwise labeled (see Figure 8.1).

C 085
S 10.0

Figure 8.1 Labeling speed on a course line *(F. J. Larkin).*

How to Calculate Time

Time (T) is expressed in minutes in the DR formula. Solve by dividing both sides of the formula by the speed. This isolates time to one side of the formula:

$$60 \times D \ = \ S \times T$$

$$\frac{60 \times D}{S} = \frac{\cancel{S} \times T}{\cancel{S}} \quad \text{or } T \quad \frac{60 \times D}{S}$$

Or, Time equals 60 times the Distance divided by the Speed. For example, if your distance is 21 nm and your speed is 12 kt, what is your TOT—time of travel?

$$60 \times D \ = \ S \times T$$

$$\frac{60 \times 21}{12} = \frac{\cancel{12} \times T}{\cancel{12}} \quad \text{or } T = \frac{60 \times 21}{12} \quad \text{or } 105 \text{ minutes.}$$

Your total TOT is 105 minutes, which equals 1 hour and 45 minutes.

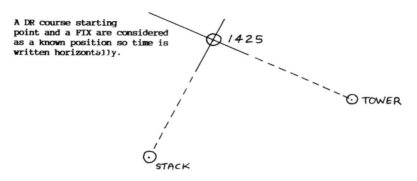

Figure 8.2   Labeling time for DR (calculated) and fixed (known) positions *(F. J. Larkin).*

HOW TO LABEL A FIXED POSITION ALONG A COURSE LINE

The method for writing time depends on whether a position is calculated (a DR position) or known (a fixed position).

DR Positions.   Dead reckoning positions are calculated or projected positions. Calculated time is written at a 45-degree angle to the course line at the reckoned position point, that is, the point where you have calculated you'll be at the end of that given time. Also record time on a Navigation Worksheet and a Trip Log.

Fixed Positions.   Your starting point in dead reckoning navigation must always be a known position. Fixes are considered known positions. Time is written horizontally at known positions.

Figure 8.2 shows examples of labeling time for DR (calculated) positions and fixed (known) positions along a course line.

Labeling Your DR Position

Mark a DR position on your course line with a heavy dot. Draw a semicircle over the dot. Since this is the symbol for a calculated position, write time at a 45-degree angle to the course line. Use four digits to express time. In navigation, expressing time in the 24-hour clock format is preferred and is more accurate. The top part of Figure 8.2 shows a labeled DR position.

When Should You Plot a DR Position?

It is prudent to plot a DR position at specific times while you are under way. A DR position should be plotted:

- Every 30 minutes at a minimum.
- Each time you change a course heading.
- Each time you change speed.
- Each time you fix your position.
- In confined waters, each time that you pass close aboard an aid to navigation.

By following these suggestions, you will remain aware of your probable position. These are also good suggestions for establishing waypoints in your GPS set.

> CAUTION: *The closer you are to hazards, the more frequently you should check your position.*

Be aware of the effects of wind and current on your boat because they are constantly changing your position. Enter obstructions and hazards into your GPS as waypoints. When you are approaching a hazard, press the GOTO key and your GPS will provide continuous warning of the heading and distance to the hazard. As a firm rule, always stay well clear of obstructions and hazards to navigation.

NAVIGATION EXERCISE FOUR: CALCULATING DR TIMES

1. Calculate the dead reckoning times for the six legs of the Navigation Exercise using the Navigation Worksheet that you started in Chapter 6. Use a speed of 12.5 kt for Legs 1, 2, 3, and 4. Due to reduced visibility, use a speed of 6 kt for Legs 5 and 6.

2. Update the Trip Log you started in Chapter 6 for each leg of the cruise.

Figures 8.3 and 8.4 show the calculations and answers. Note that, once again, these figures also show the answers for the Navigation Exercises from the previous chapters.

Navigation Worksheet | **60D=ST** | **TVMDC** Add West Down

Date:	Trip Name: *NAVIGATION EXERCISE FOUR – DR*

Leg *1*   T *095*   DEP ___:___:___

Dist: *0.767* nm   Speed *12.5* kts.   V _____   TURN ___:___:___

60 x D = S x T   M _____   TOT ___:___:___

$$\frac{60 \times 0.767}{12.5} = \frac{12.5 \times T}{12.5} = 3.6816$$

D _____   ___:___:___

C _____   ETA ___:___:___

0.6816 × 60 = 40.896 OR 41s   3m 41s

Leg *2*   T *309*   DEP ___:___:___

Dist: *1.217* nm   Speed *12.5* kts.   V _____   TURN ___:___:___

60 x D = S x T   M _____   TOT ___:___:___

$$\frac{60 \times 1.217}{12.5} = \frac{12.5 \times T}{12.5} = 5.8416$$

D _____   ___:___:___

C _____   ETA ___:___:___

0.8416 × 60 = 50.496 OR 51s   5m 51s

Leg *3*   T *068*   DEP ___:___:___

Dist: *0.883* nm   Speed *12.5* kts.   V _____   TURN ___:___:___

60 x D = S x T   M _____   TOT ___:___:___

$$\frac{60 \times 0.883}{12.5} = \frac{12.5 \times T}{12.5} = 4.2384$$

D _____   ___:___:___

C _____   ETA ___:___:___

0.2384 × 60 = 14   4m 14s

Leg *4*   42-21.120N = 042° 21'07"N   T *230*   DEP ___:___:___
          071-00.250W = 071° 00'15" W

Dist: *0.683* nm   Speed *12.5* kts.   V _____   TURN ___:___:___

60 x D = S x T   M _____   TOT ___:___:___

$$\frac{60 \times 0.683}{12.5} = \frac{12.5 \times T}{12.5} = 3.2784$$

D _____   ___:___:___

C _____   ETA ___:___:___

0.2784 × 60 = 17   3m 17s

Leg *5*   WPT 042° 20'05"N / 071° 00'12"W   T *136*   DEP ___:___:___
          #12

Dist: *0.833* nm   Speed *6.0* kts.   V _____   TURN ___:___:___

60 x D = S x T   M _____   TOT ___:___:___

$$\frac{60 \times 0.833}{6.0} = \frac{6.0 \times T}{6.0} = 8.33$$

D _____   ___:___:___

C _____   ETA ___:___:___

0.33 × 60 = 19.8 OR 20s   8m 20s

Leg *6*   WPT 042° 20'00"N / 071° 00'43"W   T *257*   DEP ___:___:___
          #13

Dist: *0.400* nm   Speed *6.0* kts.   V _____   TURN ___:___:___

60 x D = S x T   M _____   TOT ___:___:___

$$\frac{60 \times 0.400}{6.0} = \frac{6.0 \times T}{6.0} = 4.0 m$$

D _____   ___:___:___

C _____   ETA ___:___:___

Figure 8.3   Completed Navigation Worksheet for
Navigation Exercise Four *(F. J. Larkin).*

TRIP LOG			TRUE Heading	DIST nm	SPEED KTS RPM	TOT hr:min:sec	DEP hr:min:sec	Turn Time hr:min:sec	ETA hr:min:sec	COMP Heading	Actual	
				Date:				Page 1		Boat:	IDYLL TIME	
Leg/ WPT	To	Waypoint									DEP	ETA
Start Point	Fl R 6s "SH" Gong											
LEG 1	Fl G 2.5s "GP" Bell *Off Great Point.*		095	0.767	12.50 3300	0:03:41						
Notes												
LEG 2	Fl R 4s "6" Buoy		309	1.217	12.50 3300	0:05:51						
Notes												
LEG 3	Fl G 4s Bell *Near Hog Island*		068	0.883	12.50 3300	0:04:14						
Notes	*Fishing for 2 hours.*											
LEG 4	Fl R 4s "6"		230	0.683	12.50 3300	0:03:17						
Notes												
LEG 5	42 20.08N / 071 00.20W	WPT 12	136	0.833	06.00 2500	0:08:20						
Notes												
LEG 6	42 20.00N / 071 00.72W	WPT 13	257	0.400	06.00 2500	0:04:00						
Notes												

Figure 8.4   Completed Trip Log for Navigation Exercise Four
(F. J. Larkin).

Reader Study Note

I like to write the DR formula, $60 \times D = S \times T$, each time I make a DR calculation. This formula is preprinted on the Navigation Worksheet form. Using this single formula, you can solve for distance, speed, or time. The math is simple when you follow the rules. Try not to complicate it for yourself. Do all of the practice Navigation Exercises on a Navigation Worksheet and record the results on a Trip Log.

Reader Progress Note and GPS Suggestions

You can now compute time, speed, and distance on a true course line, which allows you to calculate your DR position along a course line. Don't forget that you are still operating in a perfect world. Corrections for wind, weight, or current have not yet been addressed. Unfortunately, many students stop at this point and ignore wind and current calculations. If you have a fairly fast powerboat and you are using a good GPS set with waypoints and routes, this may not be too much of a problem. However, if you have a sailboat, you must calculate for current. Also, check the procedure for setting up danger bearings on your GPS in Chapter 11.

NINE

Converting True Courses to Compass Courses

W┊hile true courses work well on a nautical chart, they can never be used as a heading for your boat's compass until they have been converted to compass courses and that is what this chapter is all about. The difference between a true course and a compass course is caused by magnetic attractions over the earth's surface and onboard your boat.

One magnetic influence is geographical and is called *variation error*. The magnetic disturbances aboard your boat are called *deviation error*. Both of these types of magnetic disturbances affect the readings you get from your boat's compass. Therefore, you must learn to understand them, to compensate for them, or to eliminate them in order to use your compass effectively and safely.

VARIATION ERROR

Variation is a predictable magnetic influence on your compass that is directly related to your position on the earth's surface and the current location of the magnetic North Pole. Magnetic compasses are attracted to the magnetic North Pole and not the geographic North Pole.

Magnetic north and true north are two distinct locations. The difference, or *variation error*, is the angular measurement between these two points from your location on the earth's surface. True north is located at the axis point on which the earth spins, whereas magnetic north is one end of a large magnetic force through the earth's surface. The position of magnetic north has moved about, albeit slowly, over the centuries. The good news is that variation error is predictable and you will find it in the center of every compass rose. Figure 1.5 back in Chapter 1 displays a typical compass rose. The other good news is that most of the newer GPS sets are able to compensate for variation error automatically. Check your GPS operating manual.

Variation error is expressed in degrees and minutes east or west of true north. The compass rose in Figure 1.5 has a variation error of 004 deg. 15 min. W. This means that magnetic north is located 4 degrees, 15 minutes west of true north at this charted position on the earth's surface. Check your local chart for the variation error in your area. New England is currently 016 degrees West.

To navigate your boat effectively, you must realize that:

- You can only plot true courses on a nautical chart.
- You can only steer a boat using a compass course.
- You must always know and calculate the difference between these two directions for accurate navigation.

Annual Increase or Decrease of Variation Error

The magnetic north pole is constantly moving. The annual increase or decrease is printed in the center of a compass rose under the variation error. In Figure 1.5, the annual increase is 8 minutes in 1985— obviously an old chart. Note that on a small boat it is virtually impossible to hold a course to 1 degree since most small boat compasses are graduated in 5- or 10-degree increments. In other words, forget about this change. You couldn't steer the correction if you wanted to. Just use current nautical charts and you will never have a variation error problem.

> GPS NOTE: *Every GPS set will have an adjustment screen for variation error. Read your GPS operating manual to learn about this correction. Most new GPS sets have a feature that automatically corrects for variation all over the world as you move about. This adjustment determines how your set will display headings. You usually have the option to select either true or magnetic headings. Since I have an electronic compass, I have selected true on my GPS. My compass has a compensating feature that eliminates all of the deviation error. I use an installation-offset feature to adjust for local variation so that the compass always displays true courses. Whatever method you decide to use, be sure that you are aware of how your GPS is calibrated.*

DEVIATION ERROR

Magnetic influences found aboard your boat that prevent your compass card from pointing directly to magnetic north are termed *deviation error*. Before you start to track down the magnetic problems, be sure that your compass is installed correctly. Here are a few simple steps to help you:

1. Check that your compass has no built-in error. Appendix 2 explains this process. Most new compasses are adjusted for built-in error at the factory.

2. Check that your compass is installed parallel with the keel or centerline of your boat. Appendix 1 will help you through this process.

3. Check for magnetic disturbances near your compass:

   a. Tie your boat to a dock so that the compass heading is steady and shut off all electrical and electronic equipment near the compass (within, say, a three-foot circle). Record the compass heading.

   b. Turn on each piece of electronic equipment one at a time and note whether the heading on the compass changes. Don't forget the windshield wiper overhead and any radios or speakers mounted beneath the compass on a bulkhead. Place the microphone handset for your marine radio and your cell phone in the position that you normally use when you are under way. If the compass card does not move, you have no local magnetic disturbance near your compass. If the card does move, you have magnetic problems. You must eliminate this error by moving the piece of equipment. If the magnetic disturbance is caused by direct current wiring, simply twisting the wires often eliminates the problem.

   c. Once you have completed steps a and b above, you will be ready to develop a *deviation table* for your boat. Appendixes 3, 4, and 5 explain the procedure. Personally, I have found that it is virtually impossible to develop an accurate deviation table on a small boat. It is so difficult to hold headings within five degrees and, unless it is an absolutely perfect day—no wind, no current, and no other boats making waves—the results are usually bogus. My electronic compass has a great attribute called an *automatic compensating* feature. You press a button called "COMP" and slowly turn your boat in a full circle and all of the deviation error is removed from the compass. "Don't leave home without one!" For the first time, I am able to deal with deviation error on a boat. A friend with the same compass recently complained that his compass wasn't operating correctly. I found out that he had installed a large GPS next to the compass. With the "COMP" button and a single tight turn, the deviation error was gone and the compass was reading accurately again. I highly recommend electronic compasses for small boats. Some people have cautioned, "What are you going to do if you lose power? You won't have a compass." Without power, my boat is dead in the water and it is too big to row. I would simply anchor and call for assistance on my hand-held radio.

Checking for Deviation Error

After you have performed the above verifications, check for deviation error using the following steps:

Step 1. Align your boat on two fixed, charted objects for which you were able to measure true bearings on a nautical chart. In Figure 9.1, the tower and the stack have a true bearing of 060 degrees.

Step 2. Determine your magnetic heading by applying variation from the nearest compass rose. In Figure 9.1, the variation of 004 degrees West is taken from the nearest compass rose.

Step 3. Record the actual compass heading of your boat when you align it on the range formed by the Stack and the Tower while under way. In Figure 9.1, the compass heading is 065 degrees.

Step 4. The difference between the magnetic heading and the compass heading is the deviation error:

Compass heading	065
Magnetic heading	064
Deviation error	001 W

To develop a full deviation table, take bearings on fixed and charted ranges at 8 to 12 different points of the compass. Plot your findings on a graph and use your deviation table when you convert courses from true to compass and vice versa.

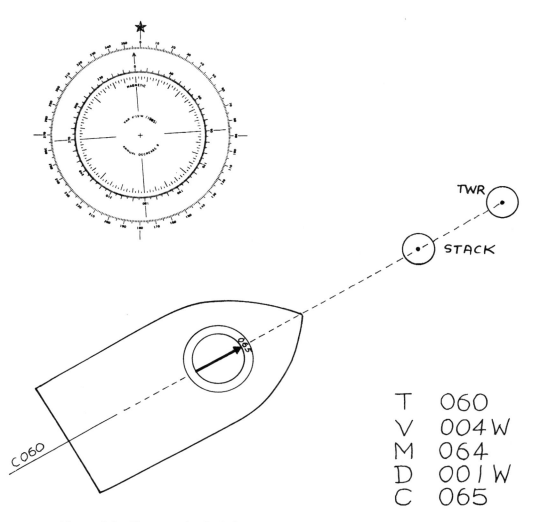

Figure 9.1 Diagram of a deviation table development process *(F. J. Larkin).*

GPS NOTE: *You can use your GPS set to develop a deviation table by comparing the data on your Trip Log to the GPS readouts. If you use this technique, remember that GPS output is often averaged and, therefore, you need to be running on a heading for a period of time before the GPS heading averages down to an actual heading. Here are a few simple steps to take:*

1. Plot the true course heading between two verified waypoints on a nautical chart. The waypoints should be loaded into your GPS set. Both waypoints must be visible to each other.

2. Convert the true heading to a magnetic heading and record it on a Trip Log form.

3. Using your GPS as a guide, run your boat between the waypoints keeping the starting waypoint directly off the stern and the destination waypoint in line with the steering post on the bow of your boat. Steering posts were explained in Chapter 4.

4. After you feel the GPS has had time to settle down and the Course Made Good—CMG—matches the magnetic course recorded on your Trip Log, record the compass reading.

5. The difference between the recorded magnetic course and the compass course is the deviation error.

THE COURSE CONVERSION FORMULA

MEMORY AID: *"T V M D C, Add West Down."*

I find that the vertical presentation of the course conversion formula, TVMDC, helps me to remember when to add and subtract variation and deviation errors. Proceed down the formula when you convert a true course to a compass course so that the "Add West Down" instruction works graphically. Remember that if you "Add West Down," you must "Subtract East Down." The Navigation Worksheet (Form 2 in Appendix 7) provides an area for making this conversion.

This is how the conversion process works down from a True to a Compass course:

1.   Read the true course from the nautical chart.

2.   Read the variation error from the compass rose nearest to your plotted course line.

3.   Calculate the magnetic course by adding westerly variation

error to or subtracting easterly variation error from the true course.

4. Take the deviation error from the boat's deviation table.

5. Compute the compass course by adding westerly deviation error to or subtracting easterly deviation error from the magnetic course.

Reread these steps a few times until you completely understand the process.

EXAMPLE: Convert a true course of 090 degrees to a compass course. Use the compass rose shown in Figure 9.1. Deviation is 005 E.

T	True	090	(Given)
V	Variation Error	004 W	(Add West down)
M	Magnetic course	094	(090 + 004 = 094)
D	Deviation Error	005 E	(Subtract East down)
C	Compass course	089	(094 − 005 = 089)

We now look at how the conversion process works upward from a compass to a true course:

1. Read the course from your compass.

2. Take the deviation error from the boat's deviation table.

3. Compute the magnetic course by subtracting westerly deviation error from or adding easterly deviation error to the compass course.

4. Take the variation from the compass rose nearest to your position on the nautical chart.

5. Compute the true course by subtracting westerly variation error from and adding easterly variation error to the magnetic course.

Reread these steps until you fully understand them.

EXAMPLE: Convert a compass course of 280 degrees to a true course. Use the compass rose in Figure 9.1. Deviation is 003 E.

T	True	279	(283 − 004 = 279)
V	Variation Error	004 W	(Subtract West up)
M	Magnetic course	283	(280 + 003 = 283)
D	Deviation Error	003 E	(Add East up)
C	Compass course	280	(Read from your compass)

The Navigation Worksheet (Form 2 from Appendix 7) shows the course conversion formula as a reference. Record your TVMDC course conversions on this document. You will be able to find errors quicker when you use this form to record navigation data and computations.

NAVIGATION EXERCISE FIVE: CONVERTING TRUE COURSES TO COMPASS COURSES

1. Convert all of the true courses to compass courses for the six legs contained in the Navigation Exercises that you have been working on in the previous chapters. Use the following deviation errors to perform the TVMDC computations using your Navigation Worksheet. The variation error for the Navigation Practice Chart is 009W.

Leg 1	001E
Leg 2	005W
Leg 3	004W
Leg 3	004W
Leg 5	004E
Leg 6	003E

2. Update your Trip Log by adding the calculated compass courses to it.

Figures 9.2 and 9.3 show the calculations for the correct compass courses.

Reader Study Note

Remember that you must correct for two magnetic errors that make your compass read incorrectly. Variation error is always provided on the nearest compass rose. If you operate your boat in one area without taking long trips, variation error will probably not change. Deviation error is another story because it is extremely difficult to compute for a small boat. The electronic compass has been the best solution that I have found for correcting deviation errors. Don't forget that each time that you change or add electronic equipment to your boat, you have to recheck and perhaps redo your deviation table.

Navigation Worksheet | **60D=ST** | **TVMDC** Add West Down

| Date: | Trip Name: | *NAVIGATION EXERCISE FIVE – TVMDC* |

Leg 1

Dist: *0.767* nm Speed *12.5* kts.

60 x D = S x T

$$\frac{60 \times 0.767}{12.5} = \frac{12.5 \times T}{12.5} = 3.6816$$

$0.6816 \times 60 = 40.896$ OR $41s$ $3m \ 41s$

T _095_   DEP __:__:__
V _009 W_   TURN __:__:__
M _104_   TOT __:__:__
D _001 E_   __:__:__
C _103_   ETA __:__:__

Leg 2

Dist: *1.217* nm Speed *12.5* kts.

60 x D = S x T

$$\frac{60 \times 1.217}{12.5} = \frac{12.5 \times T}{12.5} = 5.8416$$

$0.8416 \times 60 = 50.496$ OR $51s$ $5m \ 51s$

T _309_   DEP __:__:__
V _009 W_   TURN __:__:__
M _318_   TOT __:__:__
D _005 W_   __:__:__
C _323_   ETA __:__:__

Leg 3

Dist: *0.883* nm Speed *12.5* kts.

60 x D = S x T

$$\frac{60 \times 0.883}{12.5} = \frac{12.5 \times T}{12.5} = 4.2384$$

$0.2384 \times 60 = 14$ $4m \ 14s$

T _068_   DEP __:__:__
V _009 W_   TURN __:__:__
M _077_   TOT __:__:__
D _004 W_   __:__:__
C _081_   ETA __:__:__

Leg 4 42-21.120N = 042° 21'07"N
071-00.250W = 071°00'15"W

Dist: *0.683* nm Speed *12.5* kts.

60 x D = S x T

$$\frac{60 \times 0.683}{12.5} = \frac{12.5 \times T}{12.5} = 3.2784$$

$0.2784 \times 60 = 17$ $3m \ 17s$

T _230_   DEP __:__:__
V _009 W_   TURN __:__:__
M _239_   TOT __:__:__
D _004 W_   __:__:__
C _243_   ETA __:__:__

Leg 5 WPT #12 042° 20'05"N / 071°00'12"W

Dist: *0.833* nm Speed *6.0* kts.

60 x D = S x T

$$\frac{60 \times 0.833}{6.0} = \frac{6.0 \times T}{6.0} = 8.33$$

$0.33 \times 60 = 19.8$ OR $20s$ $8m \ 20s$

T _136_   DEP __:__:__
V _009 W_   TURN __:__:__
M _145_   TOT __:__:__
D _004 E_   __:__:__
C _141_   ETA __:__:__

Leg 6 WPT #13 042° 20'00"N / 071°00'43"W

Dist: *0.400* nm Speed *6.0* kts.

60 x D = S x T

$$\frac{60 \times 0.400}{6.0} = \frac{6.0 \times T}{6.0} = 4.0 m$$

T _257_   DEP __:__:__
V _009 W_   TURN __:__:__
M _266_   TOT __:__:__
D _003 E_   __:__:__
C _263_   ETA __:__:__

Figure 9.2 Completed Navigation Worksheet for Navigation Exercise Five
(F. J. Larkin).

Leg/ WPT	To	Waypoint	TRUE Heading	DIST nm	SPEED KTS RPM	TOT hr:min:sec	DEP hr:min:sec	Turn Time hr:min:sec	ETA hr:min:sec	COMP Heading	DEP	ETA
TRIP LOG Date									Page	Boat Name:		
Start Point	FI R 6s "SH" Gong											
LEG 1	FI G 2.5s "GP" Bell		095	0.767	12.50 3350	0:03:41				103		
Notes												
LEG 2	FI R 4s "6" Buoy S. of Sunken Ledge		309	1.217	12.50 3350	0:05:51				323		
Notes												
LEG 3	FI G 4s "3" Bell SW of Hog Island		068	0.883	12.50 3350	0:04:14				081		
Notes												
LEG 4	FI R 4s "6" Buoy 42 21.120N / 071 00.250 W		230	0.683	12.50 3350	0:03:17				243		
Notes												
LEG 5	Waypoint 12 042-20-05 N / 071-00-12 W	WP 12	136	0.833	06.00 1600	0:08:20				141		
Notes												
LEG 6	FL R 6s "SH" Gong	WP 13	257	0.400	06.00 1600	0:04:00				263		
Notes												

Figure 9.3   Completed Trip Log for Navigation Exercise Five
(F. J. Larkin).

Reader Progress Note

Now you should be able to plot a true course on a nautical chart, measure distance, compute time of travel (TOT), speed, or distance, and convert true courses to compass courses and back again. Also, you should have started to formulate a plan for handling deviation on your boat.

REVIEW QUESTIONS

9.1 _____ influences affect your compass.

9.2 The compass card on your compass is attracted to _____ north.

9.3 Because variation is _____, it is printed in the center of the compass rose.

9.4 The magnetic North Pole is constantly _____.

9.5 When converting a true course to a compass course, you must _____ easterly error downward when using the _____ formula vertically.

9.6 The annual increase or decrease of variation is found at the center of the _____ _____.

9.7 True or False?

   a. _____ The magnetic influence called deviation error is always found printed on the nautical chart.

   b. _____ The annual increase or decrease of variation is critical to the accuracy of a small boat's compass heading.

   c. _____ The difference between a true course and a magnetic course is called variation error.

   d. _____ The deviation error is the same for all boats.

   e. _____ When converting a compass course up to a true course, add easterly deviation error.

ANSWERS

9.1 MAGNETIC influences affect your compass.

9.2 The compass card on your compass is attracted to MAGNETIC north.

9.3 Because variation is PREDICTABLE, it is printed in the center of the compass rose.

9.4 The magnetic North Pole is constantly MOVING.

9.5 When converting a true course to a compass course, you must SUBTRACT easterly error downward when using the TVMDC formula vertically.

9.6 The annual increase or decrease of variation is found at the center of the COMPASS ROSE.

9.7 True or False?

   a. FALSE. You must create a deviation table that is unique for your own boat's magnetic problems.

   b. FALSE. It is minimal since it is virtually impossible to hold a true course within a single degree on a small boat.

   c. TRUE.

   d. FALSE. The local magnetic influences are different on every boat.

   e. TRUE.

TEN

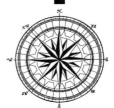

The 24-Hour Clock, or Military Time

Time is defined as the hours, minutes, and seconds that it takes to travel from your point of departure—DEP—to a destination point—ETA (estimated time of arrival). The 24-hour clock, or military time, is commonly used to express time in navigation. It is easy to make errors when projecting time. Here are a few important tips to remember:

- Hours have *sixty (60) minutes*, not 100.
- Minutes have *sixty (60) seconds*, not 100.
- Time is always expressed in *minutes* in the DR formula.

The 24-hour clock's day starts at one second after midnight. Military time is usually written in four digits without a colon; for instance, 1330 would represent 1:30 PM. GPS units, however, most often use the hh:mm or the hh:mm:ss format:

- The first two digits—hh—express the hour of the day (01 through 24).
- The second two digits—mm—express the minute within the hour (01 through 59).
- The third two digits—ss—express the second within the minute (01 through 59).

GPS NOTE: *Check your GPS set for a screen that allows you to select a specific format for expressing time. Smaller GPS sets show only hours and minutes. Newer and larger sets show hours, minutes, and seconds. If you feel comfortable with it, select the 24-hour clock option.*

Table 10.1   The 24-Hour Clock

STD Time	24-Hour Clock Time	STD Time	24-Hour Clock Time
1 AM	0100	1 PM	1300
2 AM	0200	2 PM	1400
3 AM	0300	3 PM	1500
4 AM	0400	4 PM	1600
5 AM	0500	5 PM	1700
6 AM	0600	6 PM	1800
7 AM	0700	7 PM	1900
8 AM	0800	8 PM	2000
9 AM	0900	9 PM	2100
10 AM	1000	10 PM	2200
11 AM	1100	11 PM	2300
12:00 NOON	1200	12 PM MIDNIGHT . . .	2400

HOW TO ADD TIME

The secrets for adding time correctly are:

Step 1. Add the minutes first.

Step 2. Convert the minutes over fifty-nine to hours by subtracting increments of 60 from the minutes column and adding whole hours to the hours column.

Step 3. Add the hours.

If you are using seconds, follow the same process that is described for minutes.

━━━━━━━

EXAMPLE: Add 45 minutes to 1430.

		hrs.	min.
		14	30
Add the 45 minutes.	+	00	45
(30 + 45 = 75 minutes)	Total	14	75
Convert the excess minutes to hours	−	00	60
(75 − 60 = 15 minutes)		00	15
Add the hours.	+	01	00
Total Hours and Minutes		15	15

In effect, you added 0115 (1 hr, 15 min) to 1400 to get 1515.

━━━━━━━

HOW TO SUBTRACT TIME

The secrets for subtracting time are:

Step 1. Subtract the minutes first.

Step 2. When you are subtracting more from less (i.e., 55 from 25) bring a whole hour (60 minutes) over from the hours column to the minutes column. Don't forget that a whole hour has 60 minutes, *not* 100. This is the most common mistake made.

Step 3. Subtract the hours.

If you are using seconds, follow the same process that is described by minutes.

━━━━━━━

EXAMPLE: Subtract 47 minutes from 1430.

		hrs.	min.
First bring a whole hour over to the minutes column.		14	30
	−	01	00
(14 − 1 = 13)	+	00	60
(30 + 60 = 90)	Total	13	90
Subtract the 47 minutes.	−	00	47
Total Hours and Minutes		13	43

━━━━━━━

NAVIGATION EXERCISE SIX:
TIMING THE SIX LEG CRUISE

1. Using the TOT—Time of Travel—that you calculated in Chapter 8 in Navigation Exercise Four and recorded on your Navigation Worksheet and Trip Log, determine the ETA—Estimated Time of Arrival—for each leg of the cruise on the Navigation Worksheet.

Use the following starting times:

For Leg 1, start at 08:45:00. On Legs 2 and 3, use the ETA from the previous legs. On Leg 4, depart at 12:21:00. On Leg 5, depart at 12:40:00. For Leg 6, use the ETA for the previous leg as the starting point.

You'll note that both the Navigation Worksheet and Trip Log have a place to enter your *turning time.* Chapter 14 provides details about turning times, but for now, suffice to say that it's the time required to turn your boat around a buoy.

For turning times, use the following:

Leg 1	None, you are starting
Leg 2	8 sec.
Leg 3	6 sec.
Leg 4	None, you are restarting
Leg 5	None, you are restarting
Leg 6	6 sec.

2. Update your Trip Log.

The solutions are shown in Figures 10.1 and 10.2

Reader Study Note

Timing errors are very common in navigation. Take your time and double-check your results. It is always best to time a trip after all other navigation calculations have been completed. I always wait until just before I get under way to record the final times for a trip. Too many things happen to change the game plan—weather, traffic delays, delays at the gas pump, late guests, and so on.

Navigation Worksheet

60D=ST	**TVMDC** Add West Down

| Date: | Trip Name: NAVIGATION EXERCISE SIX - TIMING THE TRIP |

Leg *1*

Dist: *0.767* nm Speed *12.5* kts.

60 x D = S x T

$$\frac{60 \times 0.767}{12.5} = \frac{12.5 \times T}{12.5} = 3.6816$$

0.6816 × 60 = 40.896 OR 41s 3m 41s

T	095	DEP	08:45:00
V	009W	TURN	00:00:00
M	104	TOT	00:03:41
D	001E		: :
C	103	ETA	08:48:41

Leg *2*

Dist: *1.217* nm Speed *12.5* kts.

60 x D = S x T

$$\frac{60 \times 1.217}{12.5} = \frac{12.5 \times T}{12.5} = 5.8416$$

0.8416 × 60 = 50.496 OR 51s 5m 51s

T	309	DEP	08:48:41
V	009W	TURN	00:00:08
M	318	TOT	00:05:51
D	005W		: :
C	323	ETA	08:54:40

Leg *3*

Dist: *0.883* nm Speed *12.5* kts.

60 x D = S x T

$$\frac{60 \times 0.883}{12.5} = \frac{12.5 \times T}{12.5} = 4.2384$$

0.2384 × 60 = 14 4m 14s

T	068	DEP	08:54:40
V	009W	TURN	00:00:06
M	077	TOT	00:04:14
D	004W		: :
C	081	ETA	08:59:00

Leg *4*

42-21.120N = 042° 21'07"N
071-00.250W = 071°00'15" W

Dist: *0.683* nm Speed *12.5* kts.

60 x D = S x T

$$\frac{60 \times 0.683}{12.5} = \frac{12.5 \times T}{12.5} = 3.2784$$

0.2784 × 60 = 17 3m 17s

T	230	DEP	12:21:00
V	009W	TURN	00:00:00
M	239	TOT	00:03:17
D	004W		: :
C	243	ETA	12:24:17

Leg *5* WPT #15 042° 20'05"N /071°00'12"W

Dist: *0.833* nm Speed *6.0* kts.

60 x D = S x T

$$\frac{60 \times 0.833}{6.0} = \frac{6.0 \times T}{6.0} = 8.33$$

0.33 × 60 = 19.8 OR 20s 8m 20s

T	136	DEP	12:40:00
V	009W	TURN	00:00:00
M	145	TOT	00:08:20
D	004E		: :
C	141	ETA	12:48:20

Leg *6* WPT #13 042° 20'00"N / 071°00'43"W

Dist: *0.400* nm Speed *6.0* kts.

60 x D = S x T

$$\frac{60 \times 0.400}{6} = \frac{6 \times T}{6} = 4.0m$$

T	257	DEP	12:48:20
V	009W	TURN	00:00:06
M	266	TOT	00:04:00
D	003E		: :
C	263	ETA	12:52:26

Figure 10.1 Completed Navigation Worksheet for Navigation Exercise Six
(F. J. Larkin).

TRIP LOG				Date:				Page	1	Boat:	IDYLL TIME	
Leg/ WPT	To	Waypoint	TRUE Heading	DIST nm	SPEED KTS RPM	TOT hr:min:sec	DEP hr:min:sec	Turn Time hr:min:sec	ETA hr:min:sec	COMP Heading	Actual DEP	ETA
Start Point	Fl R 6s "SH" Gong											
LEG 1	Fl G 2.5s "GP" Bell — Off Great Point.		095	0.767	12.50 / 3300	0:03:41	8:45:00	0:00:00	8:48:41	103		
Notes												
LEG 2	Fl R 4s "6" Buoy		309	1.217	12.50 / 3300	0:05:51	8:48:41	0:00:08 PORT	8:54:40	323		
Notes												
LEG 3	Fl G 4s Bell — Near Hog Island		068	0.883	12.50 / 3300	0:04:14	8:54:40	0:00:06 STBD	8:59:00	081		
Notes	Fishing for 2 hours.											
LEG 4	Fl R 4s "6"		230	0.683	12.50 / 3300	0:03:17	12:21:00	0:00:00	12:24:17	243		
Notes												
LEG 5	42 20.08N / 071 00.20W	WPT 12	136	0.833	06.00 / 2500	0:08:20	12:40:00	0:00:00	12:48:20	141		
Notes												
LEG 6	42 20.00N / 071 00.72W	WPT 13	257	0.400	06.00 / 2500	0:04:00	12:48:20	0:00:06	12:52:26	263		
Notes												

Figure 10.2   Completed Trip Log for Navigation Exercise Six *(F. J. Larkin).*

Reader Progress Note

By completing this chapter, you have also completed all of the calculations for the six-leg Navigation Exercise. Do you feel more confident? Can you perform all of the calculations correctly without looking at the answer sheets? Would it help for you to replot and calculate the cruise again? Since navigation is a practiced art, the more you practice, the more proficient you will get.

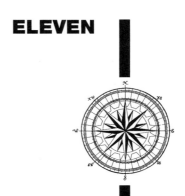

ELEVEN

Taking and Plotting Bearings

NEW TERMINOLOGY

Here are a few new terms with which you must become familiar before tackling bearings.

Heading

A *heading* is the direction in which the bow of your boat is pointed and moving. Headings are expressed in degrees—000 through 360. Figure 11.1 illustrates a heading. A compass heading must be converted to a true course in order to plot it on a nautical chart. Use the conversion formula TVMDC that was explained in Chapter 9 for this purpose.

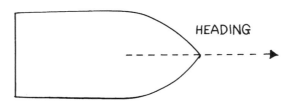

Figure 11.1 Illustration of a heading *(F. J. Larkin).*

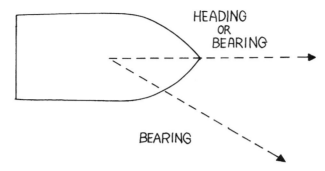

Figure 11.2 Illustration of a bearing *(F. J. Larkin)*.

Bearing

A *bearing* is a line of position—LOP—sighted from your boat to another object. A heading can be a bearing, but a bearing does not always have to be a heading. Figure 11.2 illustrates this concept. Normally, bearings are taken with a hand-held compass or may be taken by aiming the bow of your boat at an object.

When using a hand-held compass, it is good practice to determine if there are any magnetic disturbances in the area where you take the bearing on your boat. Try to find a spot on your boat where there are no magnetic disturbances and use this location when taking bearings from your boat. It makes sense that magnetic influences—deviation error—that affect your boat's compass would also affect a hand-held compass.

Line of Position

The line that you plot on a nautical chart for a bearing is called a *line of position* or LOP. A single LOP tells you that you are located somewhere along the line. Two LOPs from two different objects or targets provide you with a position or location on a chart. Ideally these objects will be 60 to 90 degrees apart from your position. Such a position is termed a *fix*. Your position is said to be where two LOPs intersect. Figure 11.3 illustrates some LOPs. A LOP is labeled with the time when the fix was taken above the plotted line.

Fix

A *fix* is the intersection of two or more plotted lines. An ideal fix contains bearings that intersect at 90-degree angles. Three LOPs define your position more accurately and should have at least 60 degrees between LOPs. The intersecting lines often form a small triangle. Your position is said to be at the center of this triangle. Label a fix with a black dot

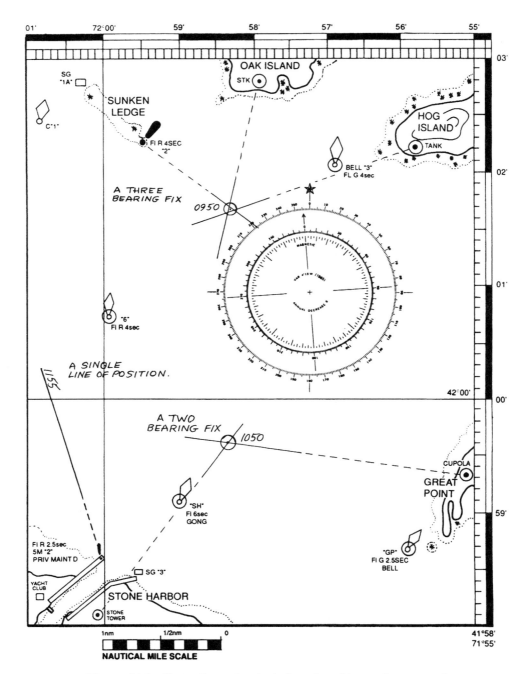

Figure 11.3   Illustrations of a single line of position and a two- and three-bearing fix *(F. J. Larkin).*

surrounded by a circle. Since a fix is considered a high-quality position, write the time when the fix was taken horizontally to the circled dot.

From a practical aspect, there are simpler ways to obtain a fix, which is needed at the beginning of every DR plot. First, every aid to navigation is considered a fix. No bearings need to be taken when you are close aboard an aid to navigation. By virtue of your proximity, you have a fix. Your GPS also provides accurate fix data in reduced visibility as long as it is calibrated correctly. Radar is another good tool for taking fixes when used with a current nautical chart. If there is enough visibility to take bearings, you should be able to see the aids to navigation and use them for fixes. With all of the other means available, in most cases, you can avoid having to take manual bearings to fix your position.

Beam Bearing

A *beam bearing* is a line sighted from your boat to an object located at a 90-degree angle from your boat's heading. Beam bearings are easy to take and are a quick method for verifying the progress of your boat along your DR line. Figure 11.4 shows a beam bearing.

Plan for many beam bearings targets along your DR course line as a check on your progress and position. Unlike regular bearings, beam bearings are plotted directly from the DR course line at a 90-degree angle to the object. This position is considered of higher quality than a DR plot and is called an *estimated position*—EP. Label an EP with a black dot surrounded by a square. Figure 11.5 illustrates the proper labeling for a beam bearing. EP positions are commonly associated with positions that are corrected for current.

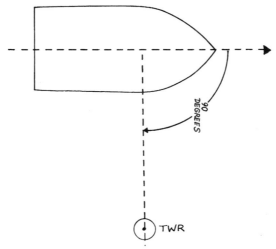

Figure 11.4   An illustration of a beam bearing *(F. J. Larkin).*

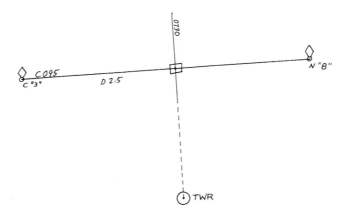

Figure 11.5   Labeling an estimated position based on a beam bearing
(F. J. Larkin).

TAKING BEARINGS

Bearings are always taken to fixed, surveyed, and charted objects that are printed on a nautical chart. The best objects are identified with the chart symbol of a circle with a center dot. Floating aids to navigation, while not as accurate as a fixed object, are useful for taking bearings. Use a hand-held compass or the boat's compass to take bearings. With the exception of beam bearings, bearings are plotted *back from* the charted object. The logic is that the object is positioned on the nautical chart and your boat is not.

To plot a bearing on a nautical chart, you must first convert it to true. Use the TVMDC formula explained in Chapter 9 to complete this conversion. Here is a simple procedure that should help you understand the process:

Step 1.   Take a bearing from your boat to a charted object using a hand-held compass. Record the angle—i.e., 020 degrees.

Step 2.   Convert the bearing to true using the TVMDC formula. Assume there is no deviation in the location on your boat where the bearing was taken. The variation is 016 W.

T	004	(020 – 016 = 004)
V	016 W	From nearest compass rose
M	020	Bearing with hand-held compass
D	000	
C	020	

Here is how it worked:

- The compass course is the bearing that you read on your hand-held compass.

- There was no deviation because you stood on a location on your boat where there was no deviation error. If you use the boat's compass to take the bearing, use the deviation from your boat's deviation table.

- Variation is taken from the nearest compass rose.

- Because you are moving from compass to true, you move up the conversion formula (CDMVT instead of TVMDC) and subtract westerly error and add easterly error.

Step 3. Calculate the reciprocal (opposite) angle of your bearing by adding or subtracting 180 degrees.

True bearing		004
Plus	+	180
Reciprocal true bearing		184

Step 4. Plot the reciprocal bearing back from the charted object on the nautical chart. Your position is located somewhere along this LOP.

LABELING BEARING LOPS

As mentioned above, a single bearing that crosses a DR course line is considered an EP—an estimated position. Label it with a black dot surrounded with a square. Bearing LOPs are often drawn with a dashed line. The time when you took the bearing is written using four-digit 24-hour clock time above the plotted LOP. The true bearing from the object can be written under the LOP using three digits. The figures in this chapter illustrate the proper labeling for bearings.

RELATIVE BEARINGS

A relative bearing is a line sighted from your boat to another object in relationship to the compass heading of your boat. The bearing shown in Figure 11.2 is a relative bearing. Relative bearings are taken with a pelorus, which most small boaters do not own. However, you can perform a few good tricks with relative bearings by marking angles on your bow rails. Place a mark on your bow rails at 045, 090, 270, and 315 degrees. This will allow you to take beam bearings and doubling-the-angle-on-the-bow bearings while sitting at your helm.

DOUBLING THE ANGLE ON THE BOW

Doubling the angle on the bow is a quick and easy technique for determining your distance off a fixed-charted object. Here is a quick method for performing this navigation operation:

Step 1. As you cruise along the coast on your DR course line, pick out a fixed-charted object on the shore.

- Take a bearing using the 45-degree bow rail mark.

- Record the time of the bearing.

Step 2. Continue along your planned DR course line until the charted object is abeam.

- Use the 090-degree mark for determining when you are abeam.

- Record the time of the beam bearing.

Step 3. Using the DR formula, $60 \times D = S \times T$, which, of course, assumes you know your boat's speed, calculate the distance run. The distance run is equal to the distance off the fixed-charted object.

Step 4. Draw a LOP from your DR line to the object.

Step 5. Measure back from the object toward the DR course line using the distance computed in step 3. This point is considered your estimated position, which is of a higher quality than your DR position. Continue plotting your cruise from this new EP position. If you find that you have a wide discrepancy from your DR position, you may want to question your speed curve unless you can explain the difference with other phenomena such as the action of wind, waves, or current.

Figure 11.6 illustrates a relative bearing and the doubling-the-angle-on-the-bow technique.

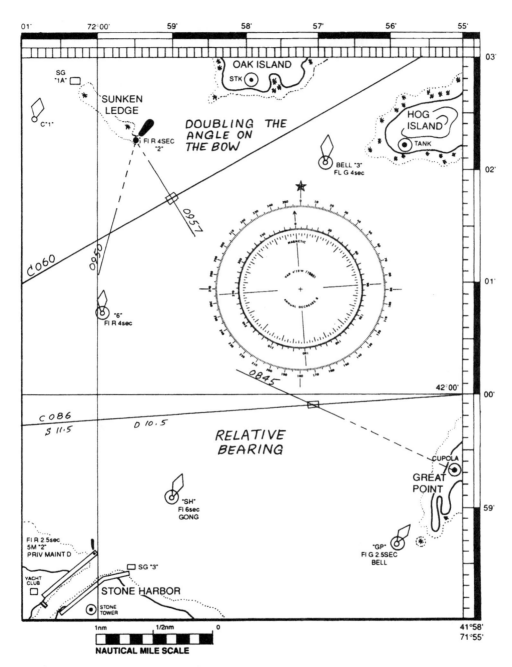

Figure 11.6 A relative bearing and an illustration of doubling the angle on the bow *(F. J. Larkin).*

> GPS NOTE: *If your boat is tracking on a GPS route, you never need to take bearings. Simply plot the LAT/LON readout from the GPS display. Taking bearings is only necessary when you let the batteries in your GPS run low and you haven't packed away any spares for such an emergency. To avoid the battery problem, always buy a GPS that can be plugged into the direct current on your boat.*

DANGER BEARINGS

When there is an obstruction near your course line, some great techniques are available to help you stay clear of it. First, you can actually plot the obstruction as a waypoint. When you get near it, use the GOTO key on your GPS to that waypoint. Your GPS will immediately begin telling you the heading and the DTG—Distance to Go—to the obstruction. Use this information to steer clear and stay safe.

Another technique is to plot a line back from the waypoint on the leg where the obstruction is located to the obstruction—i.e., your course heading is 060 degrees and the LOP from the obstruction to the same waypoint is 020 degrees allowing some room for safety. Make note of this danger bearing in your Trip Log—i.e., NLT (no less than) 020 deg. Now, while transiting this leg, if the elements push you to starboard so that your compass approaches 020 degrees, you will know enough to make a large correction to port or else you could strike the obstruction. This is another good reason to pay close attention to your compass when operating a boat and keep it on course. Don't let yourself be distracted. Figure 11.7 illustrates this technique.

Danger bearings can be written on charts in a manner similar to the technique explained above. However, unlike with the GPS, the waypoint must be visible to the eye for the danger bearing to work effectively.

Reader Study Note

You always have the option of using three distinct positioning techniques: a DR position, an estimated position, and a fix. Study these positioning techniques carefully until you acquire an appreciation of the utility of each technique. Also, be aware that the elements are constantly affecting your course and position. Prudent mariners continuously verify and recheck their positions in order to maintain accurate headings. Make full use of all of the alarms provided on your GPS set. Check your GPS operating manual for the availability of these

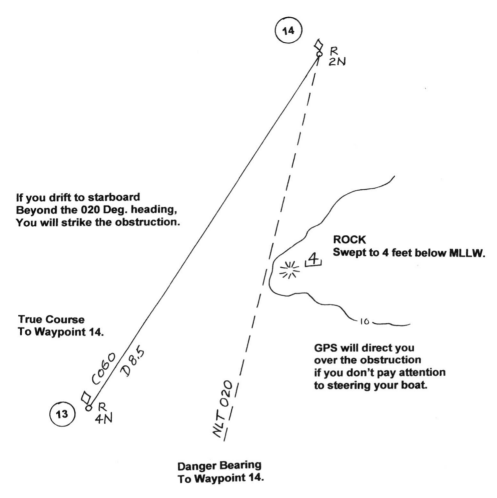

Figure 11.7   Illustration of the danger bearing technique *(F. J. Larkin).*

alarms on your set and for the procedure for setting them. Use every tool that you have to keep yourself and your guests safe while under way on your boat.

Reader Progress Note

By now you should have a good understanding of dead reckoning and be able to plot a course, convert it for use on your compass, and track it between buoys while under way. You should also be able to prepare a Trip Log.

REVIEW QUESTIONS

11.1   The direction in which your boat's bow is pointing is called a _____.

11.2   True or false: A compass heading can be plotted directly on a nautical chart. _____

11.3   Bearings are taken to _____ and _____ objects.

11.4   A bearing, plotted on a chart, indicates that your boat is _____ _____ along the LOP.

11.5   Another name for a bearing is a _____ or LOP.

11.6   The intersection of _____ or more _____ or bearings is called a fix.

11.7   A _____ _____ is a line sighted at a 90-degree angle from your boat's heading.

11.8   When doubling the angle on the bow, the _____ run is equal to the _____ from the object.

11.9   A _____ _____ is a line sighted from your boat to another object in relationship to your boat's _____ _____.

11.10   Relative bearings are usually taken with an instrument called a _____.

11.11   You should have a _____ chart aboard your boat that is corrected with the latest _____ _____ ___ _____ information.

11.12   A fix is labeled with a position dot surrounded by a _____.

11.13   A beam bearing is considered an _____ and is labeled with a position dot surrounded by a square.

11.14   A DR position is labeled with a position dot and a _____.

ANSWERS

11.1   The direction in which your boat's bow is pointing is called a HEADING.

11.2   FALSE. A compass heading must be converted to true before it can be plotted directly on a nautical chart.

11.3   Bearings are taken to FIXED and CHARTED objects.

11.4   A bearing, plotted on a chart, indicates that your boat is LOCATED SOMEWHERE along the LOP.

11.5   Another name for a bearing is a LINE OF POSITION or LOP.

11.6   The intersection of TWO or more LOPs or bearings is called a fix.

11.7   A BEAM BEARING is a line sighted at a 90-degree angle from your boat's heading.

11.8   When doubling the angle on the bow, the DISTANCE run is equal to the DISTANCE from the object.

11.9   A RELATIVE BEARING is a line sighted from your boat to another object in relationship to your boat's COMPASS HEADING.

11.10   Relative bearings are usually taken with an instrument called a PELORUS.

11.11   You should have a NAUTICAL chart aboard your boat that is corrected with the latest LOCAL NOTICE TO MARINERS information.

11.12   A fix is labeled with a position dot surrounded by a CIRCLE.

11.13   A beam bearing is considered an EP and is labeled with a position dot surrounded by a square

11.14   A DR position is labeled with a position dot and a SEMICIRCLE.

TWELVE

How to Use a GPS Navigation System on a Small Boat

Without getting into many technical details, GPS is operated from 24 orbiting satellites that are continuously rising and setting overhead. These satellites are positioned so that we receive signals from 6 of them nearly 100 percent of the time, which provides excellent position information to our GPS set. Satellites are equipped with precision clocks that keep time to within 3 nanoseconds—or three billionths of a second.

LORAN systems operate from land-based stations. If you are making a decision about what type of electronic navigation system to buy for coastal navigation, the answer is simple: Buy a GPS set. However, if you own a late-model LORAN, don't throw it away. As long as the Coast Guard supports this navigation system, continue to use your LORAN, especially if you have a lot of verified waypoints and routes in its database.

In general, I find that LORAN is a simpler system to operate, basically because it doesn't have all of the bells and whistles that you find on a GPS set and because LORAN sets have bigger keys and more of them. Theoretically, from a repeatable accuracy viewpoint, LORAN is more accurate than GPS. The ability of an electronic navigation system to return you to a location (waypoint) that you verified by actually visiting the position is called *repeatable accuracy*. But, lately this accuracy argument has been favoring the GPS side, as new technology is developed and made available on the latest GPS sets. No such development is being focused on LORAN.

The purpose of this chapter is to help you simplify the use of your GPS set and to greatly increase its effectiveness as a quality and accurate navigation tool.

THE QUESTION OF ACCURACY: SELECTIVE AVAILABILITY

Selective availability (SA) is a term used to describe a transmission error that can be built into the GPS satellite signal output. Because the selective availability error has been shut off, any standard GPS set will position you within a 25- to 35-meter target circle 98 percent of the time. That's the equivalent of having your boat in the middle of a football gridiron with you looking for the goal posts. A more capable type of GPS set, a Differential Global Positioning System (DGPS) set, doubles your investment but drops the error to a 30-foot circle, putting your position inside the footprint of a normal small boat.

Newer GPS sets provide additional accuracy capability called *wide-angle augmentation system* (WAAS), which was developed to provide precision guidance for aircraft. WAAS takes GPS sets to a higher level of accuracy. I have experienced accuracy to within six to eight feet using WAAS in Boston Harbor. With WAAS, your GPS advises you of the level of accuracy that it is attaining—which is another great GPS feature. When you buy your next GPS set, be sure that it has WAAS capability.

THINGS TO CONSIDER WHEN BUYING A GPS SET

Intended Use

When you get ready to buy a GPS unit, consider the worst case scenario under which it will be used. If it is difficult to use the set in the calm atmosphere of a dealer's showroom, imagine what it will be like in stormy conditions when waves are beating against your hull, your boat is bouncing back and forth, and the windshield is covered with salt spray. In these conditions, you will not be able to let go of the helm without losing control of the boat and you certainly will not be able to key data into a GPS set or read a small-size screen. A GPS set with a large navigation display is your best bet.

Let's look now at some other important features you should consider.

Mounting Capability

Your GPS should be mounted near the steering station (helm) rather than just laying the set somewhere on the dashboard. Your GPS set should come with a mounting system or be compatible with stock mounts. I also recommend that the mount have a swivel capability both to adjust the position of the screen up and down to get rid of glare and to be able to swing the face of the GPS left or right so that a second person can read it if necessary in stormy conditions. I notice that many GPS screens can only be viewed directly from the front.

When mounting a GPS set near your compass, don't forget its magnetic impact on the accuracy of your compass. Most sets will affect your compass. As mentioned in an earlier chapter, the benefit of having an electronic compass is that they have a compensation feature that eliminates deviation error—magnetic influence near your compass. The accuracy of your compass should never be compromised. Your dilemma is to get your GPS set positioned as closely as possible to your helm so you can clearly view the display, while at the same time not changing the accuracy of your compass, which you need for steering your boat. A GPS is not a compass. However, many GPS manufacturers are starting to bundle an electronic compass into the newer GPS sets.

Be sensitive to the potential distraction factor that a GPS set can present to a boat operator. The operator must maintain a continuous view of the area and the other boats operating in the area. Looking at a GPS or computerized chart display can easily compromise this need. For safety's sake, you should keep your GPS display close to your helm in a position that doesn't require the user/operator to look away from the surrounding area where the boat is transiting.

Screen Size

Screen size will be dictated by economics. You want a screen that has a large enough display that can easily be read, keeping the worst case scenario in mind. Older boat operators with bifocals may find it difficult to view the smaller screens found on many GPS sets. Also, many larger screens use tiny letters and numbers. Some sets sacrifice the readability of the navigation data—headings, speed, time, etc.—in order to provide more chart area on their screens. You will not be able to lean over and focus your eyes on a small GPS screen while trying to keep your eyes on the waves that are rushing at your boat. Take a quick look at the screen graphic shown later in Figure 12.14 and note how the navigation data is displayed at the top of the screen. Even on this screen, you can see how this data is confusing to read. Imagine the difficulty you would have in a heavy wave and wind situation.

For a practical demonstration of the problem, hold a GPS set at about an arm's length and jump up and down. If you can still read the display, buy the set. (Also, by now, you should be drawing the conclusion that more than one person on your boat should be trained in navigation and seamanship. In stormy situations, steering and navigation must be performed by at least two persons who switch off periodically to avoid becoming exhausted.)

Waterproof versus Submergible

Waterproof means that the device will generally survive a little dampness. Submergible means that the device will survive a dunking in the ocean. If you have a small open boat, water will get on the GPS set. Although nothing is ever waterproof when exposed to extensive soaking, opt for the submergible label and always store your GPS set in a dry area when you are not using your boat.

Display Lighting

Buy a GPS set that has a backlit display so that you can view it at night and during periods of reduced visibility. Avoid bright white lights at night because they destroy your night sight. Color displays are easier to read than black and white but are much more expensive. From the other aspect, your GPS screen has to be visible in bright sunlight, which means that it always must display a clear image and reflect glare from bright sunlight. Have the dealer place a bright light behind the GPS set to simulate the sun. Check whether you can read the data on the GPS display. Most black-and-white sets are almost impossible to read and interpret when the sun is shining brightly behind the set. Try viewing the screen when the bright light is shining in your eyes. If you can't distinguish the data on the screen, don't buy the set. Because GPS sets need direct access to the satellites, for those sets that do not have a remote antenna, there is a good chance they will be in direct sunlight on your boat.

Access to Your Boat's Electrical System

Don't buy a GPS that does not come with a power cord that can be plugged into your boat's 12-volt electrical system. Also, your GPS set should have a battery backup system. There is nothing worse than losing GPS navigation capability in the middle of a harrowing navigation situation. To use waypoints and routes for navigating your boat, the GPS set has to be in continuous operation. Some portable sets have a specific procedure and time limit for changing batteries. Learn and follow this procedure so that you don't lose data when you change batteries, and always keep spare batteries aboard your boat.

Keyboard and Key Size

Keyboard size is becoming a problem on many GPS sets. Because many sets are designed for automotive usage, waypoint navigation is not a problem and, as a result, the numeric keys are being eliminated on these sets. For proper coastal navigation, you need to use waypoints and routes. Therefore, you want the ability to easily enter these waypoints. Waypoints can be entered into GPS sets in many different ways:

1. Actually keying the data into a waypoint list. Many low-end and portable sets no longer provide this option. This is a desirable and convenient GPS feature.

2. Using a cursor on a chart display screen. GPS sets with chart displays offer this feature.

3. Actually visiting the waypoint with your boat and recording the waypoint. This is called *verifying a waypoint.* I recommend that you verify every waypoint that you enter into your GPS set.

4. Using a remote computer to enter data into your GPS set.

Key size can also be a problem. It is becoming difficult at best to enter data on some sets without striking double keys or the wrong key. On some sets, you are instructed to hold one key down while data is entered with another key. Being able to enter data in such a way in stormy conditions may be virtually impossible. Try the jumping up and down exercise again and see how difficult it can be to enter accurate data in the GPS set. This condition is certainly a positive argument for entering waypoints and routes in advance.

By now, you should be getting an appreciation for the use of LAT/LON data as waypoints in an effective GPS system plan. Therefore, buy sets with larger keys, numeric keys, and simple data input menus. Read the operating manual to determine how many keystrokes are required for entering data in a set. Choose the simpler systems. Unfortunately, you may have to trade off features against price when considering the GPS sets being offered today. To minimize your investment in electronic navigation equipment, you may need to select the option of preplanning your trips back in port in calm conditions so that you will need only a minimal interaction with your GPS set while under way. This is obviously the most economic approach.

Used GPS Set and Processor Size

The age of a GPS set is important due to the rapid advancement of GPS technology. If you're considering buying a used GPS, note that older GPS sets have smaller computing capability and may be slow to initialize and process data. When searching for a set, pay more money for increased processing power rather than for bells and whistles. The faster processing sets deliver more accurate navigation data sooner. Most of the numbers delivered by a GPS are averages or means—that is, they use older data to project the future. The faster a GPS set processes data, the sooner this average or mean will reflect reality. Good sets reprocess positions at least once per second. Older sets may reprocess every 20 to 30 seconds.

As mentioned earlier, besides the obvious slowness that you may experience with an older set and the lack of some navigation features, you should have the opportunity to operate the set before you buy it and, perhaps, get a little free instruction about its operation from the previous owner. Never buy any set without its operating manual.

Many older GPS sets have memory batteries that are hard wired to a PC memory board. The shelf life on these batteries is three to five years. You may not be able to get this battery replaced.

The best price for a used set is free. Avoid sets that just provide LAT/LON data. With the ever-decreasing prices for new sets with their advanced technology and performance, it makes sense to buy new. Shop around for the best price but don't scrimp on the navigational features and capabilities.

Chart Plotter Capability

If you want chart-plotting capability, the cost of your GPS will be increased considerably. You have two display options—black and white and color. Color sets are on the high end of the price scale, but I have two basic problems with black-and-white sets:

1. They are very difficult to view when they are installed in a sunny place near the helm of your boat. Color is a definite plus for resolving this problem. If you can keep the black-and-white display out of well-lighted areas, however, it should work fine.

2. In an effort to provide more space to display nautical charts on the screen, the navigational data readouts are kept very small and very difficult to read from any distance from the display. This is also true for color sets but the color enhances the readability.

Gazing at a GPS chart display in order to check your position continuously is not a safe boating practice. On busy boating days, it can become a very dangerous practice. As the helmsperson, you must keep an eye on all of the boating traffic as you keep the boat on its course. The prudent operator uses a trip log for steering information and a compass for direction—not the GPS.

If you are able to plot courses on a chart and enter waypoints and routes into a GPS or LORAN, you really do not need chart-plotting capability. The GPS navigation screens show you all of the information that you need to know to navigate safely and you have a paper nautical chart backup for quick reference. Paper charts are not problem to read in the bright sun!

Display Clutter

Too much information displayed on a screen is what I call *clutter.* This problem is especially true of GPS sets with chart displays. As you focus in on a single area, the data presented on the GPS screen can become very confusing. Often, you have to adjust your screen or chart attributes to eliminate some of this data, such as depths or aids to navigation. What you eliminate in a large-detail screen, you lose in the small-scale views where you need it.

Screen Capabilities

The ease of switching from one screen to another is as important as the data that is presented on the various navigation screens that a GPS set offers. When buying, look at a few select screens that provide the most important navigational data and make sure the data is presented in a clear and readable manner. You shouldn't have to jump around a series of screens in order to view basic navigation output. This also applies to data entry screens. On the low-end GPS models you have less of a choice, if any.

Minimize your dependency on a GPS screen and focus your attention on the handling and safety of your boat. Save your money. Preplot your courses on a nautical chart and prepare a trip log. Steer your boat by your compass. Use your current nautical chart for referencing obstructions and shoals, plotting your course, and referencing your waypoints and routes. Use your GPS as the quality control check for this process.

Remote Antenna Capability

GPS sets need a clear view of the satellites in order to operate. Be alert to the visual and audible alarms provided by your GPS when it loses navigation accuracy. This problem can be caused by operating near tall buildings, large structures, bridges, or under the overhead cover in your helm area where your GPS is mounted. A remote antenna installation will resolve this problem. Be sure that your GPS has remote antenna capability before you buy it.

Multiplexing versus Parallel GPS Receivers

Multiplexed receivers have a few—sometimes only one—channels. This means that they tune in satellites one at a time. Parallel GPS receivers acquire and process several satellites simultaneously. They come in 3-, 5-, 8-, and 12-channel versions, which means more accurate processing and quicker start-up. Buy a parallel receiver.

GPS Sensor Design

GPS sensor capability provides navigational data interfaces to other navigational equipment, such as radar, chart plotters, and depth sounders. Trends appear to be heading toward bundled navigation systems that combine many different features and functions. Not all sensors are compatible with other manufacturers' equipment despite their claims. The standard interface is NNME—National Marine Electronics Association. It is often best to buy all of your navigational equipment from one manufacturer to avoid compatibility problems between different brands.

SETTING UP AND NAVIGATING WITH A TYPICAL GPS SET

Because it is virtually impossible to explain how every different GPS set operates, I have devised a suggested procedure to walk you through the initial phases of getting a GPS set operating correctly in a maritime mode and then using it to navigate your boat. You will find the process is very simple and the navigation techniques are easy to use. Here are a few suggestions to get you started:

1. Always keep your GPS operating manual handy so you can find the specific instructions for a particular GPS function.

2. Take your time and practice the GPS functions as they are explained in this chapter on your own GPS. *Practice* is the keyword to gaining GPS proficiency.

3. Do not digress from this process. Do not jump ahead. Stay with the step-by-step procedure as it is described. Do not

become distracted by the other nice-to-have features that may be available on your GPS set. If your GPS does not have a feature that is being explained, simply move on to the next step.

4.   Write procedures to help you operate your own GPS set as you are introduced to different data displays and screens. Procedures are a great learning aid for a GPS user since it often takes a while to become familiar with and memorize the menus and displays available with your set. Keep your GPS procedures on your boat next to your GPS—ready for quick reference. Most people will have to go through a familiarization process each spring after a winter layoff. Don't guess. Save time by following your tested procedures.

Phase One: Familiarization and Setup

Turning On Your GPS Set.   Check your GPS operating manual for the proper method for turning on your GPS. Read about data acquisition and learn to recognize when your set is ready to provide accurate navigation data.

Getting Acquainted with the GPS Keyboard.   While you are just starting to learn the functions of a new GPS, keep a copy of the "Quick Guide" beside your set. Quick Guides or similar publications are usually provided with or part of the operating manual. Don't expect to remember all of the key functions right away. It will be necessary to look them up for a period of time and a Quick Guide is often a handy reference document. Figure 12.1 shows a sample Quick Guide card, and Figure 12.2 shows a Quick Guide menu list card. Cards like this provide you with a quick reference to the functions that you need to master the operation of your GPS.

If your GPS set does not come with a Quick Card, develop your own keyboard procedure for your GPS set. Just by performing this exercise, you will gain a clearer understanding of the functions available with your GPS and you will start to familiarize yourself with any operating peculiarities. Most GPS sets do pretty much the same thing. Your problem will be to discover whether your set has a certain function and just how your set performs that function. Figure 12.3 shows a home-made "Quick Guide" procedure card that explains the typical keyboard layout for a GPS set.

Quick Guide

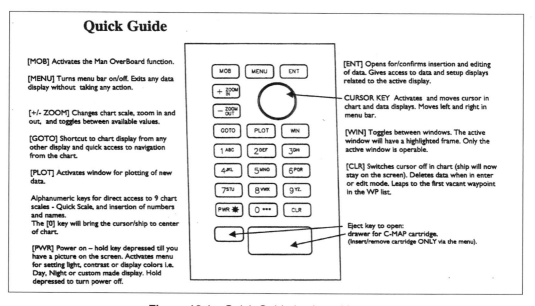

[MOB] Activates the Man OverBoard function.

[MENU] Turns menu bar on/off. Exits any data display without taking any action.

[+/- ZOOM] Changes chart scale, zoom in and out, and toggles between available values.

[GOTO] Shortcut to chart display from any other display and quick access to navigation from the chart.

[PLOT] Activates window for plotting of new data.

Alphanumeric keys for direct access to 9 chart scales - Quick Scale, and insertion of numbers and names.
The [0] key will bring the cursor/ship to center of chart.

[PWR] Power on – hold key depressed till you have a picture on the screen. Activates menu for setting light, contrast or display colors i.e. Day, Night or custom made display. Hold depressed to turn power off.

[ENT] Opens for/confirms insertion and editing of data. Gives access to data and setup displays related to the active display.

CURSOR KEY Activates and moves cursor in chart and data displays. Moves left and right in menu bar.

[WIN] Toggles between windows. The active window will have a highlighted frame. Only the active window is operable.

[CLR] Switches cursor off in chart (ship will now stay on the screen). Deletes data when in enter or edit mode. Leaps to the first vacant waypoint in the WP list.

Eject key to open:
drawer for C-MAP cartridge.
(Insert/remove cartridge ONLY via the menu).

Figure 12.1   Quick Guide keyboard layout.

MENU
Press the [MENU] key to toggle the menu on/off. The individual menus are selected by keying the number next to the menu name or by using the multi-direction cursor key to highlight the menu, and pressing [ENT].

C-MAP cartridge (standby)
Press [MENU], [1], [2] whenever inserting or removing a cartridge.

Chart orientation
1. Press [MENU], [1], [5] to load Chart setup 2.
2. Move cursor to 'Orientation', and use +/- keys to toggle between NORTH UP, HEAD UP and NAV UP.
3. Move cursor to 'Motion', and toggle between TRUE or RELATIVE.
☞ The cursor must be turned off (press [CLR] from chart display) to enable chart rotation.

Navigate to cursor
- point and go.
1. Press [GOTO] to load chart in display.
2. Place cursor on the destination where you want to go.
3. Press [GOTO] and [ENT].
A course line will be drawn from

actual position (ship's position) to destination (cursor's position).
Press [MENU], [4], [1] to call up the graphical steering display with all relevant information: course over ground, bearing, speed over ground and distance to waypoint, etc.

Make route by waypoint plots
1. Press [GOTO] to load chart in display.
2. Place cursor on the position for the first waypoint.
3. Press [PLOT], [3] Make route.
4. Move cursor to next destination, and press [PLOT], etc. etc.
5. Press [ENT] when ready to save the route.
6. You can give the route a name, or choose a different route number than the one suggested.
7. Press [ENT] to store the route in the memory.

Route navigation
1. Press[GOTO], [3] from chart display.
2. Key in route number
3. Move around in display with cursor key, and change values with +/- key e.g. forward or reverse direction in route.
4. Press [ENT] to start navigating.

5. A graphical steering display ([MENU], [4],[1]) will provide all relevant information to use for navigation.

Advance or stop navigation
• Press [GOTO], select 'Waypoint advance'.
• Press [GOTO], select 'Turn NAV OFF'.

Plot ship's position as WP
1. Press [PLOT] from chart display (cursor should be off [CLR]), or press [PLOT] from any other display.
2. Press 1 to plot and save the ship's position as a waypoint, or...
3. Press 2 to plot the ship's position as a waypoint with name, etc.
4. Press the alphanumerical keys to key in a name, move back and forth with cursor key.
5. Press [ENT] to save the waypoint in the WP list.

Plot cursor's position as WP
Follow same procedure as for plotting the ship's position, except for point 1, which should be:
1. Place cursor on the position you wish to plot as a waypoint and press [PLOT].
Continue with point 2 to 5.

Delete mark/waypoint
1. Press [GOTO] to load chart in display.
2. Place cursor on mark/waypoint.
3. Press [ENT], [GOTO] to open for editing.
4. Press [CLR], [CLR] to delete mark/waypoint.

Delete mark/waypoint via the WPlist:
1. Press [MENU], [3], [1] to load Waypoint list.
2. Key in WP no. or scroll through the list by means of the +/- keys.
3. Press [ENT] to open for editing.
4. Press [CLR], [ENT] to delete waypoint.

Dual speed display
Dynamic and steady speed readout Press [MENU] [2] [3].

Information on chart objects
1. Place cursor on C-MAP object (light, buoy, etc.) or own recordings (mark, waypoint, etc.), and press [ENT].
2. Repeat pressing [ENT] to scroll through all available information.
3. Press [CLR] or move cursor to exit.

Figure 12.2   Sample Quick Guide menu list.

Key	Key Function
+ / −	Either the Plus or Minus key may be applied.
0–9	Numeric keys used for the entry of numbers. Inserts and selects data in data displays. Keys 1 thru 9 are also Quick Scales that select fixed chart scales in the chart display. Key 0 centers the cursor or your boat's position in the center in a display.
A–Z	Alpha keys for the insertion of letters. Inserts and selects data in data displays.
ENT	Turns the cursor on or off. Opens for/confirms insertion on marks, waypoints, etc., on the chart.
MENU	Turns the Menu Bar on and off. Exits any data display without taking action.
MOB	Press this key for two seconds to activate the Man Overboard function.
+ Zoom In	Zoom in to see more charted details—smaller scale chart. + and − toggle between available values on the screen.
− Zoom Out	Zooms out to see a larger overview of the chart—a larger scale chart. + and − toggle between available values on the chart.
O	Cursor key—Use the multidirectional cursor key to move around the menus, displays, and charts. Activates the cursor on the chart.
GOTO	Activates pop-up window "Select NAV mode."
PLOT	Activates pop-up window "Select PLOT mode."
WIN	Toggles between four preselected windows. Hold for two seconds for automatic rotation of the preselected displays. Press WIN to return to manual operation.
CLR	Turns off the Menu Bar. Turns off the Cursor. Deletes data. Leaps to first vacant waypoint position in your waypoint list.
PWR	Turns the GPS program on. Calls up an info window where you can adjust light/contrast for the screen and the background light on the keypad. Adjusts contrast on black-and-white sets. Turns the GPS program off.

Figure 12.3   Typical "homemade" keyboard orientation procedure.

> GPS TASK 1: *Review the keyboard functions for your GPS set. If you do not have a Quick Card, prepare one by reviewing your set's operating manual. Compare your keyboard procedure with the procedure shown in Figure 12.3 so that you don't miss any functions.*

Unit of Measure Definitions. To make your GPS operate accurately, you will need to make a series of important decisions that define the units that your GPS will use to perform its calculations. Your GPS data output must reflect a maritime environment. Figure 12.4 shows a typical GPS display screen that allows you to record a series of decisions about the units of measure the GPS will use. Table 12.1 provides an explanation and commentary on each of these decision fields. The decisions shown in this display are considered one-time decisions because they are made once when you first set up your GPS and do not have to be changed unless you decide to do so.

Units of Measure

Setup for Units

Depth/Altitude in: FEET
Distance in: NAUTICAL MILES
Speed in: KNOTS
Temperature in: FAHRENHEIT
Software Version: XXXXXXXXXXXX
WIN Change Interval: 05 sec MANUAL
Display Text in: ENGLISH (US)

Figure 12.4   Units of measure setup screen.

> GPS TASK 2: *Check your GPS operating manual and set all of the unit of measure parameters so that your GPS set is ready for navigation in a marine environment. Use the following checklist:*

Check		Date Entered	Parameter
	Depth		
	Distance		
	Speed		
	Temperature		
	Text		

Table 12.1   Explanation of the Options Shown in Figure 12.4

Option	Functionality of Option
Depth/Altitude In:	Defines any interface with a depth sounder or altimeter. Must reflect feet rather than meters but actually depends on the nautical chart that you are using. If you have a chart display feature on your GPS, be sure that if the chart program doesn't update this unit of measure automatically, you do it manually.
Distance In:	Distances must be calculated in nautical miles, rather than statute miles, which would be proper if you were using your GPS in a motor vehicle. Many portable GPS sets come preset to statute miles.
Speed In:	Speeds must be calculated in knots—nautical miles per hour—rather than MPH or KPH. Many portable GPS sets come preset to MPH—statute miles per hour.
Temperature In:	Defines how temperatures will be reported for any interface with depth sounders that provide surface temperature of the water. Fahrenheit and centigrade are typical options.
Software Version:	The revision of the GPS software used on your GPS appears here. Check your GPS operating manual for software options. This feature is often updated automatically when the software is loaded into your GPS set.
WIN Change Interval:	Shows the time interval at which the preselected window or display is presented. Check your operating manual for this feature. Many smaller sets may not have this feature.
Display Text In:	Your GPS may have multiple language options. Select "ENGLISH (US)."

Phase Two: Navigation Setup Decisions

A series of decisions regarding chart interfaces and navigation are all necessary when using a GPS. Most of these options have been discussed in previous chapters. Figure 12.5 shows a sample update screen that addresses these decisions. An explanation of each option is given in Table 12.2.

Navigation Setup

Datum000:

Datum Name: World Geodetic System
   1984

Delta Position: 0-00.000N 0-00.000W

Course & Bearings as: TRUE

Navigation Mode: RHUMBLINE

Auto Waypoint Shift: WP-line

WP Circle Alarm: ON 0.10 nm

XTE Alarm Distance: ON 0.10 nm

Anchor Alarm: OFF 0.10 nm

Figure 12.5   Navigation setup screen.

Table 12.2   Explanation of the Options Shown in Figure 12.5

Option	Functionality of the Option
Datum Name (This refers to horizontal datum. Check your horizontal datum each time you change nautical charts. Horizontal datum is usually printed in the General Information Block on your chart.)	This is a key GPS field. Most GPS sets come preset to the WGS84 Horizontal Datum. As discussed in Chapter 1, you must set the horizontal datum in your GPS to the horizontal datum used by the nautical chart that you are using. If you have a chart plotter on your GPS, the software loading process generally updates the horizontal datum. However, check your operating manual to be certain. Failure to make this match can result in faulty data and position projections by your GPS.
Delta Position (Check your Delta position offset each time you change your nautical chart.)	Some paper charts do not indicate a datum. They contain a notation to an offset or difference (delta) of the chart positions to the WGS84 survey. Load this difference in this field.
Course & Bearings as	Select MAGNETIC or TRUE. If you have an electronic compass, you can choose TRUE when you offset your compass for local variation error. Be sure that your electronic compass is also set to read TRUE.
Navigation Mode	Unless you do your boating on the Great Lakes, select RHUMBLINE. Reference the General Information Block on your nautical chart. If the chart is a Mercator projection, select RHUMBLINE navigation. If your chart is a polyconic projection, select GREAT CIRCLE navigation.
Auto Waypoint Shift (One time update)	In AUTO WAYPOINT mode, the system will automatically shift to the next waypoint in a route after you pass the WP Circle Alarm perimeter. Check your operating manual to be certain how your GPS handles this operation. You should find the answer in the Routes section. If you have this option, use it.
WP Circle Alarm (One time update)	0.01 to 9.99 nm limits are usually available. 0.01 is suggested. Selection of a distance establishes a warning perimeter around each waypoint. When your boat crosses this line, an alarm or action is triggered. Most sets shift and start to display the navigation data for the next leg in the route. This is a desirable navigational feature. Check your operating manual and set this alarm. You should find the instructions in either the Waypoint section or the Alarm section.
XTE Alarm Distance (Cross-track error)	0.01 to 9.99 nm limits are available. 0.01 is suggested. Select whatever distance fits the navigational situation. Sailboats can use this function to set the limits on which to tack the boat. A special navigation display screen is usually available that graphically shows the preset limits and your boat position in relationship to these limits. Many also display your track line. (See Figure 12.26 later in this chapter.)
Anchor Alarm (Set when anchored only)	0.01 to 9.99 nm limits are available. 0.01 is suggested. Use this option when you anchor. When your boat drifts over the preset alarm perimeter, an alarm is tripped. This is a desirable GPS feature.

GPS TASK 3: *Read your GPS operating manual and set all of the navigational features explained above on your GPS set before proceeding to Phase Three. Use the following checklist:*

Check		Date	NAV Feature
	Datum (Horizontal) Name		
	Delta Position		
	Course & Bearings		
	Navigation Mode		
	Auto Waypoint Shift		
	Waypoint Circle Alarm		
	XTE (Cross-Track) Alarm Distance		

Physical GPS Characteristics and Position Data. Your GPS set must be adjusted to reflect the height of your GPS antenna, its starting position, and other interface information. Figure 12.6 presents an example of this screen. Table 12.3 explains the options shown on this screen and Table 12.4 presents a procedure often used in GPS sets for changing the data input on a position setup screen.

Position Setup

Manual Antenna Altitude: 2 m

Altitude Mode: MANUAL

Display Depth in POS Display: YES

DGPS Input Format: RTCM 1.04

DGPS: data 0, max 2, test 1860

Speed and Course Filter Level: 3

Start Position: LAT _____ LON_____

Figure 12.6 Position setup screen.

Table 12.3   Explanation of the Options Shown in Figure 12.6

Option	Functionality of the Option
Manual Antenna Altitude	GPS sets usually come with a preset height of 5 meters or approximately 15 feet. Measure the distance from the waterline to the top of your GPS antenna, convert it to meters, and enter it in this field. If you have a portable GPS, enter the distance from the waterline to the dashboard where you mount the GPS set. Antenna height has an effect on the accuracy of your set. Check the GPS operating manual for instructions on how to set the height for your GPS antenna.
Altitude Mode	Set to MANUAL for boats. Check your GPS operating manual for instructions.
Display Depth	Enter YES if your have an NMEA connection to your depth sounder. Many new GPS sets have a built-in depth sounder.
DGPS Input Format	If you do not have DGPS, leave the factory setting as is. With the selective availability error currently being shut off, a DGPS feature is not really needed on a small boat.
DGPS Speed and Course Filter Level	If you do not have a DGPS, leave the factory setting as is. A 10-step speed and course filter may be provided with your GPS set where 0 = fast response and 9 = stable readings. Check your GPS operating manual for this setting. Remember that the data that you receive from your GPS set is always an average or mean. This selection affects how quickly the averages reflect reality. Read your GPS operating manual carefully on this subject.
Start Position	This entry is commonly initiated by your GPS set when you turn it on. Check your GPS operating manual for any special instructions regarding this feature.

Table 12.4   Typical Procedure for Changing Data Input on a Position Setup Screen

Action	Procedure
ENT	Opens the field for change.
O	Use cursor to go to the function that you wish to change.
+ / – Zoom	Make your selection.
0–9 Keys	Insert figures as needed to make the change.
ENT	Confirm data entry.

GPS TASK 4: *Read your operating manual about position setup and set the parameters for these GPS features if your set provides them. Use the following checklist:*

Check		Date	Position Parameter
	Manual Antenna Altitude		
	Altitude Mode		
	Display Depth		
	DGPS Input Format		
	DGPS		
	Speed and Course Filter Level		

Phase Three: GPS Navigation Validation Process

Before you use any electronic instrument, common sense says that you should check to ensure that it is providing good and accurate data. Each GPS set will have a screen that shows you the status of the satellites that it is currently using. Learn to interpret this data or you can be directed into hazards if your GPS suddenly goes off-line. A blinking screen is a typical warning of a problem. Other sets display a special message when they go off-line.

Figure 12.7 shows a screen that depicts the conditions of the various satellites being used by the GPS set. The status of each satellite is displayed using a code. Check your GPS operating manual for a similar screen, read the explanation for the screen, and review all of the coding symbols so that you are clear about their meaning. This is always good information to include in a GPS procedure. Explanations of the position setup codes and satellite reception codes used in Figure 12.7 are given in Tables 12.5 and 12.6, respectively.

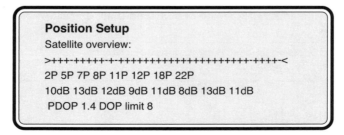

Figure 12.7 Satellite status screen.

**Table 12.5   Explanation of the Position Setup Codes
Used in Figure 12.7**

Symbol	Meaning
+	Satellite is healthy.
−	Satellite is excluded or a nonexisting satellite.
0	Satellite data is faulty.
*	Satellite is manually excluded. You may want to exclude a satellite manually when a particular satellite is disturbing your navigation.
PDOP (Position Dilution of Position)	PDOP is the equivalent of 3D positioning. The values usually stay between 1.3 and 8. The lower the PDOP value, the higher the quality of the position capability of your GPS.
DOP Limit	DOP limit is preset at the factory to 8. When the DOP limit shows an asterisk (*), it causes the position updating capability of your GPS to stop until it is reset within the present limit of 8. The DOP limit can be changed but should not be set higher than 8, at which point poor accuracy and false positions are generated by the GPS set.

**Table 12.6   Explanation of the Satellite Reception Status Codes Used
in Figure 12.7 (Example: 5P, 13dB)**

5	This is the number for the satellite that your GPS set is viewing.
P	Status codes: 　S = Search of satellites 　C = Code lock 　F = Frequency lock 　P = Phase lock Check your GPS operating manual for the codes and their meaning on your GPS set. Include these codes in your homemade procedure manual.
13	Signal-to-noise indicator. Typically it is 18 to 31.
dB	Decibels.

Tables 12.7 and 12.8 list the steps used to exclude or reinstate a satellite, respectively. You may want to exclude a satellite

Table 12.7   Typical Procedure for Excluding a Satellite

ENT	Open for the change.
O	Move the cursor to the left or right to locate the satellite that you want to exclude.
– Zoom Out	The minus key excludes the satellite.
ENT	Confirms the entry.

Table 12.8   Typical Procedure for Reinstating a Satellite

ENT	Open for the change.
O	Move the cursor left or right to locate the satellite that you want to reinstate.
+ Zoom In	The plus key will reinstate the satellite.
ENT	Confirms the entry.

> GPS TASK 5: *Read your GPS operating manual about the verification process provided for your set. Be sure that you understand when your set is operating properly and when it is not. Do not proceed to Phase Four until you have verified that your GPS is producing accurate data.*

Phase Four: Entering Waypoints

A *waypoint* is a position expressed in LAT/LON that is used for navigation in a GPS set. The best objects to use as waypoints are aids to navigation because they provide visual confirmation that coincides with the electronic directions received from your GPS. Sounding aids are great for periods of reduced visibility. Lighted aids are best for nighttime running.

Most GPS sets offer multiple methods for creating and updating waypoints into their memory files:

1. *Manually loading the waypoint coordinates into a data screen.* Some of the smaller sets do not provide this option but offer a cable as an interface to a PC. You can recognize these sets by their lack of number (0–9) keys.

2. *Using the chart cursor.* Obviously you need a good computer chart capability to use this feature effectively. Many low-end sets with charting capability do not provide numeric key functions and this is the sole method for loading waypoints.

3. *Recording the actual LAT/LON at the waypoint site.* You can accomplish this by physically visiting the waypoint's location with your boat and recording the LAT/LON. Most sets offer this feature. This process is called *waypoint verification.*

4. *Remotely entering waypoints with a computer.* You will need special software to accomplish this entry mode. If you are computer literate, you may prefer this mode.

Be sure that you fully understand the various capabilities provided with the GPS set that you are buying. The ease of waypoint entry is an important aspect in the purchasing process for a GPS set since, without waypoints, you will not able to navigate your boat with your GPS.

When using GPS for navigating your boat:

- Think about how the GPS set will operate in the worst case scenario rather than on those quiet idyllic boat trips.

- Keep your waypoint definitions simple for ease of entry and for ease of screen and option selection.

- Always preplan your trips with a paper chart and enter the waypoints into your GPS before you start out to sea.

- Use routes to organize the sequence of when waypoints are used.

- Remember that a GPS set is not a compass. A GPS only reflects events that are in progress. Navigate your boat with a good compass, preferably an electronic compass.

- Reference your paper nautical charts while you are under way.

Entering Waypoint Data Using a Waypoint List.   Every GPS set will have some kind of a waypoint list. Often, there will be a screen that allows you to record waypoints by simply adding them to a list. As I have indicated before, don't just enter waypoints at random. Plan ahead. Check your GPS operating manual to learn whether you can enter waypoints to a listing. A typical procedure for updating waypoints to a list is shown in Figure 12.8.

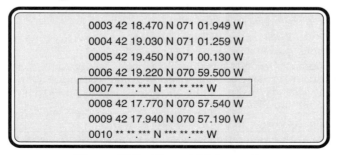

Figure 12.8 Waypoint list screen.

Table 12.9   Typical Procedure for Updating a Waypoint List

MENU	Load Waypoint List. Part of the Waypoint List will be displayed in numerical order. The actual waypoint that you select will be displayed between two horizontal lines. The bottom line indicates how many vacant waypoints are left in your waypoint memory bank.
New WP	Select.
0–9	Key in the waypoint number that you desire—a good reason for keeping waypoint identification simple.
+ / –	Scroll through the Waypoint List to the desired number, or . . .
CLR	The CLR key will place you at the first empty waypoint number. Check your GPS operating manual for such an option.
ENT	Opens the waypoint position for entry of data.
0–9	Insert latitude. A new data entry usually overwrites any existing figures. Enter the letter "N" for North in the Northern Hemisphere. Use "S" in the Southern Hemisphere. Latitude is entered as degrees, minutes, and seconds—fractionalized as minutes. It will look like this: 41 23.417 N *Special Note:* Many government publications and latitude readings taken from nautical charts show latitude as degrees, minutes, and seconds. *Degrees of latitude:* Latitude is normally expressed with three digits as I have explained in earlier chapters. However, when entering latitude into an electronic device, it is expressed as only two digits in order to save file space; that is, 041 degrees is entered as 41. *Seconds:* Seconds are often expressed as fractions of minutes when entered into an electronic device. To make the conversion, simply divide the seconds by 60; that is, 25 seconds equals 25/60, which converts to 0.417 minutes.
0–9	Insert longitude. New data usually overwrites any existing data. Enter the letter "W" for West as a suffix in the Western Hemisphere and "E" in the Eastern Hemisphere. Longitude is entered in degrees, minutes, and seconds—fractionalized as minutes. It will look like this: 071 45.750 W *Special Note:* Many government publications and longitude readings taken from nautical charts show longitude as degrees, minutes, and seconds. *Degrees of longitude:* Unlike latitude, longitude is expressed with three digits; that is, 071 degrees is entered as 071. *Seconds:* Seconds are often expressed as fractions of minutes when entered into an electronic device. To make the conversion, simply divide the seconds by 60; that is, 45 seconds equals 45/60 which converts to 0.750 minutes.
O	Use the cursor to move around the screen.
+ / –	Choose a symbol. This is the symbol that will appear on the chart display as the waypoint.

Table 12.9 continued

	Special Note: I select a unique symbol for identifying waypoints that are not yet verified. Verification is the process of physically visiting the waypoint with my boat and checking the LAT/LON.
A–Z	You can name your waypoint. Remember, "KISS—Keep It Simple, S_____."
+ / –	You can change the color of the symbol.
ENT	Complete the waypoint entry. This action places the waypoint on your Waypoint List.
Excel	Enter the waypoint on your Excel spreadsheet. Figure 12.9 shows an example of an Excel Waypoint List.

WPT	RTE	LL No.	*Waypoint Listing* Description	TRUE HDG	DTG	Latitude Deg Mins	Longitude Deg Mins	Type of Mark
1	1		Float at Dorchester Yacht Club	122	0.233	042 18.31 N	071 03.13 W	Dock
2	1		Morrissey Blvd Bridge	070	0.700	042 18.22 N	071 02.83 W	Outer Bridge Pier - South
3	1	11230	Dor. Bay Lighted Buoy 12	043	0.767	042 18.47 N	071 01.94 W	Lighted Red Buoy
4	1	11210	Dor. Bay Lighted Buoy 5	068	0.917	042 19.03 N	071 01.25 W	Lighted Green Buoy
5	1	11200	Dor. Bay Buoy 3	122	0.383	042 19.45 N	071 00.13 W	Green Can
6	1	11579	Western Way Buoy 9	136	0.967	042 19.22 N	070 59.70 W	Green Can
7	1		Right Pier Long Island Bridge	140	0.983	042 18.52 N	070 58.82 W	Right Pier of Bridge
8	1	11554	Western Way Lighted Buoy 4	073	0.567	042 17.77 N	070 57.94 W	Lighted Red Buoy
9	1	11514	Peddocks Is, Channel Buoy 2P	064	1.020	042 17.94 N	070 57.19 W	Red Nun

Figure 12.9   A sample Excel Waypoint List.

Note that the waypoints shown on the sample Excel Waypoint List in Figure 12.9 match the waypoints that were entered in Figure 12.8, the GPS's Waypoint List screen.

> GPS TASK 6: *Review your GPS operating manual and write a procedure for entering waypoints into your GPS set. Also, enter all of the waypoints that are necessary to make a boat trip from your dock or mooring position to a location that you normally visit on one of your weekend trips.*

Waypoint Verification Using the GPS Chart Cursor Feature.   Portable GPS sets may not have a feature that allows you to verify waypoints using the chart cursor. However, there will be some sort of process to accomplish validation in your GPS set. Check your GPS operating manual for instructions for your particular GPS set.

Table 12.10 lists a typical procedure for updating a waypoint using the chart cursor, while Figure 12.10 shows a graphic procedure for doing this.

Table 12.10   Typical Procedure for Updating a Waypoint Using the Chart Cursor

O	Activate the cursor and locate the waypoint.
ENT	Open the waypoint for editing.
	A pop-up window will advise when you have found the waypoint and will list the options that are available.
	WP 32 found Move: Cursor + GOTO Edit: GOTO Delete from Route: CLR Exit: MENU
	In every possible case, select an aid to navigation to use for the position of a waypoint. This provides a visual check on the waypoint when you are under way, which further enhances your safety on the water. Move the cross symbol until it is exactly over the position of the aid. Changing the position of the waypoint may also update the position data on the Waypoint List in your GPS. Check your GPS operating manual.
	Deleting a waypoint from a route may or may not delete the waypoint from your GPS Waypoint List. Again, check your operating manual.
ENT	Confirms the entry of the waypoint.

Create route by cursor

Waypoints entered by cursor plottings are stored in the WP list starting from the highest vacant WP number.

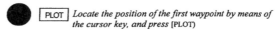

● | PLOT | *Locate the position of the first waypoint by means of the cursor key, and press* [PLOT]

| 3 | *Select '3. Make route' from 'Select PLOT mode' window*

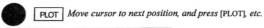

● | PLOT | *Move cursor to next position, and press* [PLOT], *etc.*

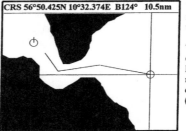

CRS 56°50.425N 10°32.374E B124° 10.5nm

The example shows that route point no. 4 is about to be made.

The top line will show cursor's position in lat/long (or decca lanes/Loran TDs) plus bearing and distance from position (or last plot) to cursor.

If you plot a wrong position by mistake:

| CLR | *Delete the last plotted position*

| ENT | *Press* [ENT] *when ready to save the Route*

Figure 12.10   A typical graphic procedure for updating a waypoint with a chart cursor.

Verifying Every Waypoint Position Entry in Your GPS.   Verify each waypoint by physically visiting the waypoint's location on your boat. A typical procedure for manually validating a waypoint is given in Table 12.11. Portable GPS sets will always have a similar procedure; check your GPS operating manual. You may want to write a similar procedure for your homemade GPS procedure manual.

The act of actually visiting the position of the waypoint confirms that you have not made a data entry error when you entered the waypoint into your GPS and also allows you to adjust the LAT/LON so that it is near the aid and not right on top of the aid.

Table 12.11   Typical Procedure for Validating a Waypoint Position Entry

MENU 3,1	Load Waypoint List.
0–9	Enter a Waypoint Number or …
CLR	Go to next vacant waypoint number on the GPS Waypoint List.
ENT	Open for entry.
	The system will suggest use of the boat's present position as the LAT/LON entry for the waypoint. If you are located at the geographical position of the waypoint, verify the LAT/LON against your Excel Waypoint List.
	Set up waypoint:
	Display position as:
	LAT/LON 42 23.417N 071 45.750W
+ / –	Enter the symbol that you use to designate that a waypoint has been verified.
ENT	Completes the waypoint entry.

Deleting a Waypoint Using the Chart Cursor.   Waypoints used in one or more routes often cannot be deleted from your GPS's Waypoint List. You usually have to delete them from the routes before the system will allow you to delete them from the Waypoint List. However, some sets do allow you to delete waypoints from a route. Check your GPS operating manual for instructions as to the deletion of waypoints on your set.

Chart plotters usually provide a simple means for deleting a waypoint. Table 12.12 provides a typical procedure for deleting a waypoint using a chart cursor. Check your GPS operating manual for instructions for your set.

**Table 12.12   Typical Procedure for Deleting a Waypoint
from a Chart Display**

GOTO	Activates the chart display.
O	Activates the cursor.
	Locate the waypoint.
ENT	Opens the waypoint for editing.
CLR-CLR	Deleted the waypoint.

Deleting Waypoints Using a Waypoint List.   Table 12.13 shows a typical procedure for deleting waypoints using the Waypoint List in your GPS. Check your GPS operating manual for this feature and then write a procedure for your custom GPS procedure manual.

**Table 12.13   Typical Procedure for Deleting a Waypoint
from a Waypoint List**

MENU	Load Waypoint List.
0–9	Key in waypoint number or scroll through the Waypoint List using the + / – key.
ENT	Open waypoint for editing.
CLR	Delete waypoint.
	LAT/LON is replaced with an asterisk (*).
ENT	Confirms edit.
MENU	Exit the delete function without deleting the waypoint.

These examples are provided to show you some processes commonly used for loading and deleting waypoints in a GPS set. Obviously, your set will be slightly different.

GPS TASK 7: *Write a procedure for verifying waypoints with your GPS. Verify every waypoint that you have entered into your GPS set in GPS Task 6. Reference your GPS operating manual for the correct procedure. Use this task list to manage this project.*

Check	Task No.	Task Description
	1.	*Select aids to navigation or other physical locations as your waypoints. Select waypoints for courses that you run in your everyday boating.*

Check	Task No.	Task Description
	2.	Plot the waypoints on your nautical chart. Measure the LAT/LON for each waypoint.
	3.	Plot courses to each waypoint on your nautical chart.
	4.	Develop a trip log.
	5.	Visit each waypoint position and verify the LAT/LON. Never trust a waypoint until you have actually verified it.

Phase Five: Establishing Routes

Routes are formed by linking a series of waypoints into a chain (Table 12.14). They are a key element for navigating with a GPS. The newer GPS systems can hold up to 50 routes, each with a 99-waypoint capacity. Routes can often be named with up to 27 characters, but simple, clear route names are suggested. On some systems, each leg within a route can be assigned a special XTE alarm distance corridor. Here are some features that you may find available in your GPS set:

- Waypoints used within a route are assigned a route point number in addition to their waypoint number.
- Waypoints used in routes can be edited when they are not being used for navigation.
- Existing waypoints can be deleted from the route and new waypoints can be added to a route.
- A waypoint cannot be deleted from the waypoint list as long as it is part of a route or is being used for navigation.
- Routes are identified with a four-digit numeric codes. The first two digits are the route number and the last two digits are the waypoint point number.
- The course line and the XTE corridor can be set to ON/OFF on each leg. The color of the course line can be changed in some sets.

Figure 12.11 shows a typical method for creating a route in a GPS set. Read your GPS operating manual for the procedure for creating a route in your GPS set.

```
Set up route 00.01
Name
Course Line_____OFF  XTE_____OFF
** **.*** N *** **.*** W
** **.*** N *** **.*** W
** **.*** N *** **.*** W
** **.*** N *** **.*** W
New WP XTE: 0.50nm Nav: RHUMBLINE
0001 42 18.310N 071 03.310W
Insert: PLOT Replace: GOTO
Delete: CLR Delete route: WIN
Accept: ENT Exit: MENU
```

Figure 12.11   Typical GPS screen for setting up a route.

Table 12.14   Typical Procedure for Setting Up a Route Using a Waypoint List

MENU	Select a route number.
0–9	Enter a vacant route number or leaf through the routes in memory.
ENT	Open the route for data entry.
0–9	Key in the first waypoint or scroll through the Waypoint List to select an existing waypoint.
0–9	If desired, go to and set the XTE limit for each leg.
+ / –	If desired, go to and set the navigation mode. Toggle between RHUMBLINE and GREAT CIRCLE. Check the General Information Block for the nautical chart that you are using for this information.
PLOT	Insert this waypoint into the route. Repeat this procedure until all of the waypoints are included in the route.
ENT	Confirm and save the route.

> GPS TASK 8: *Check your GPS operating manual for the procedure for setting up a route. Establish the route using the waypoints that you established in GPS Tasks 6 and 7. Write a procedure for setting up a route in your GPS for your customized procedure manual.*

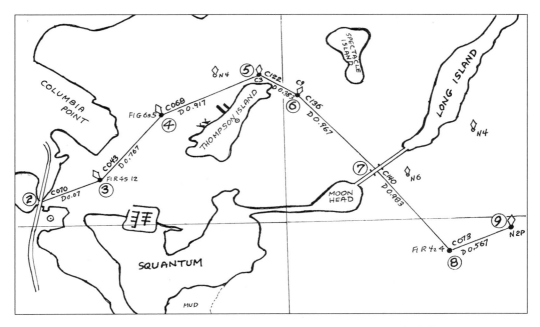

Figure 12.12   Labeling waypoints and routes on your nautical chart.

You can avoid a large investment for a chart plotter with your GPS system by using the technique shown in Figure 12.12 for labeling waypoints and routes. As you study this figure, note the following:

1.   Select aids to navigation as waypoints. This practice adds a visual dimension to your navigation and a physical start and end point for each leg in a route.

2.   Designate waypoints with simple numbers.

3.   If possible, number waypoints within a route in numerical order.

4.   Use a small round dot label to identify each waypoint on your nautical chart. Write the waypoint number on the label for quick reference while under way. Each waypoint can always be used with a GOTO command whenever needed.

Running a Trip Using a GPS.   Now that you have set up your GPS and learned how to enter waypoints and routes, you are ready to use your GPS to navigate your boat. Tables 12.15 and 12.16 show checklists of my recommendations for using your GPS in an effective and accurate manner for navigating your boat.

Table 12.15   Start of Operation: One-Time Setup Checklist

Task	Check	Item to Check
1		Depth—unit of measure—feet, meters, or fathoms. Reference the nautical chart that you are using for the correct vertical datum—depth and height. Usually does not change unless you move out of your normal area of operation.
2		Distance—unit of measure—nautical miles.
3		Speed—unit of measure—knots.
4		Temperature—unit of measure—Fahrenheit or centigrade. Needed if there is an interface to depth sounder.
5		Text Display—English (US).
6		Horizontal Datum—Reference the General Information Block of the nautical chart that you are using. Latest is probably WGS84.
7		Course and Bearing—unit of measure—true or magnetic. Match your GPS to your compass.
8		Navigation Mode—rhumb line or great circle. Reference the General Information Block on the nautical chart that you are using. Select RHUMBLINE for Mercator projections and GREAT CIRCLE for polyconic projections.
9		Auto Waypoint Shift—Turn on so that the navigation system automatically shifts to the next waypoint after passing the Waypoint Circle Alarm perimeter.
10		Waypoint Circle Alarm—Establish a warning circle by setting a distance in this feature.
11		Cross-Track Error Alarm (XTE)—Establish a warning distance-off-course limit corridor.
12		Anchor Alarm—Set this perimeter alarm when at anchor.
13		GPS Antenna Altitude—Set the height of the top of the GPS antenna from the waterline in your GPS.

When every item on these checklists is prepared and operating correctly, you are ready for a day at sea. The best time to practice and develop your navigation skills is when the sea is calm and the sun is shining. Errors are easy to correct when you can clearly see errors evolving and can make quick corrections. Every trip that you make in the daylight is an opportunity to hone your navigation skills. These practice trips will prepare you for the worst case scenarios of blinding rain, high winds, or fog. With practice, you will welcome the chance to

Table 12.16   Pre-Trip Checklist

Task	Check	Item to Check
1		Load the waypoints for your trip. Your Excel Waypoint List should be updated, printed, and added to your procedure manual. Waypoints should be validated. Unvalidated waypoints should be highlighted so that you will take extra caution when using them. Safe navigation calls for validating every waypoint.
2		Set up route(s) for your trip.
3		Waypoints and routes are labeled on your nautical chart.
4		Trip Log is prepared for your trip.

Additional checks prior to getting under way

5		Validate that satellite navigation is working.
		Check the position setup screens.
6		Check to ensure that the GPS procedure manual and GPS operating manual are on board.
7		Check to ensure that the Excel waypoint and route list is on board.
8		Make sure a current nautical chart is on board.
9		Make sure you have spare batteries for your GPS on board.

demonstrate your new skills when the time comes. With validated routes loaded in your GPS, you will be ready to handle any problem like a professional.

NAVIGATION SCREENS

Many GPS sets have a GOTO or similar function that allows the user to:

- Have direct access to the chart display.
- Select, change, or stop navigation.
- Select a Home function to center the cursor or boat on a screen.

The set may also have the capability to allow the user to select different modes for navigation such as those shown in Table 12.17.

Table 12.17   Various Navigation Modes Offered by Some GPS Sets

Cursor Navigation	Usually the cursor function must be turned on. Function provides the ability to: • Plot a mark—save a position as a waypoint. • Make a route. • Plot a target. • Determine bearing and distance from point A to point B. • Determine distance and TTG—Time to Go—from one route point to another.
Waypoint Navigation	Navigate to the next waypoint.
Route Navigation	Options may include: • Call up a route number. • Use cursor to establish a route. • Navigate along a route.
Track Navigation	Options may include: • Record the track of your boat. • Save the track similar to a route. • Use the track similar to a route.

Figure 12.13 shows a sample screen that would be used when navigating while using a route. Route navigation is the most common mode used with a GPS. Once a route is completely validated and saved in memory, the navigator can feel secure about using it any time in the future. Using an established route is a simple process, as laid out in Table 12.18.

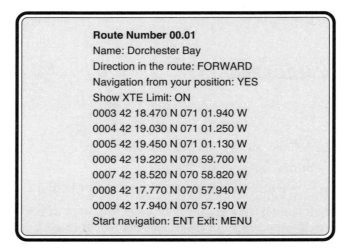

Route Number 00.01

Name: Dorchester Bay

Direction in the route: FORWARD

Navigation from your position: YES

Show XTE Limit: ON

0003 42 18.470 N 071 01.940 W

0004 42 19.030 N 071 01.250 W

0005 42 19.450 N 071 01.130 W

0006 42 19.220 N 070 59.700 W

0007 42 18.520 N 070 58.820 W

0008 42 17.770 N 070 57.940 W

0009 42 17.940 N 070 57.190 W

Start navigation: ENT Exit: MENU

Figure 12.13   Route navigation screen.

Table 12.18   Typical Procedure for Navigating with a GPS Route

MENU	Select Route Navigation from menu.
0–9	Key in the route number or select from a list.

If desired, scan the waypoints used in the route for unverified waypoints. These should be marked with a special symbol, per earlier discussions, so that you can easily recognize unverified waypoints. You must take extra caution on those legs that have unverified waypoints and remember to verify the waypoint when you are on site.

ENT	Start navigating.

GPS TASK 9: *Now that you have set up a route in your GPS, get under way and verify each waypoint by running the route in the daylight on a clear, calm day. Check your work with routes and waypoints as you go:*

- *Bring your nautical chart and your Trip Log along. As your GPS set suggests heading and distances for each leg, sanity check them against your Trip Log. Do they point you to the next waypoint? If not, make the necessary corrections and proceed.*

- *Does the waypoint's LAT/LON on your Trip Log match the actual LAT/LON reading at the waypoint's position? Remember that the Coast Guard from time to time moves the position of aids to navigation for a number of reasons. Reset the LAT/LON of a waypoint as necessary.*

- *Repeat this process until you have completed the verification process of each leg in the route.*

You now have a verified route that you can use in any kind of weather. For practice, run this verified route every time you go out on your boat. Practice makes perfect. This adage is especially true in navigation.

The screen shown in Figure 12.14 is reporting only data about your current position. Table 12.19 provides a brief explanation of the data outputs shown in Figure 12.14.

Figure 12.15 shows a screen that is reporting navigation data and the status of the helmsperson's ability to stay on course. Table 12.20 provides a brief explanation of the data outputs shown in Figure 12.15.

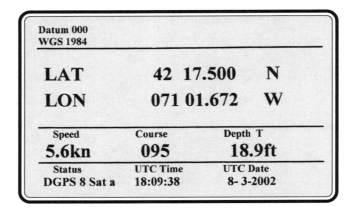

Figure 12.14 Position display screen.

Table 12.19 Explanation of the Information Shown in Figure 12.14

Data Output	Explanation
Datum	Shows that the GPS set is calibrated to WGS84.
LAT/LON	Shows the position of the boat.
Speed	This is the SOG—average speed that the boat is making over the ground.
Course	Can be magnetic or true. This is the average course that the boat is heading from the point where the last position was reviewed by the computer. This is not a compass course.
Depth	Obviously, this GPS is connected to a depth sounder or has a built-in depth capability. The depth is measured from the position of the transducer on your boat to the seabed.
Status	This GPS set has DGPS capability and is operating in that mode. Also shows that eight satellites have been selected and the grade of the signal.
UTC Time	Universal Time Coordinates. Usually, this field can be adjusted to show local time.
UTC Date	Shows the date.

It is very common for position and navigation output to be combined into a single navigation screen. Check your GPS operating manual for this type of screen. This is the type of screen display that you would use to navigate your boat when using GPS.

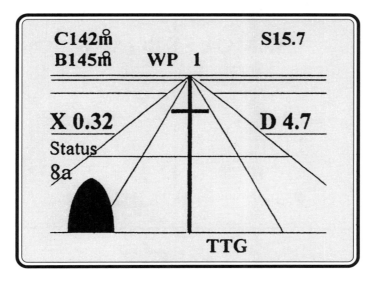

Figure 12.15 XTE—cross-track error navigation screen.

Table 12.20   Explanation of the Information Shown in Figure 12.15

Data Output	Explanation
C142m	Indicates that the average course that you are currently making is 142 degrees magnetic.
B145m	Indicates that the course or bearing to Waypoint 1 is 145 degrees magnetic.
WP1	Indicates that the GPS is directing you to Waypoint 1 (WP 1) on your Waypoint List.
S15.7	Indicates that your boat is making 15.7 knots over the ground on average.
X0.32	Indicates that you are 0.32 nm—nautical miles—off the bearing to WP 1.
D 4.7	Indicates that the current distance to WP 1 is 4.7 nm.
Status 8a	Indicates that the GPS is operating from 8 satellites and that the status is "a."
Black Bow	The graphic of the black bow indicates that you are off your course to port.
TTG	Indicates the TTG—Time to Go—to WP 1, based on the SOG and the DTG. Based on the data displayed, the TTG would be: $60 \times 4.7 = 15.7 \times T$ or 17.96 minutes or 17 min. 58 sec.

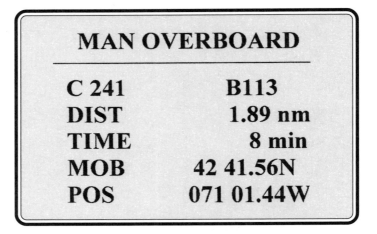

Figure 12.16 Man Overboard (MOB) screen.

Every GPS seems to have a Man Overboard feature. Learn how to use the screen shown in Figure 12.16 and include it as part of your man overboard procedure. Most sets provide a separate key for this function. Check your GPS operating manual for this function.

When activated, the MOB function brings up a screen that displays data that will bring you back to the position in which your boat was located when you pressed the MOB button. This feature is most important if anyone falls overboard at night or during heavy weather when it is so difficult to find a person in the water. As a secondary precaution, if you operate your boat at night, equip every life jacket with a small white strobe light. This will increase your odds for recovering anyone who falls overboard during periods of reduced visibility.

Table 12.21 provides a brief explanation of the data outputs found on the MOB display screen shown in Figure 12.16.

Table 12.21 Explanation of the Information Shown in Figure 12.16

Data Output	Explanation
C241 B113	Indicates the average course that your boat is making. Shows the bearing to the position of your boat when you pressed the MOB key on your GPS.
DIST 1.89 nm	Shows the distance to the position of your boat when you pressed the MOB key on your GPS.
Time	Elapsed time in minutes since you activated the MOB key on your GPS.
MOB POS	LAT/LON of the position of your boat when you pressed the MOB key on your GPS.

Here are a few more safety tips to remember if you ever have a man overboard accident:

1. Toss a Type IV PFD into the water. This can assist the person in the water or act as a physical datum for his or her position.

2. Assign a crewperson to be the pointer. This person keeps pointing to the person in the water while you are maneuvering the boat.

3. Broadcast a Pan-Pan-Pan radio message to alert other boats in the area to assist you.

4. If you don't find the person in the water right away, search downwind or down current.

5. Have your crew break out towels, blankets, and dry clothes to warm the person who went overboard when retrieved.

6. Never put another person in the water unless he or she is tethered with a line to your boat.

GPS NAVIGATION SUMMARY

If you have studied all five phases and completed all nine GPS tasks, you should be well schooled on the operation of your GPS. Now is the time to install routes that you will be using this season so you can start to feel confident about your ability to safely navigate your boat. Here are a few tips that can enhance that feeling:

1. Always use GPS with a nautical chart. It is often easier to reference a paper chart rather than a small chart display unless you have top-of-the-line equipment.

2. Always steer your boat by the compass—not your GPS. I like the electronic compass option. It is more accurate, easier to adjust for deviation error, and a quality check on my GPS readouts.

3. Preplot all of your trips on a paper nautical chart and use a Trip Log with verified waypoints. The Trip Log acts as another quality check on your GPS readouts.

4. Label all your waypoints on your nautical chart.

5. Train other crewpersons to navigate using your charts and GPS so that they can take over the navigating function during periods of heavy weather.

6. Train other crewpersons to operate your boat so that they can relieve you during periods of heavy weather.

INTERFERENCE PROBLEMS

Powered TV Antennas

The U.S. Coast Guard and the FCC have determined that certain VHF/UHF marine television antennas can cause degradation in the performance of GPS receivers, which can result in the inaccurate display of position information or a complete loss of GPS acquisition and tracking ability. This problem has been reported up to 2,000 feet from the interference site (or one-third of a nautical mile). Some problems were associated with temperature extremes or proximity to a television broadcast site.

If you are experiencing reoccurring outages or degradation of your GPS receiver, the problem could be caused by one of the antennas on or nearby your boat. If you have such an antenna on your boat and are experiencing problems with your GPS, perform a simple ON/OFF test. If turning off the antenna solves the problem, the antenna is the source of the problem. In that case, you should contact the manufacturer of the antenna and identify the symptoms. If the test is not positive and the interference persists, you should contact the Coast Guard Navigation Information Service at 703-313-5900, or via e-mail at nisws@navcen.uscg.mil, or visit their website at http://www.navcen.uscg.gov.

Cell Phone Antenna Interference

GPS users have noted problems with the operation of their GPS systems in the vicinity of cell phone towers. The interference is a geographic problem that is related to your boat's proximity to the antenna. The interference should disappear as you move away from the antenna's position. Smaller, portable GPS sets appear to be less affected by this interference.

THIRTEEN

The Height of the Tide at Any Time

I estimate that there may be five situations when you need to know the exact depth of the water; 99 percent of the time, the depth printed on the chart is sufficient for the average boater. The question asked most often by the boater is "When is high tide?" Unfortunately, most new boaters don't realize that the depths marked on their charts refer to the low water mark and that their greatest concern should be for the time of lowest water. Here is a list of the five situations.

First, you will want to know the times of high or low water. This is the simplest solution because all you have to do is read Table 1 in the *Tide Tables* and then adjust the time to your local time. The tide tables are not adjusted for daylight saving time.

Tide data from Table 1 is often printed in your daily newspaper. Most newspapers correct the times to local time. Also, many local marinas and bait stores offer free tide calendars, which provide this basic information. Many of these tide tables are corrected to local time. The good news is that most new GPS sets provide a screen that displays the times of high and low water. Check your GPS operating manual for this capability.

Second, you may need to know the height of the tide at a specific point in time. Most new GPS sets show this information.

Third, you may want to know the depth of the water at various points of time over an extended period. Setting up a tide graph will supply you with this information. The use of the tide graph is explained later in this chapter.

Fourth, you may want to determine the height (distance) from the waterline to the span of a bridge for a specific point in time. This simple calculation is made after you determine the height of the tide. It is also explained later in this chapter.

Fifth, you may want to know the time when you have a certain clearance of depth over an obstruction such as a shoal or bar.

CAUTION: *Remember that shoals and bars are always subject to change and shifting depths. Also understand that certain weather conditions can change the predicted depth of a tide significantly. As I have stated before, navigation appears to be a perfect science that is trying to predict events in an imperfect environment. Never trust any depth without verifying your predictions by more than one navigational technique.*

TERMINOLOGY

Before you do the depth and height calculations, you need to understand a few new terms.

Tide Tables

The term *tide tables* usually refers to Table 1 in the *Tide Tables,* which gives daily predictions of the times and heights of high and low water for a reference station. The actual *Tide Tables,* however, is a book that contains all three tables for predicting tide times and heights.

Reference Station

A reference station is a fixed tide station for which independent daily predictions of high and low tides are given in the *Tide Tables.* Reference stations appear in Table 1 of the *Tide Tables.* This is also true of your GPS set.

Substation

A substation is a fixed location for which tide predictions are determined by applying correction data to predictions for a reference station. Substations appear in Table 2 of the *Tide Tables.* Your GPS set will also display alternative substations. Select the substation nearest your position.

Range of Tide

The range of tide is the vertical difference in feet or meters of the depth of the water from the point of high water to the point of low water or vice versa.

Duration of Tide

The duration of tide is the predicted time interval in hours and minutes from the time of high water to the time of low water or vice versa.

THE TIDE TABLES

Before you become completely confused about tides, familiarize yourself with Tables 1, 2, and 3 of the *Tide Tables.* Sample pages from each are reproduced as figures in this chapter. As you read about each table, refer to its corresponding figure until you have a firm picture in your mind about the information provided by each table.

A brief description of the three tables that are used in calculating the height of the tide follows.

Table 1: Table of Daily Tide Predictions

Table 1 (see Figure 13.1) contains the predictions of the time and height of high and low water for every day of the year for reference stations. The predictions in Table 1 change yearly. You will have to buy a new *Tide Tables* each year to get the latest time and height predictions. Nevertheless, there are other sources for these data. Here are a few samples:

- Daily newspaper
- *Eldridge Tide and Pilot* book
- Local bait stores and marina calendars.

The reference stations used in the *Tide Tables* for the East Coast of the United States are:

Argentia, Newfoundland	Eastport, ME
Pictou, Nova Scotia	Boston, MA
Harrington Harbour, Quebec	Newport, RI
Quebec, Quebec	New London, CT
Halifax, Nova Scotia	Bridgeport, CT
St. John, New Brunswick	Willets Point, NJ

BOSTON, MASS.

Times and Heights of High and Low Waters

JANUARY

Day	Time h m	Height ft	m		Day	Time h m	Height ft	m
1 Su	0537	8.9	2.7		16 M	0556	10.3	3.1
	1154	1.7	0.5			1223	0.2	0.1
	1805	8.0	2.4			1838	8.7	2.7
2 M	0006	1.9	0.6		17 Tu	0035	0.9	0.3
	0627	9.0	2.7			0657	10.3	3.1
	1249	1.5	0.5			1328	0.2	0.1
	1902	7.9	2.4			1942	8.6	2.6
3 Tu	0057	1.9	0.6		18 W	0135	1.1	0.3
	0716	9.2	2.8			0758	10.3	3.1
	1344	1.2	0.4			1430	0.0	0.0
	1954	8.0	2.4			2045	8.6	2.6
4 W	0148	1.8	0.5		19 Th	0235	1.1	0.3
	0805	9.5	2.9			0856	10.4	3.2
	1435	0.8	0.2			1528	-0.1	0.0
	2045	8.2	2.5			2142	8.7	2.7
5 Th	0237	1.5	0.5		20 F	0328	1.0	0.3
	0853	9.9	3.0			0949	10.4	3.2
	1522	0.3	0.1			1617	-0.2	-0.1
	2135	8.5	2.6			2231	8.9	2.7
6 F	0325	1.2	0.4		21 Sa	0417	0.9	0.3
	0939	10.4	3.2			1036	10.5	3.2
	1609	-0.2	-0.1			1703	-0.3	-0.1
	2221	8.9	2.7			2329	9.0	2.7
7 Sa	0413	0.8	0.2		22 Su	0503	0.8	0.2
	1026	10.8	3.3			1121	10.5	3.2
	1654	-0.6	-0.2			1744	-0.3	-0.1
	2307	9.2	2.8			2358	9.1	2.8
8 Su	0500	0.4	0.1		23 M	0549	0.7	0.2
	1112	11.1	3.4			1203	10.3	3.1
	1740	-1.0	-0.3			1822	-0.2	-0.1
	2353	9.6	2.9					
9 M	0549	0.1	0.0		24 Tu	0036	9.2	2.8
	1200	11.3	3.4			0631	0.7	0.2
	1826	-1.2	-0.4			1242	10.1	3.1
						1901	0.0	0.0
10 Tu	0039	9.9	3.0		25 W	0113	9.2	2.8
	0637	-0.2	-0.1			0712	0.8	0.2
	1249	11.3	3.4			1324	9.8	3.0
	1912	-1.3	-0.4			1938	0.3	0.1
11 W	0126	10.2	3.1		26 Th	0151	9.2	2.8
	0727	-0.3	-0.1			0754	0.9	0.3
	1338	11.1	3.4			1404	9.4	2.9
	1958	-1.2	-0.4			2018	0.6	0.2
12 Th	0215	10.4	3.2		27 F	0231	9.2	2.8
	0822	-0.3	-0.1			0839	1.1	0.3
	1431	10.7	3.3			1448	9.0	2.7
	2049	-0.9	-0.3			2057	1.0	0.3
13 F	0307	10.5	3.2		28 Sa	0313	9.1	2.8
	0918	-0.2	-0.1			0924	1.3	0.4
	1527	10.3	3.1			1534	8.5	2.6
	2141	-0.4	-0.1			2140	1.3	0.4
14 Sa	0401	10.5	3.2		29 Su	0356	9.0	2.7
	1017	0.0	0.0			1014	1.4	0.4
	1628	9.6	2.9			1625	8.1	2.5
	2237	0.1	0.0			2227	1.7	0.5
15 Su	0457	10.4	3.2		30 M	0445	8.9	2.7
	1119	0.1	0.0			1108	1.6	0.5
	1730	9.1	2.8			1718	7.8	2.4
	2335	0.6	0.2			2318	2.0	0.6
					31 Tu	0537	8.9	2.7
						1205	1.5	0.5
						1816	7.7	2.3

FEBRUARY

Day	Time h m	Height ft	m		Day	Time h m	Height ft	m
1 W	0014	2.0	0.6		16 Th	0118	1.5	0.5
	0630	9.1	2.8			0745	9.7	3.0
	1302	1.3	0.4			1419	0.5	0.2
	1915	7.7	2.3			2037	8.3	2.5
2 Th	0109	1.9	0.6		17 F	0221	1.4	0.4
	0726	9.4	2.9			0846	9.8	3.0
	1358	0.9	0.3			1515	0.4	0.1
	2011	8.0	2.4			2131	8.6	2.6
3 F	0205	1.6	0.5		18 Sa	0317	1.2	0.4
	0821	9.9	3.0			0938	10.0	3.0
	1451	0.3	0.1			1603	0.2	0.1
	2106	8.5	2.6			2219	8.8	2.7
4 Sa	0258	1.1	0.3		19 Su	0405	1.0	0.3
	0914	10.4	3.2			1024	10.1	3.1
	1542	-0.3	-0.1			1643	0.1	0.0
	2154	9.0	2.7			2257	9.1	2.8
5 Su	0351	0.4	0.1		20 M	0448	0.7	0.2
	1005	11.0	3.4			1106	10.1	3.1
	1630	-0.9	-0.3			1720	0.1	0.0
	2242	9.7	3.0			2334	9.3	2.8
6 M	0440	-0.2	-0.1		21 Tu	0529	0.5	0.2
	1052	11.4	3.5			1143	10.1	3.1
	1716	-1.4	-0.4			1756	0.1	0.0
	2329	10.3	3.1					
7 Tu	0529	-0.7	-0.2		22 W	0008	9.5	2.9
	1142	11.6	3.5			0608	0.4	0.1
	1802	-1.6	-0.5			1220	9.9	3.0
						1829	0.2	0.1
8 W	0015	10.8	3.3		23 Th	0042	9.6	2.9
	0619	-1.1	-0.3			0645	0.4	0.1
	1231	11.6	3.5			1257	9.7	3.0
	1848	-1.7	-0.5			1904	0.4	0.1
9 Th	0101	11.1	3.4		24 F	0117	9.6	2.9
	0710	-1.2	-0.4			0725	0.5	0.2
	1322	11.3	3.4			1335	9.4	2.9
	1935	-1.4	-0.4			1941	0.7	0.2
10 F	0149	11.2	3.4		25 Sa	0153	9.5	2.9
	0802	-1.1	-0.3			0806	0.7	0.2
	1415	10.8	3.3			1415	9.0	2.7
	2023	-0.9	-0.3			2018	1.0	0.3
11 Sa	0239	11.1	3.4		26 Su	0231	9.4	2.9
	0857	-0.8	-0.2			0848	0.9	0.3
	1510	10.1	3.1			1458	8.6	2.6
	2116	-0.3	-0.1			2100	1.4	0.4
12 Su	0332	10.8	3.3		27 M	0311	9.2	2.8
	0956	-0.4	-0.1			0935	1.1	0.3
	1608	9.4	2.9			1545	8.1	2.5
	2211	0.4	0.1			2145	1.7	0.5
13 M	0430	10.4	3.2		28 Tu	0358	9.1	2.8
	1057	0.1	0.0			1027	1.4	0.4
	1712	8.7	2.7			1639	7.8	2.4
	2310	1.0	0.3			2237	2.0	0.6
14 Tu	0533	10.0	3.1					
	1204	0.4	0.1					
	1821	8.3	2.5					
15 W	0014	1.4	0.4					
	0638	9.8	3.0					
	1313	0.6	0.2					
	1932	8.2	2.5					

MARCH

Day	Time h m	Height ft	m		Day	Time h m	Height ft	m
1 W	0453	9.0	2.7		16 Th	0619	9.4	2.9
	1123	1.4	0.4			1253	1.0	0.3
	1736	7.7	2.3			1913	8.2	2.5
	2335	2.1	0.6					
2 Th	0549	9.1	2.8		17 F	0102	1.8	0.5
	1223	1.3	0.4			0728	9.3	2.8
	1838	7.8	2.4			1400	0.9	0.3
						2017	8.4	2.6
3 F	0035	1.9	0.6		18 Sa	0206	1.6	0.5
	0651	9.4	2.9			0827	9.4	2.9
	1323	0.9	0.3			1453	0.8	0.2
	1938	8.2	2.5			2109	8.7	2.7
4 Sa	0135	1.5	0.5		19 Su	0259	1.3	0.4
	0750	9.9	3.0			0920	9.6	2.9
	1421	0.3	0.1			1538	0.7	0.2
	2035	8.8	2.7			2153	9.0	2.7
5 Su	0233	0.8	0.2		20 M	0346	1.0	0.3
	0849	10.5	3.2			1003	9.7	3.0
	1512	-0.4	-0.1			1615	0.5	0.2
	2126	9.6	2.9			2231	9.3	2.8
6 M	0328	0.0	0.0		21 Tu	0427	0.7	0.2
	0941	11.0	3.4			1044	9.8	3.0
	1603	-1.0	-0.3			1650	0.5	0.2
	2215	10.4	3.2			2303	9.6	2.9
7 Tu	0420	-0.8	-0.2		22 W	0506	0.4	0.1
	1033	11.5	3.5			1120	9.8	3.0
	1649	-1.4	-0.4			1724	0.5	0.2
	2303	11.1	3.4			2335	9.8	3.0
8 W	0510	-1.4	-0.4		23 Th	0543	0.3	0.1
	1122	11.7	3.6			1155	9.7	3.0
	1736	-1.7	-0.5			1757	0.6	0.2
	2348	11.6	3.5					
9 Th	0600	-1.8	-0.5		24 F	0009	9.9	3.0
	1213	11.6	3.5			0620	0.2	0.1
	1823	-1.6	-0.5			1231	9.5	2.9
						1832	0.9	0.3
10 F	0034	11.8	3.6		25 Sa	0042	9.9	3.0
	0650	-1.9	-0.6			0658	0.3	0.1
	1304	11.2	3.4			1309	9.2	2.8
	1909	-1.2	-0.4			1909	1.0	0.3
11 Sa	0123	11.8	3.6		26 Su	0117	9.8	3.0
	0742	-1.6	-0.5			0737	0.4	0.1
	1356	10.6	3.2			1346	8.9	2.7
	1959	-0.7	-0.2			1946	1.2	0.4
12 Su	0212	11.5	3.5		27 M	0155	9.7	3.0
	0836	-1.1	-0.3			0819	0.6	0.2
	1451	9.9	3.0			1428	8.6	2.6
	2051	0.0	0.0			2028	1.5	0.5
13 M	0308	10.9	3.3		28 Tu	0237	9.5	2.9
	0934	-0.4	-0.1			0903	0.9	0.3
	1549	9.2	2.8			1516	8.3	2.5
	2147	0.8	0.2			2114	1.8	0.5
14 Tu	0406	10.3	3.1		29 W	0324	9.3	2.8
	1035	0.2	0.1			0956	1.1	0.3
	1654	8.6	2.6			1608	8.0	2.4
	2249	1.4	0.4			2206	2.0	0.6
15 W	0512	9.8	3.0		30 Th	0419	9.3	2.8
	1143	0.7	0.2			1051	1.2	0.4
	1804	8.2	2.5			1706	8.0	2.4
	2354	1.7	0.5			2305	2.0	0.6
					31 F	0519	9.3	2.8
						1152	1.0	0.3
						1806	8.2	2.5

Time meridian 75° W. 0000 is midnight. 1200 is noon.
Heights are referred to mean lower low water which is the chart datum of soundings.

Figure 13.1   Table 1: Table of Daily Tide Predictions
(Source: The Tide Tables).

New York (The Battery), NY   Savannah River Entrance, GA
Albany, NY   Savannah, GA
Sandy Hook, NJ   Mayport, FL
Breakwater Harbor, DE   Miami Harbor Entrance, FL
Reedy Point, DE   Key West, FL
Philadelphia, PA   St. Petersburg, FL
Baltimore, MD   St. Marks River Entrance, FL
Washington, DC   Pensacola, FL
Hampton Roads, VA   Mobile, AL
Wilmington, NC   Galveston, TX
Charleston, SC   Tampico Harbor, Mexico

Figure 13.1 shows a sample page from Table 1. Take a moment to review this figure so that you fully understand how to read this table and understand what the data means.

Figure 13.2 shows the tide predictions for Saturday, March 4, taken from Figure 13.1. For the purpose of presenting an example of tide in some of the following figures, note that morning high tide is predicted to be at 7:50 AM with a height of 9.9 feet and afternoon low tide is predicted to be at 2:21 PM with a height of 0.3 feet.

MARCH		
Day	Time h m	Height ft
4	0135	1.5
Sa	0750	9.9
	1421	0.3
	2035	8.8

Figure 13.2   Sample data from Table 1.

Table 2: Tidal Differences and Other Constants

Table 2 (see Figure 13.3) lists substations that are associated with specific reference stations. This table shows the position (LAT/LON) of the substation along with the time and height differences of high and low tide from the predictions of their associated reference stations shown in Table 1. Table 2 remains fairly constant year to year. You can't use data from Table 2 without the appropriate base data from Table 1.

CAUTION: *The time and height differences listed in Table 2 are average differences calculated from comparisons of simultaneous tide observations at the reference stations and the substation. Because Table 2 figures are constant, they do not make provision for the daily variances of the actual tide at a substation's location.*

The predictions at the substations are not as accurate as the predictions at the reference stations. Table 2 should only be used to approximate the times and heights of high and low water at the substations. This means that you should expect to have some error or difference from your calculated depth to the actual depth at the location. Act accordingly. Figure 13.3 shows a sample of the substations associated with the various reference stations near Labrador.

Table 3: Height of Tide at Any Time

Table 3 provides a means to correct the height of tide based on the duration of the tide, the time from the nearest high or low water, and the range of the tide. These terms were explained earlier in this chapter. Figure 13.4 shows a complete Table 3. Follow these simple steps to find the height of tide for 6:55 AM on Saturday, March 4, from Figure 13.2 and Table 3 in Figure 13.4:

Step 1.   Enter Table 3 at the top section at the time in the left-hand column that is nearest to the duration of the tide.

- Time of high tide: 0750

- Time of low tide: 1421

- Duration of tide: 0631 (1421 – 0750 = 0631)

Enter Table 3 at the "6 40," which is closest to 06 31.

Step 2.   Follow horizontally across the "6 40" row to the column that is closest to the desired time difference from the nearest high water or low water prediction for the day.

- Time of nearest high or low tide: 0750

- Time height is desired: 0655

- Time differential: 0055

Move across to the "0 53" column, which is closest to 0055.

TABLE 2. — TIDAL DIFFERENCES AND OTHER CONSTANTS

NO.	PLACE	POSITION Lat.	Long.	DIFFERENCES Time High water	Low water	Height High water	Low water	RANGES Mean	Spring	Mean Tide Level
		° ' N	° ' W	h. m.	h. m.	ft	ft	ft	ft	ft
	BAFFIN BAY, etc., West Side Time meridian, local				on HALIFAX, p.20					
101	Fort Conger, Discovery Harbor..........	81 44	64 44	+3 48	+3 25	-1.4	-1.3	4.3	5.9	3.0
103	Cape Lawrence..........................	80 21	69 15	+3 46	+3 40	-0.2	-1.3	5.5	7.2	3.6
105	Payer Harbour, Cape Sabine.............	78 43	74 25	+3 36	+3 30	+1.7	-0.9	7.0	9.4	4.7
107	Cape Adair.............................	71 33	71 30	+3 06	+3 06	+0.4	-1.2	6.0	7.8	3.9
109	Cape Hewett............................	70 16	67 47	+2 56	+2 56	+0.6	-0.5	5.5	7.2	4.4
	DAVIS STRAIT, West Side Time meridian, 60°W				on PICTOU, p.8					
111	Cape Hooper, Baffin Island.............	68 23	66 45	-5 52	-5 41	*0.47	*0.43	1.6	1.9	1.8
113	Kivitoo, Baffin Island.................	67 56	64 56	-5 17	-5 10	*0.51	*0.43	1.8	2.4	1.9
					on SAINT JOHN, N. B., p.24					
115	Cape Dyer, Baffin Island...............	66 34	61 40	-6 19	-6 21	*0.31	*0.45	5.8	7.3	4.7
117	Clearwater Fiord, Cumberland Sound......	66 36	67 20	-5 36	-5 38	-5.5	-0.6	15.9	20.6	11.4
119	Frobisher Bay..........................	63 29	68 02	-4 13	-4 15	+5.5	+3.3	23.0	29.8	18.8
	HUDSON STRAIT and BAY									
121	Pikyulik Island, Payne River...........	60 00	69 55	-2 15	-1 54	+3.7	+3.2	21.3	26.8	17.9
	Time meridian, 75°W									
123	Sorry Harbor, Resolution Island........	61 37	64 44	-5 30	-5 30	-8.3	-0.9	13.4	17.6	9.8
125	Lower Savage Islands...................	61 46	65 51	-4 46	-4 55	-1.2	+2.0	17.6	25.4	14.8
127	Ashe Inlet, Big Island.................	62 33	70 35	-3 46	-3 43	+4.2	+2.2	22.8	30.9	17.6
129	Schooner Harbour, Baffin Island........	64 24	77 52	-0 49	-0 44	-6.2	+0.4	14.2	18.9	11.5
131	Winter Island, Foxe Basin..............	66 11	83 10	+1 02	+1 10	-12.1	-0.8	9.5	12.4	8.0
	Time meridian, 90°W									
133	Coral Harbour, Southampton Island.......	64 08	83 10	-0 25	+0 04	-14.4	-1.5	7.9	10.3	6.5
135	Chesterfield Inlet.....................	63 20	90 42	-8 17	-8 20	-12.4	-0.8	9.2	11.8	7.8
137	Churchill.............................	58 47	94 12	-4 25	-4 36	-11.5	-1.4	10.7	13.4	7.9
					on QUEBEC, p.16					
139	Port Nelson, Nelson River entrance......	57 05	92 36	+3 56	+4 35	-3.1	-0.9	11.5	12.9	6.4
	Time meridian, 75°W									
141	Moosonee, James Bay....................	51 17	80 38	+9 29	+9 32	*0.48	*1.81	4.5	5.4	5.2
143	Moose Factory, James Bay...............	51 16	80 35	+9 33	+10 37	*0.42	*1.56	4.0	5.4	4.5
145	Charlton Island, James Bay.............	51 57	79 16	+8 00	+6 38	*0.39	*1.06	4.3	5.3	3.9
					on SAINT JOHN, N. B., p.24					
147	Digges Harbour.........................	62 30	77 42	-2 11	-2 05	*0.39	*0.62	7.1	9.3	6.1
149	Port de Boucherville, Nottingham Island.	63 12	77 28	-2 07	-2 02	-11.6	-1.2	10.4	14.0	8.0
151	Wakeham Bay...........................	61 43	71 57	-3 52	-3 55	-0.4	+2.2	18.2	27.0	15.3
153	Stupart Bay...........................	61 35	71 32	-4 10	-4 17	0.0	+2.4	18.4	27 2	15.6
155	Diana Bay.............................	60 52	70 04	-4 00	-4 03	+2.8	+3.1	20.5	26.8	17.4
157	Hopes Advance Bay, Ungava Bay..........	59 21	69 38	-3 59	-4 00	*1.44	*2.20	27.0	34.4	22.3
159	Leaf Bay, Ungava Bay...................	58 55	69 00	-4 00	-4 00	*1.49	*2.25	28.0	36.0	23.0
161	Leaf Lake, Ungava Bay..................	58 45	69 40	-3 00	-3 00	(*1.54+5.8)		32.0	40.0	28.0
163	Koksoak River entrance.................	58 32	68 11	-3 50	-3 53	*1.47	*2.00	28.5	36.4	22.3
165	Port Burwell, Ungava Bay...............	60 25	64 52	-4 13	-4 13	-6.5	-0.9	15.2	19.9	10.7
	LABRADOR Time meridian, 52°30'W									
167	Button Islands........................	60 37	64 44	-2 38	-2 38	-9.5	-0.3	11.6	15.4	9.5
169	Williams Harbour......................	60 00	64 19	-3 07	-3 27	*0.32	*0.30	6.8	8.2	4.6
					on HALIFAX, p.20					
171	Eclipse Harbour.......................	59 48	64 09	+0 25	+0 02	-2.4	-1.0	3.0	3.7	2.6
173	Kangalaksiorvik Fiord..................	59 23	63 47	+1 00	+0 42	-2.6	-1.5	3.3	4.1	2.2
175	Nachvak Bay...........................	59 03	63 35	+0 04	-0 20	-1.5	-1.1	4.0	5.0	3.0
177	Port Manvers..........................	56 57	61 25	-0 55	-0 55	-2.3	-1.2	3.3	4.2	2.6
179	Hebron, Hebron Fjord...................	58 12	62 38	-0 49	-1 05	-1.4	-0.9	3.9	4.7	3.2
181	Nain..................................	56 33	61 41	-0 32	-0 54	+0.3	-0.5	5.2	6.5	4.2
183	Hopedale Harbour......................	55 27	60 13	-0 46	-1 09	-0.4	-0.3	4.3	5.6	4.0
185	Webeck Harbour........................	54 54	58 02	-1 07	-1 38	-1.3	-0.8	3.9	5.0	3.3
	Hamilton Inlet and Lake Melville									
187	Indian Harbour......................	54 27	57 12	-0 37	-1 33	-1.0	-0.9	4.3	5.7	3.4
189	Ticoralak Island....................	54 17	58 12	-0 35	-0 55	-0.9	-0.5	4.0	4.9	3.7
191	Rigolet.............................	54 11	58 25	-0 02	-0 17	-1.9	-1.0	3.5	4.5	2.8
193	Goose Bay...........................	53 21	60 24	+4 22	+4 24	(*0.27+0.4)		1.2	1.7	1.6

Figure 13.3 Table 2: Tidal Differences and Other Constants
(Source: The Tide Tables).

Step 3. Staying in this column, follow down vertically to the intersection of the row in the lower table that is closest to the range of the tide.

- Height of tide at high water: 9.9 feet
- Height of tide at low water: 0.3 feet
- Range of the tide: 9.6 feet

Enter the lower table at 9.5 feet and move to the intersection point. Read the correction in height of 0.4 feet.

Step 4. Since the tide is falling (the period you're concerned with falls within a period when a high tide is going toward a low tide), *subtract* this correction in height from the depth reading from the chart for your position. If the chart depth was 8.9 feet:

- Depth of water on the chart: 8.9 feet
- Minus the correction in height: 0.4 feet
- Corrected depth of water: 8.5 feet

(If the tide were rising, you would *add* the correction in height to the depth reading.)

The *Tide Tables* publication provides a full explanation for using these three tables. Due to the dynamic nature of tides, it is often better to use graphs to depict the changes in the depth of water over the duration of a tide cycle. Computer programs that perform this task are available for your PC. Many larger vessels follow the standard practice of printing out and posting a height of tide curve for each watch. Two simple graphing techniques are provided in this chapter.

TIDE GRAPH: "ONE-QUARTER/ONE-TENTH RULE"

This is another simple method for determining the height of tide at any time. Use this tide graph technique when you want to know the depth of the water at various times on the same day or during a tide cycle. This technique is also called the one-quarter/one-tenth rule.

Note that you must develop a curve graphic for each substation where you may be operating during the day.

Time from the nearest high water or low water

Duration of rise or fall, see footnote (h.m.)	h.m.	h.m.	h.m.	h.m.	h.m.	h.m.	h.m.	h.m.	h.m.	h.m.	h.m.	h.m.	h.m.	h.m.	h.m.
4 00	0 08	0 16	0 24	0 32	0 40	0 48	0 56	1 04	1 12	1 20	1 28	1 36	1 44	1 52	2 00
4 20	0 09	0 17	0 26	0 35	0 43	0 52	1 01	1 09	1 18	1 27	1 35	1 44	1 53	2 01	2 10
4 40	0 09	0 19	0 28	0 37	0 47	0 56	1 05	1 15	1 24	1 33	1 43	1 52	2 01	2 11	2 20
5 00	0 10	0 20	0 30	0 40	0 50	1 00	1 10	1 20	1 30	1 40	1 50	2 00	2 10	2 20	2 30
5 20	0 11	0 21	0 32	0 43	0 53	1 04	1 15	1 25	1 36	1 47	1 57	2 08	2 19	2 29	2 40
5 40	0 11	0 23	0 34	0 45	0 57	1 08	1 19	1 31	1 42	1 53	2 05	2 16	2 27	2 39	2 50
6 00	0 12	0 24	0 36	0 48	1 00	1 12	1 24	1 36	1 48	2 00	2 12	2 24	2 36	2 48	3 00
6 20	0 13	0 25	0 38	0 51	1 03	1 16	1 29	1 41	1 54	2 07	2 19	2 32	2 45	2 57	3 10
6 40	0 13	0 27	0 40	0 53	1 07	1 20	1 33	1 47	2 00	2 13	2 27	2 40	2 53	3 07	3 20
7 00	0 14	0 28	0 42	0 56	1 10	1 24	1 38	1 52	2 06	2 20	2 34	2 48	3 02	3 16	3 30
7 20	0 15	0 29	0 44	0 59	1 13	1 28	1 43	1 57	2 12	2 27	2 41	2 56	3 11	3 25	3 40
7 40	0 15	0 31	0 46	1 01	1 17	1 32	1 47	2 03	2 18	2 33	2 49	3'04	3 19	3 35	3 50
8 00	0 16	0 32	0 48	1 04	1 20	1 36	1 52	2 08	2 24	2 40	2 56	3 12	3 28	3 44	4 00
8 20	0 17	0 33	0 50	1 07	1 23	1 40	1 57	2 13	2 30	2 47	3 03	3 20	3 37	3 53	4 10
8 40	0 17	0 35	0 52	1 09	1 27	1 44	2 01	2 19	2 36	2 53	3 11	3 28	3 45	4 03	4 20
9 00	0 18	0 36	0 54	1 12	1 30	1 48	2 06	2 24	2 42	3 00	3 18	3 36	3 54	4 12	4 30
9 20	0 19	0 37	0 56	1 15	1 33	1 52	2 11	2 29	2 48	3 07	3 25	3 44	4 03	4 21	4 40
9 40	0 19	0 39	0 58	1 17	1 37	1 56	2 15	2 35	2 54	3 13	3 33	3 52	4 11	4 31	4 50
10 00	0 20	0 40	1 00	1 20	1 40	2 00	2 20	2 40	3 00	3 20	3 40	4 00	4 20	4 40	5 00
10 20	0 21	0 41	1 02	1 23	1 43	2 04	2 25	2 45	3 06	3 27	3 47	4 08	4 29	4 49	5 10
10 40	0 21	0 43	1 04	1 25	1 47	2 08	2 29	2 51	3 12	3 33	3 55	4 16	4 37	4 59	5 20

Correction to height

Range of tide, see footnote (Ft.)	Ft.	Ft.	Ft.	Ft.	Ft.	Ft.	Ft.	Ft.	Ft.	Ft.	Ft.	Ft.	Ft.	Ft.	Ft.
0.5	0.0	0.0	0.0	0.0	0.0	0.0	0.1	0.1	0.1	0.1	0.1	0.2	0.2	0.2	0.2
1.0	0.0	0.0	0.0	0.0	0.1	0.1	0.1	0.2	0.2	0.2	0.3	0.3	0.4	0.4	0.5
1.5	0.0	0.0	0.0	0.1	0.1	0.1	0.2	0.2	0.3	0.4	0.4	0.5	0.6	0.7	0.8
2.0	0.0	0.0	0.0	0.1	0.1	0.2	0.3	0.3	0.4	0.5	0.6	0.7	0.8	0.9	1.0
2.5	0.0	0.0	0.1	0.1	0.2	0.2	0.3	0.4	0.5	0.6	0.7	0.9	1.0	1.1	1.2
3.0	0.0	0.0	0.1	0.1	0.2	0.3	0.4	0.5	0.6	0.8	0.9	1.0	1.2	1.3	1.5
3.5	0.0	0.0	0.1	0.2	0.2	0.3	0.4	0.6	0.7	0.9	1.0	1.2	1.4	1.6	1.8
4.0	0.0	0.0	0.1	0.2	0.3	0.4	0.5	0.7	0.8	1.0	1.2	1.4	1.6	1.8	2.0
4.5	0.0	0.0	0.1	0.2	0.3	0.4	0.6	0.7	0.9	1.1	1.3	1.6	1.8	2.0	2.2
5.0	0.0	0.1	0.1	0.2	0.3	0.5	0.6	0.8	1.0	1.2	1.5	1.7	2.0	2.2	2.5
5.5	0.0	0.1	0.1	0.2	0.4	0.5	0.7	0.9	1.1	1.4	1.6	1.9	2.2	2.5	2.8
6.0	0.0	0.1	0.1	0.3	0.4	0.6	0.8	1.0	1.2	1.5	1.8	2.1	2.4	2.7	3.0
6.5	0.0	0.1	0.2	0.3	0.4	0.6	0.8	1.1	1.3	1.6	1.9	2.2	2.6	2.9	3.2
7.0	0.0	0.1	0.2	0.3	0.5	0.7	0.9	1.2	1.4	1.8	2.1	2.4	2.8	3.1	3.5
7.5	0.0	0.1	0.2	0.3	0.5	0.7	1.0	1.2	1.5	1.9	2.2	2.6	3.0	3.4	3.8
8.0	0.0	0.1	0.2	0.3	0.5	0.8	1.0	1.3	1.6	2.0	2.4	2.8	3.2	3.6	4.0
8.5	0.0	0.1	0.2	0.4	0.6	0.8	1.1	1.4	1.8	2.1	2.5	2.9	3.4	3.8	4.2
9.0	0.0	0.1	0.2	0.4	0.6	0.9	1.2	1.5	1.9	2.2	2.7	3.1	3.6	4.0	4.5
9.5	0.0	0.1	0.2	0.4	0.6	0.9	1.2	1.6	2.0	2.4	2.8	3.3	3.8	4.3	4.8
10.0	0.0	0.1	0.2	0.4	0.7	1.0	1.3	1.7	2.1	2.5	3.0	3.5	4.0	4.5	5.0
10.5	0.0	0.1	0.3	0.5	0.7	1.0	1.3	1.7	2.2	2.6	3.1	3.6	4.2	4.7	5.2
11.0	0.0	0.1	0.3	0.5	0.7	1.1	1.4	1.8	2.3	2.8	3.3	3.8	4.4	4.9	5.5
11.5	0.0	0.1	0.3	0.5	0.8	1.1	1.5	1.9	2.4	2.9	3.4	4.0	4.6	5.1	5.8
12.0	0.0	0.1	0.3	0.5	0.8	1.1	1.5	2.0	2.5	3.0	3.6	4.1	4.8	5.4	6.0
12.5	0.0	0.1	0.3	0.5	0.8	1.2	1.6	2.1	2.6	3.1	3.7	4.3	5.0	5.6	6.2
13.0	0.0	0.1	0.3	0.6	0.9	1.2	1.7	2.2	2.7	3.2	3.9	4.5	5.1	5.8	6.5
13.5	0.0	0.1	0.3	0.6	0.9	1.3	1.7	2.2	2.8	3.4	4.0	4.7	5.3	6.0	6.8
14.0	0.0	0.2	0.3	0.6	0.9	1.3	1.8	2.3	2.9	3.5	4.2	4.8	5.5	6.3	7.0
14.5	0.0	0.2	0.4	0.6	1.0	1.4	1.9	2.4	3.0	3.6	4.3	5.0	5.7	6.5	7.2
15.0	0.0	0.2	0.4	0.6	1.0	1.4	1.9	2.5	3.1	3.8	4.5	5.2	5.9	6.7	7.5
15.5	0.0	0.2	0.4	0.7	1.0	1.5	2.0	2.6	3.2	3.9	4.6	5.4	6.1	6.9	7.8
16.0	0.0	0.2	0.4	0.7	1.1	1.5	2.1	2.6	3.3	4.0	4.7	5.5	6.3	7.2	8.0
16.5	0.0	0.2	0.4	0.7	1.1	1.6	2.1	2.7	3.4	4.1	4.9	5.7	6.5	7.4	8.2
17.0	0.0	0.2	0.4	0.7	1.1	1.6	2.2	2.8	3.5	4.2	5.0	5.9	6.7	7.6	8.5
17.5	0.0	0.2	0.4	0.8	1.2	1.7	2.2	2.9	3.6	4.4	5.2	6.0	6.9	7.8	8.8
18.0	0.0	0.2	0.4	0.8	1.2	1.7	2.3	3.0	3.7	4.5	5.3	6.2	7.1	8.1	9.0
18.5	0.1	0.2	0.5	0.8	1.2	1.8	2.4	3.1	3.8	4.6	5.5	6.4	7.3	8.3	9.2
19.0	0.1	0.2	0.5	0.8	1.3	1.8	2.4	3.1	3.9	4.8	5.6	6.6	7.5	8.5	9.5
19.5	0.1	0.2	0.5	0.8	1.3	1.9	2.5	3.2	4.0	4.9	5.8	6.7	7.7	8.7	9.8
20.0	0.1	0.2	0.5	0.9	1.3	1.9	2.6	3.3	4.1	5.0	5.9	6.9	7.9	9.0	10.0

Figure 13.4   Table 3: Height of Tide at Any Time
(Source: The Tide Tables).

Setting Up the Tide Graph

Make a copy of the Tide Graph form (Form 3) from Appendix 7 whenever you set up a tide graph. Here are a few simple steps to follow to help you make a tide graph.

Step 1.   Label the vertical scale (left-hand side of the graph) with the height of tide gradients. These are the height figures from Table 1. You may need to start with a negative number depending on the tidal predictions for the day. Start your labeling in the lower left-hand corner and increase the height upwards. In our example, the height of low tide is 0.3 feet and high tide is 9.9 feet. Start your labeling at zero and increase up the scale to ten feet (refer to Figure 13.5).

Step 2.   Label the horizontal scale (bottom of the graph) in hours. Start at the lower left-hand corner and proceed toward the right along the bottom of the graph. Example: Use the times and heights of high and low water for Saturday, March 4, from Figure 13.2.

In our example, we will be operating between 0800 and 1400. Always correct the *Tide Tables* for daylight saving time. Since the month in the example is March, daylight saving time is not in effect so we can read the time directly from Table 1.

Label the vertical scale of the tide graph from 0.0 feet to 10.0 feet. Label the horizontal scale from 0700 to 1400 hours. Figure 13.5 shows a labeled tide graph.

Plotting the Height of Tide Curve

Now that the graph is set up, you can begin to plot the tidal data. Follow these simple steps to complete this part of the graph.

Step 1.   On the tide graph, plot the height and time of the high and low water in the order of their occurrence for the day you have selected. These plotted points become the starting and ending points of your tide curve. Example: The high tide plot will be on the vertical 0750 hour line at the 9.9-ft horizontal line. The low tide plot will be on the 1421 vertical line and the 0.3-ft horizontal line. These points are plotted in Figure 13.5.

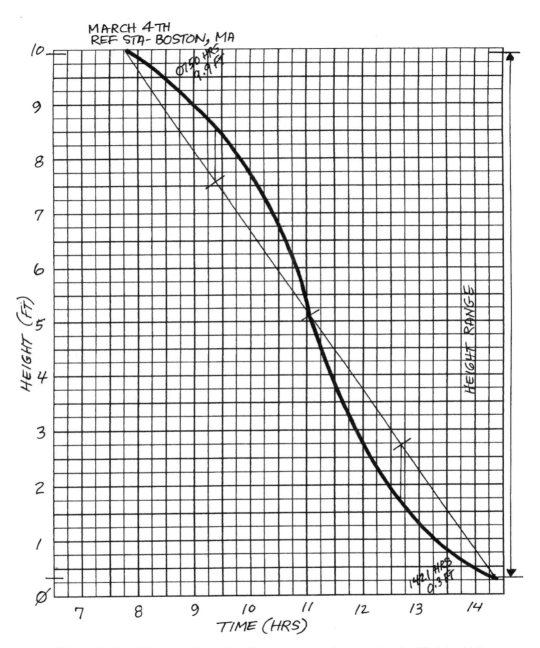

MARCH 4TH
REF STA- BOSTON, MA

0150 HRS
9.9 FT

HEIGHT RANGE

1421 HRS
0.3 FT

HEIGHT (FT)

TIME (HRS)

Figure 13.5 Tide graph illustrating the one-quarter/one-tenth rule *(F. J. Larkin)*.

Step 2.   Draw a straight line connecting the high point and the low point. You may need to plot successive high and low water lines depending on the time of day that you expect to be under way. Figure 13.5 shows this plotted line.

Step 3.   Divide your plotted line into four equal parts. The halfway point on this line is the intersecting point for your curve.

Step 4.   At the margin of your graph, measure the distance between the high and low water marks that you just plotted. This length is your height range or range of tide.

• At the upmost quarter mark on your line, draw a vertical line upward. This vertical line should be equal to one-tenth of the height range.

• At the lower quarter mark on your line, draw a vertical line downward. This vertical line should be equal to one-tenth of the height range. Figure 13.5 shows an example of these vertical lines.

Step 5.   On the plotted line, draw a smooth curve starting at the plotted high water point, tangent to the high-water quarter vertical line point, through the center point, tangent to the low-water quarter vertical line point, ending at the plotted low water point. Round the curve well.

This curve approximates the actual tide curve. The heights of tides for any time of the day can be readily scaled from this type of curve. Add or subtract the height of tide to or from the depth of water printed on your nautical chart.

EXAMPLE: Using the tide graph plotted in Figure 13.5, find the height of tide for 1130 hrs. The depth of the water printed on your chart is 5 feet at 1130 hrs. The tide graph shows the height of tide for 1130 to be 3.75 feet or 3' 8". Added to the charted depth of 5 feet, your estimated depth would be 8' 8".

CAUTION: *The one-quarter/one-tenth rule is based on the assumption that the rise and fall of tide conforms to simple cosine curves. The heights obtained will always be approximate. The roughness of the approximation will vary as the tide curve differs from the cosine curve.*

GPS NOTE: *Most newer GPS sets provide Height of Tide predictions as part of their software package. Many sets show the height correction as part of a navigation screen. Check your GPS operating manual for this feature. Figure 13.6 shows a tide tracking screen from a GPS set. It also provides the latest information on the time of high and low tides in the area.*

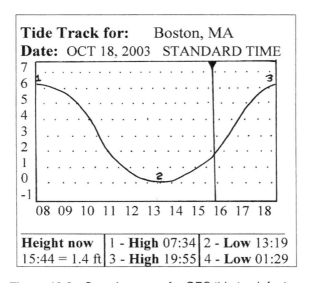

Figure 13.6 Sample screen for GPS tide track feature.

PRACTICE PROBLEMS

Use the tide graph in Figure 13.5 to solve these problems.

1. What is your estimated depth at 0930 if your charted depth is stated as 2.5 feet?

2. The charted depth is 9.3 ft. What is the estimated depth at 12 noon?

3. The charted depth is 5 ft. The MHW datum is 9.5 ft for this area. The vertical height of the bridge is 12 ft. At what time would your estimated clearance under the bridge be 15 ft?

4. The charted depth of a shoal is 2 feet. You need a minimum of 6 ft to clear the shoal with a 3-ft safety margin. What is the latest time that you should plan to cross over this shoal?

ANSWERS

1. Simply measure your estimated depth for 0930 and add it to the charted depth.

Estimated depth from graph	8.4 ft
Charted depth	+2.5 ft
Estimated depth at your position	10.9 ft

2. Find the estimated depth from the graph for 1200 hrs and add it to the charted depth.

Estimated depth from graph	2.7 ft
Charted depth	+9.3 ft
Estimated depth at your position	12.0 ft

3. You need 15 ft. The vertical clearance for the bridge is 12 ft. Subtracting 12 from 15 shows that you need an additional 3 ft. The height of tide at high water is 9.9 ft, which is 0.4 ft above the MHW datum. Subtract 3.4 ft from the high water height and find the time on the graph for that depth.

Clearance required	15.0 ft
Vertical clearance of bridge	− 12.0 ft
Additional clearance required	3.0 ft
Height of tide at high water	9.9 ft
MHW datum for place	9.5 ft
Difference over MHW datum	0.4 ft
Additional clearance required	+ 3.0 ft
Total clearance required	3.4 ft
Height of tide at high water	9.9 ft
Total clearance required	− 3.4 ft
Depth to enter graph	6.5 ft
Time when vertical clearance is 15 ft	1036 hrs

4. You need to enter the graph at the 4-ft point on the vertical scale and read the time from the horizontal scale.

Minimum depth required	6 ft
Charted depth	2 ft
Additional clearance required	4 ft
Graphed time at 4 ft	1124 hrs

THE RULE OF TWELVES

The rule of twelves is a simplified method for predicting the height of the tide at any time. This technique involves dividing the range of tide into twelve equal parts and applying the rule. The resulting data may be graphed if you need multiple height predictions during a tidal cycle. Follow these simple steps to complete the rule of twelves tidal predictions.

Step 1. Determine the range of tide. The range of tide is the difference between the high and low height predictions on a specific day for a particular tide cycle. As an example, use the data found in Figure 13.2. Because the date is March 4, you don't have to correct for daylight saving time. Use the range of tide between 1421 and 2035 hrs.

Depth at 2035 hrs	8.8 ft
Depth at 1421 hrs	– 0.3 ft
Range of tide	8.5 ft

Step 2. Divide the range of tide by twelve: 8.5 ft divided by 12 equals 0.71 ft.

Step 3. Apply the rule of twelves.

END OR START OF HIGH TIDE	RULE OF TWELVES	TIDE CHANGE IN FEET	DEPTH PREDICTION
Start 1421			0.30 ft
First Hour 1521	1/12	0.71 ft	1.01 ft
Second Hour 1621	2/12	1.42 ft	2.43 ft
Third Hour 1721	3/12	2.12 ft	4.55 ft
Fourth Hour 1821	3/12	2.12 ft	6.67 ft
Fifth Hour 1921	2/12	1.42 ft	8.09 ft
Sixth Hour 2021	1/12	0.71 ft	8.80 ft

Going from low to high water, add the tide change. Going from high to low, subtract the tide change.

Step 4. When you need to predict the height of tide for various times during a tidal cycle, plot your data on a tide graph. The vertical scale is height of tide and the horizontal scale is time. Figure 13.7 shows the data plotted for the example calculated in Step 3. Notice how, when the curve is rounded, it looks like the tide curve that was developed using the one-quarter/one-tenth rule.

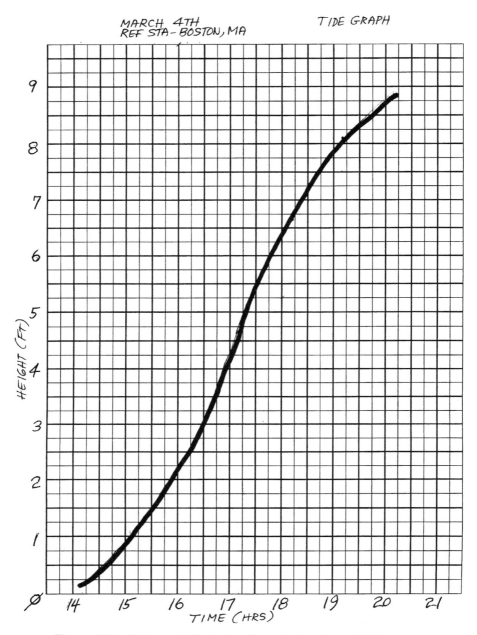

Figure 13.7   Tide graph illustrating the rule of twelves *(F. J. Larkin).*

> CAUTION: *The rule of twelves is based on the assumption that the rise and fall of tide conforms to simple cosine curves. The heights obtained will always be approximate. The roughness of the approximation will vary as the tide curve differs from the cosine curve.*

PRACTICE PROBLEMS

Use the tide graph in Figure 13.7 to solve these problems.

1. What is the estimated depth at 4:30 PM if the charted depth is 3.5 ft?
2. The charted depth is 5 ft. You need 10 ft to cross a shoal. What is the earliest estimated time that you can make this crossing?
3. At what time will the depth be 7.5 feet above the charted depth?

ANSWERS

1. Convert 4:30 PM to military time or 1630 hrs. Enter the graph at 1630 and read out the feet or 3.1 ft.

Charted depth	3.5 ft
Graph depth	+3.1 ft
Estimated depth	6.6 ft

2. You have 5 ft and need 5 more. Enter the graph at 5 ft and read out the hours: 17.3 or 1718 hours or 5:18 PM.

3. Enter the graph at 7.5 feet and read out the hours: 18.7 or 1842 hours or 6:42 PM.

HEIGHT AVAILABLE UNDER A BRIDGE

Now that you know how to find the depth of water at any time, it is a simple matter to determine the depth under a bridge at any time. There are a few facts that you need to know that will help you understand this calculation:

- Bridge heights are measured from MHW, mean high water, upward to the lowest part of the span over the navigation channel.

- The tidal information block on each nautical chart shows the height of MHW, mean high water.

Here are a few simple steps that will help complete this height calculation.

Step 1. Look up the mean high water datum from the tidal information block on your nautical chart. There may be more than one MHW datum listed so use the one closest to your position. Enter the MHW datum on your worksheet. Figure 13.8 shows the tidal information block from a Boston Harbor chart. The place nearest to Neponset is Charlestown, which has a MHW datum of 9.5 ft.

Step 2. Copy the projected height of tide for the point in time that you will be passing under the bridge. Use either of the graphing methods explained in this chapter. Using Figure 13.6, assume you plan to pass under the bridge at 1730 hours or 5:30 PM. The projected depth is 5.5 ft at that time for that day.

Step 3. Determine the additional clearance provided by the tide by subtracting the projected height of tide from the nearest MHW datum. Post the result on your worksheet. In our example, the mean high water datum is 9.5 feet.

MHW datum for nearest place	9.5 ft
Projected Height of Tide	– 5.5 ft
Additional clearance	4.0 ft

Step 4. Enter the vertical clearance listed for the bridge. These data will be found on your chart. The Bascule Bridge in the Neponset area has a vertical clearance of 12 ft.

Step 5. To compute the available height under the bridge, add the additional clearance figure to the vertical clearance listed for the bridge. For our example:

Vertical clearance of bridge	12.0 ft
Additional clearance	+ 4.0 ft
Available height under the bridge	16.0 ft

The available height under the bridge at 1730 hours on March 4th is 16.0 ft.

BOSTON INNER HARBOR

Mercator Projection
Scale 1:10,000 at Lat. 42°22′
North American 1927 Datum

SOUNDINGS IN FEET
AT MEAN LOW WATER

	Height referred to datum of soundings (MLW)			
Place	Mean High Water	Mean Tide Level	Mean Low Water	Extreme Low Water
	feet	feet	feet	feet
Charlestown	9.5	4.7	0.0	−3.5

TIDAL INFORMATION

(1279)

Figure 13.8 Sample tidal information block
(Source: NOAA nautical chart).

Reader Progress Note

What do you now know? You can correct a depth for the time of the tide and can figure the height clearance under a bridge for a specific time. However, never forget that these are *estimated* depths and heights and that you should use multiple methods to verify all data in navigation. Nothing stays the same on the sea. Weather changes the depth of the water—both high and low. Shoals are generated where they never were before. Become very suspicious and double-check everything. Above all, use common sense. If it doesn't feel right, don't go there.

FOURTEEN

Compensating Your Course for Current and Other Elements

USING GPS TO CORRECT FOR CURRENT AND OTHER ELEMENTS

The newer GPS sets recalculate their position every second or at even shorter intervals. Check your GPS operating manual to see if your set fits in that category. Newer, rapid-calculating GPS sets provide a good estimate of your boat's SOG—Speed Over the Ground—or the velocity that your boat is tracking along the surface of the earth. Bundled into this SOG is the effect of all of the elements on your boat: current, wind, water depth, weight on your boat, and the attitude angle of your boat. The GPS measures exactly what is happening to your boat at the exact time that you observe the reading. If you are operating a motorboat at a speed over 10 to 15 knots, the effect of current and the other elements is immaterial. As long as you understand the makeup of the speed reading, there is no need to reference a speed curve. When you need to travel at 15 kts, just crank up the engine RPMs until the SOG on your GPS is reading 15 kts. Think of all the mathematical transactions and calculation time that you can save. The TTG—Time to Go—readout will display the time of travel to your next waypoint based on the SOG you are achieving at the time. (Remember, however, to steer your boat with a compass and not the GPS.) On some newer sets, you can plug in the time when you want to reach a waypoint (an ETA) and the GPS will show you the SOG that you need to achieve in order to stay on schedule. Nice stuff! Columbus is rolling over in his grave!

If you have an older and slower GPS or LORAN set, you may have some problems. I had an old LORAN that calculated information every 30 seconds. Unless I made a long, straight run on a course heading, the LORAN's speed and heading were always off. Remember that speed is always being averaged and that the heading is a straight line from where the boat was 30 seconds ago to where it is now. Any turn in a course line causes erroneous headings. However, the headings to the next waypoint in a route work very well. I overcame this difficulty by using a nautical chart and staying aware of how the set is calculating its data.

Regardless, wind and current will always deflect your boat off course and you need to stay aware of this possibility. Assuming your compass and steering post are set up correctly, always keep in mind that the bearing that your GPS is displaying to the next waypoint is changing. A Trip Log is very helpful for this situation. The following simple procedure will help you handle this problem:

Step 1.   If you notice that a heading correction is required by the GPS, first assure yourself that this is not just a steering error. If you detect a steering error, bring your boat back on the correct course immediately by referencing the compass course in your Trip Log. Some GPS sets continue to reference the course heading between waypoints.

Step 2.   Hold your original compass heading from the Trip Log. Do not change it yet.

Step 3.   If, after a short run, your boat drifts off course, correct your compass heading as follows:

- Record the amount of degrees that your boat is off course from your original Trip Log heading, i.e., 6 degrees to port. For the purpose of our example, assume that your Trip Log heading is a compass course of 090 degrees. Therefore, your compass would be reading 084.

- To counteract whatever elements are pushing your boat off course, double the number of degrees that your boat is off the Trip Log course and steer it in the opposite direction. That is, your boat is off 6 degrees to port so you need to steer 12 degrees to starboard or 096 on your compass. Steer with your compass. Note that your boat will not be pointing at the next waypoint when you perform this correction.

Step 4. Hold this new course on your compass and, after a reasonable interval, recheck whether you have overcome the effect of the element. Your boat should be crabbing along the track line shown on your GPS. In other words, while your boat's steering post will not be pointing directly at the next waypoint, your boat's CMG—Course Made Good—on the GPS should start to reflect your original Trip Log compass heading. Repeat Step 3 as necessary.

GPS Safety Note: *When you use waypoints to assist with the navigation of your boat, the heading to the next waypoint that is suggested by your GPS often changes to reflect the direction from your boat's actual LAT/LON position to the waypoint. This is a dynamic process so that wherever you steer the boat, your GPS will continue to provide you with the heading back to the next waypoint. This is a wonderful GPS feature but it also has its pitfalls. Suppose there is an obstruction or shoal nearby your planned track line to the waypoint. If you are inattentive to your steering, it is highly probable that you can steer your boat off course to the point where the suggested heading on the GPS will direct your boat right over the obstruction. Stay focused when steering your boat and keep matching your CMG to your planned Trip Log heading. Keep safe out there!*

Sailors travel at a much slower speed than powerboat operators and, therefore, the effect of current on their boat is more pronounced. Sailors must be constantly aware of the effect of the elements on their boat and be able to correct for them with their navigation skills. Without their boat's engine, they are at the mercy of the wind and the other elements. The rest of this chapter is written for you hardy sailors and for those dedicated "predicted loggers" who insist on precision navigation using only a compass and a tachometer.

CORRECTING FOR CURRENT AND OTHER ELEMENTS

Unfortunately, the only time that you can use a DR heading and speed prediction is on a day when there is no wind, and the current is slack, the water depth is over 18 feet, and the weight of your boat is exactly the same as when you ran your speed curve. After many attempts at predicting an exact ETA without great success, I have isolated five elements that affect the accuracy of a DR calculation:

1. The accuracy of your DR speed prediction.
2. The presence of current along your DR course line.
3. Weight differences from your boat's baseline weight.
4. Water depth under 18 feet.
5. The presence of wind along your DR course line.

Every navigator needs to deal with DR predictions and current problems. Owners of heavy displacement vessels may find that changes in boat weight and wind velocity have minimal impact on their ETA predictions due to the large size of their boats. However, boat owners of small planing boats will soon discover that any weight change and wind will have a great effect on their navigation speed predictions.

Without any understanding of the five elements, you could be led to think that your piloting errors are due to something that you failed to understand about the DR formula, $60 \times D = S \times T$. Not so! The following five examples illustrate a complete piloting prediction and will help you understand why a DR speed prediction does not work on its own.

The DR Prediction

To illustrate the situation, suppose you are on a leg of a trip that is 2.8 nm long, on a heading of 090 degrees, and at a speed of 12.3 knots. If you started this leg at 0900, what is your ETA?

> $60 \times 2.8 = 12.3 \times T$ or 13.659 minutes or 13 m 40 s. Your ETA is 09:13:40.

Mathematical errors are the biggest problem with this first element. Get yourself a good calculator or install the formula on your computer. I use a computer to check all my navigation data when I plan a trip.

The Current Problem

Assume 0.500 kts of current is striking your boat directly on the stern. Your speed prediction must change since current at the stern will make your boat go faster. Starting this leg at the same time as the preceding example, you will find a 32-second change in your ETA due to the current.

> 12.3 kts + 0.500 kts = 12.800 kts
>
> $60 \times 2.8 = 12.800 \times T$ or 13.125 minutes or 13 m 8 s.

Your DR ETA of 09:13:40 changes to 09:13:08. If you hadn't corrected for this element, you would be 32 seconds or about 100 yards off on this leg of your trip. This could be disastrous in the fog or on a night run.

A Weighty Issue

Now presume you had been running for 5 hrs before you began this leg of your trip. Your boat is 25 feet in length, your fuel consumption is 12.5 gallons per hour, and the boat has a base weight of 4,350 lbs. The effect of this lengthy run and the resultant loss of weight due to fuel consumption would be an increase of 0.501 knots in your predicted speed because a lighter boat will go faster.

$$5 \text{ hr} \times 12.5 \text{ gal/hr} = 62.5 \text{ gals} \times 5.667 \text{ lbs/gal} = 354 \text{ lbs}/4,350$$
$$= 0.081/2 = 0.041 \times 12.3 \text{ kts} = 0.501 \text{ kts}$$

You add the weight correction in this example since it lightens the boat and a lighter boat goes faster.

(Drift correction + 0.500 kts) + (Weight correction + 0.501 kts) + (Planned speed 12.300 kts) = 13.301 kts

$60 \times 2.8 = 13.301 \times T$ or 12.631 minutes or 12 m 38 s

Assuming that the DR and current elements are the same, your ETA is now estimated to be 09:12:38. This is a 30-second difference from your previously corrected time. The weight change correction is similar to the current correction in this example—a difference often missed by the average skipper, but very important to a Predicted Logging enthusiast.

Water Depth

Water depths of under 18 feet impact the speed of your boat by approximately 0.125 knots for every foot of depth change. The effect is different for displacement and planing boats. Let's suppose that you have a planing boat and you are transiting an area that has a water depth of 15.8 feet on this leg. The effect on predicted speed would be 0.275 knots. Since planing boats speed up in shallow water, the 0.275 would be added to your predicted speed.

15.8 ft – 18.0 ft = 2.2 ft × 0.125 kts = 0.275 kts

13.300 kts + 0.275 kts = 13.575 kts

$60 \times 2.8 = 13.575 \times T$ or 12.376 minutes or 12 m 23 s

Your new ETA is 09:12:23. Each of the first four elements have caused you to reach your ETA sooner. There is a 1 minute 17 second difference from your original DR-generated ETA. That time difference would put you almost six football fields (588 yards) off your mark.

The Effect of Wind

Wind has a distinct influence on the speed of small, light boats. Presume that a 16-knot wind is blowing directly on your boat's stern. This wind velocity causes your boat to drift downwind at a rate of 1.2 knots. Assuming that the DR, current, depth, and weight are the same as calculated above, your predicted speed would be changed since your boat speed would be increased by the wind at the stern.

13.575 kts + 1.200 kts = 14.775 kts

$60 \times 2.8 = 14.775 \times T$ or 11.371 minutes or 11 m 22 s

Your ETA now is 09:11:22. Because your boat is moving faster, you get there sooner.

Normally, you won't be able to predict the effect of the wind in advance. You will experience it while under way. A technique for predicting the effect of the wind is explained later in this chapter.

Let's take a summary look at the total effect of the five elements:

Planned Speed 12.300	Change	Predicted Speed	ETA	Effect
DR calculation	0.000	12.300	09:13:40	None
Effect of drift	+0.500	12.800	09:13:08	Off the stern. ETA is 32 s sooner. Boat SOA increases.
Effect of weight	+0.501	13.301	09:12:38	Boat weight decreases. ETA is 30 s sooner. Boat SOA increases.
Effect of depth	+0.275	13.575	09:12:23	Shoal increases speed. ETA is 15 s sooner. Boat SOA increases.
Effect of wind	+1.200	14.775	09:11:22	Off the stern. ETA is 61 s sooner. Boat SOA increases.
Speed of advance	+2.476 kts	14.775	09:11:22	ETA is 2m 18 s sooner.

The point you need to understand is that your ETA prediction is often a moving target. Don't be distressed that the DR-generated ETA isn't the complete answer. Certainly, it may appear sufficient on a clear, calm day. However, it won't be accurate enough for running in fog, in rain, or at nighttime. It is important to make it a practice of calculating each element and performing test runs in clear weather. This practice is the only way to improve your navigational skills and learn how your boat operates. Only then will you be able to handle fog and night running. When you run at night, select slow speeds. It is very difficult to see floating logs or lobster trap buoys. Also at night, avoid all white light to preserve your night sight.

If, in the fifth example, the wind shifted to the bow rather than the stern, this would be a good instance of an incident when the five elements almost balance themselves out due chiefly to the wind. However, if you had not corrected for the wind, you would be 61 seconds off your ETA. When you use the DR calculation exclusively, and you arrive at your ETA close to your predicted time, you can be sure that you have experienced compensating speed adjustments from any or all of the other four elements. I hope this gives you enough incentive to learn and understand the other four elements. You should have already mastered the DR procedure in Chapter 8.

CORRECTING YOUR COURSE FOR CURRENT

Current can have a major effect on your ability to hold a course and arrive at a planned destination at a specified time. I have found over the years that most of the current that you will experience will be less than 1 knot. I have also found that the traditional current vector technique does not work well with these slow currents but is effective with currents over 1 knot. Both systems are explained for you.

To understand current, become familiar with this new terminology:

Intended track: This is the planned heading for your boat after you have compensated for current, wind, or seas. When calculated correctly, your boat's heading will be the intended track but it, actually, should crab along the DR line that you plotted on your chart assuming that none of the other four elements is present.

Track: Track is the direction of your planned (intended) track line. Track is abbreviated TR.

Speed of advance: Speed of advance is the planned (intended) rate of travel along your planned (intended) track line after you have compensated your planned speed for the other outside elements. The abbreviation for speed of advance is SOA.

Course made good: This is the net direction of the actual path of your boat. The abbreviation is CMG. Ideally, you want your DR line and your

CMG to be equal. The reason for the additional term is that often they are different due to any of the five elements.

Speed made good: This is the actual rate of travel along the track. The abbreviation is SMG. Again, it should be the same as your SOA. This skill of understanding your boat's characteristics is to make SMG and SOA equal.

Set: Set is the direction of the current or the direction to which the current is flowing. Set is expressed in degrees. This term is used for water flow only, not wind. Note that wind direction is expressed in the direction from which the wind is blowing.

Drift: Drift is the speed of the current. Drift is usually stated in knots and must always be corrected for the calendar date by a factor when using tidal current charts. This factor is related to the predicted drift for each day of the year. It is usually different for ebbs and floods.

WHERE DO YOU FIND INFORMATION ABOUT TIDES AND CURRENTS?

Obviously, you can't predict current without specific information about the speed and drift that is present in an area that you are transiting. Go back and review Chapter 2. Specifically, look over tide tables, tidal current tables, tidal current charts, and tidal current diagrams. Depending on the geographical area where you do your boating, different publications are better than others. Also review nautical publications such as Eldridge and Reeds, which may be more appropriate for your area. Each of these publications has a section that explains the use of their current charts and tables. Visit a good marine book store and ask for specific advice about your boating area.

Always keep in mind that navigation is an imperfect science that is affected by natural elements. Don't expect your calculated results to be perfect. Things constantly change on the water. The proficient navigator learns how to recognize when changes happen under way and corrects for them. This knowledge takes time to attain but it's worth the effort.

THE EFFECTS OF CURRENT

Current is the horizontal movement of water and it can affect your boat's speed and course from any angle. This effect can be separated into three conditions:

1. **Current striking your boat directly on the bow.**
2. **Current striking your boat directly on the stern.**
3. **Current coming from any other direction.**

The first two conditions can be explained easily with the following simple rules:

Rule 1. When the current is striking your boat directly on the bow, there is no effect on the direction or heading of your boat. However, your forward progress will be slowed by the drift of the current.

To compute your SOA (speed of advance), subtract the drift (speed of the current) from your planned boat speed. For example, your planned boat speed is 10 knots (by your speed curve). The drift of the current on your bow is 1.5 knots. Your SOA is 8.5 knots (10 kts – 1.5 kts = 8.5 knots).

Rule 2. When the current is striking directly on the stern of your boat, there is no effect on its direction or heading. However, the forward progress of your boat will be faster.

To compute your SOA, add the drift to your planned boat speed. For example, your planned boat speed is 10 knots (by your speed curve). The current off your stern has a drift of 1.5 knots. Your SOA is 11.5 knots (10 kts + 1.5 kts = 11.5 kts).

The third condition needs more explanation.

Current Striking Your Boat from Any Other Direction

Unfortunately, the situation where current is striking your boat's hull from a direction other than the bow and stern is the most common. This correction is accomplished by using either current vectors or simple tables:

- Tables are efficient to use with currents under 1 knot.

- Current vectors or tables can be used for currents over 1 knot.

- Canals or guts that have high-velocity currents can be very dangerous if you have a slow boat. It is prudent to plan your transit through these areas around times of slack water in order to avoid losing control of your boat and endangering yourself and crew.

Current Vectors. A current vector is simply a triangle where one side represents the set and drift, one side represents your DR course, and the third side depicts the track of your boat. When any two sides of the

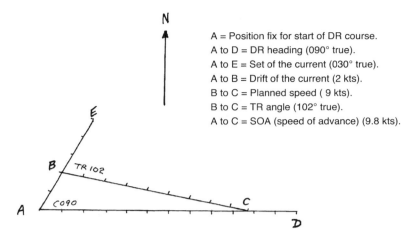

A = Position fix for start of DR course.
A to D = DR heading (090° true).
A to E = Set of the current (030° true).
A to B = Drift of the current (2 kts).
B to C = Planned speed (9 kts).
B to C = TR angle (102° true).
A to C = SOA (speed of advance) (9.8 kts).

Figure 14.1 A vector diagram *(F. J. Larkin)*.

triangle are known, the third side can be calculated or measured. I find that it is easier to draw a current vector by using speed as the controlling element.

Figure 14.1 graphically depicts the parts of a current diagram. Assume your true course is 090 degrees, your planned speed is 9 knots, the set of the current is 030 degrees, and the drift of the current is 2 knots. This current problem can be easily solved by drawing a current vector using speed in knots. Select a fixed interval to represent a knot. I use the millimeter scale on a ruler and plot on graph paper. Assume true north is at the top of the page. Draw a vector as large as possible and your angle and speed measurements will be more accurate.

Step 1. Plot the direction of your DR course line (090 degrees). Label the starting point "A" and the ending point "D." The length of the line is not important as long as it is longer than your planned speed multiplied by your selected knot interval. (That is, planned speed is 9 kts and the selected knot interval is 1 inch. The length of line A–D would be longer than 9 inches.)

Step 2. Plot the set and drift of the current. From point A, draw a line at 030 degrees. The length is not important as long as it is longer than the selected knot interval times the drift. Label the ending point "E." The line A–E is a projection of the set (direction) of the current.

Step 3. From point A, measure off the set of the current toward point E. The set is 2 knots so the distance would be equal to two of your selected knot intervals. Label this new point

"B." The line A–B is a representation of the set and drift of the current.

Step 4.   From point B, measure off the planned speed of the boat so that it intersects the A–D line. The planned speed is 9 knots so the length of the line would be equal to nine of your selected knot intervals. Label this new point "C." Draw a line from point B to point C. Line B–C represents your intended track.

Step 5.   To find the angle of your track (TR), use a plotter and measure the angle of the B–C line. (102 degrees.)

Step 6.   To find your SOA, measure the A–C line using the selected knot interval. (9.8 knots.)

Note: This current solution assumes that you know the set and drift of the current in advance. Figure 14.1 illustrates this current vector solution.

THE BEFORE AND AFTER CURRENT PROBLEM

Dealing with current is a little like "Pay me now, or pay me later." There are two ways to correct for current, *planning ahead* or *correcting afterwards*. Planning ahead was just explained.

In a "correcting afterwards" circumstance, you may want to determine the current in an area that has no current prediction, or you may discover that you are off course after a period of travel and suspect that the error is due to current. The unfortunate thing is that the effect of all of the elements will be bundled in your solution and you may not be able to attribute your solution to any single element.

A simple problem is used to explain the piloting procedure. Your DR course is 240 degrees and your planned distance is 8.0 nm. Initially, the planned speed is 12 knots and your departure time is 0900. After traveling for 15 minutes, you discover that you are off your DR course line. By taking a fix, you determine your 0915 position.

To solve this piloting problem, first, determine the set and drift of the current and, second, plot a new course to your destination point. Now we can find the set and drift:

Step 1.   Calculate and plot your DR course to your destination point.

$$60 \times 8.0 \text{ nm} = 12.0 \text{ kts} \times T \text{ or } 40 \text{ m; ETA is } 0900 + 0040$$
$$= 09 \text{ h } 40 \text{ m}.$$

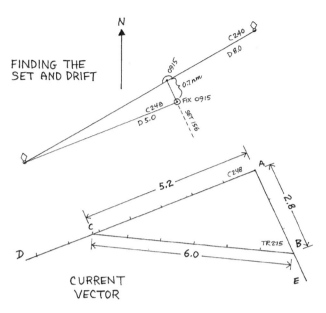

Figure 14.2 A course plot and vector diagram *(F. J. Larkin).*

Step 2. Calculate and plot your 0915 DR position. This is a simple DR formula (60*D* = *ST*) solution for distance. Time and speed are known.

$$60 \times D = 12.0 \text{ kts} \times 15 \text{ m} = 3 \text{ nm}$$

Measure 3 nm down from the departure point and label your DR position.

Step 3. Plot your 0915 fix. You can use a LORAN fix, a GPS fix, a fix obtained by plotting two or three bearings, or, if you pass close aboard an aid to navigation, you can use it as a fix. These alternatives are all considered valid position fixes.

Step 4. Measure the distance from your 0915 fix to your 0915 DR position plot. (0.7 nm.)

Step 5. Calculate the drift of the current. You know the time. You measured the distance in Step 4. Use the DR formula and solve for speed.

$$60 \times 0.7 \text{ nm} = S \times 15 \text{ m} = 2.8 \text{ kts}$$

Step 6. Using a plotter, measure the set of the current. (Set equals 156 degrees.) Figure 14.2 shows this plotted course and fix.

Correcting Your Course to Your Destination Point

Now that you have discovered your error and have calculated the set and drift of the current, you can develop a current vector for the remainder of your trip. Your new starting point is your 0915 fix since it is a higher grade position than your 0915 DR position. Draw a current vector employing the new data using the following steps. Use 6 kts as your new planned speed. Be aware that, in reality, a current may not remain constant over the entire leg of a trip. Train yourself to be alert for changes in current set and drift.

Step 1.   Measure and plot the direction of your new DR course line (248 degrees). Use your 0915 fix as the starting position because it is considered a higher level position than a DR position. Label the starting point "A" and the ending point "D." When using a vector to solve a current problem, you can draw it directly on the chart or use graph paper. The principles are the same. However, it is much neater to use graph paper. Keep the writing on your charts to a minimum, especially items that are constantly changing.

Step 2.   Plot the set of the current. From point A, draw a line at 156 degrees. Label the ending point "E."

Step 3.   Plot the drift of the current. From point A, measure off the set of the current toward point E. Set is 2.8 knots so the distance would be equal to 2.8 of your selected knot intervals. Label this new point "B." The line A–B now represents the set and drift of the current.

Step 4.   Draw a line from point B so that it intersects the A–D line at the length of your planned speed (measured with your selected space interval). Your new planned speed is 6 knots so the length would be equal to six of your selected knot intervals. Label this new point "C."

Step 5.   Find the track (TR). Use a plotter and measure the angle of the B–C line (275 degrees).

Step 6.   Find your speed of advance. Measure the A–C line using the selected knot interval (5.2 kts).

Calculating the New ETA to Your Destination Point

With the knowledge of the set and drift that originally pushed you off course, you can now calculate a new ETA.

Step 1. Measure the distance from the 0915 fix to your destination point (5.0 nm).

Step 2. Calculate your ETA. You know the new distance (5.0 nm) and have a new SOA (5.1 knots). Use the DR formula to compute your time.

$$60 \times 5.0 \text{ nm} = 5.1. \text{ kts} \times T = 58.82 \text{ m or 58 m 49 s}$$

Your new ETA is 09:15:00 + 00:58:49 or 10:13:49.

Step 3. Correct your new TR of 274 degrees for variation and deviation using TVMDC before running this course with your boat's compass.

T	274
V	016 W (from the nearest compass rose)
M	290
D	004 E (from your boat's deviation table)
C	286

You would steer your boat on a compass heading of 286. The boat would crab along your DR line toward your destination being pushed on the port bow by the 2.8-kt current. Note that just because a current affected the first half of a leg, it may not continue throughout the entire leg. However, it is a best estimate. You should always be alert for changes.

Estimated Positions

Positions calculated using current vectors and tables are called *estimated positions* (EPs). They are considered more accurate than DR positions but less accurate than fixes. Use the symbol of a position dot surrounded by a square when labeling estimated positions (Figure 14.3).

Figure 14.3 Estimated position *(F. J. Larkin)*.

USING TABLES TO CORRECT FOR CURRENT

Because most of the current drift that you will encounter will be less than a knot, you will find that tables are more convenient to use for correcting your predicted speed and heading. You will also find that predicted speed corrections are more important than corrections for headings, especially on small boats. Trying to steer a heading correction of 1 or 2 degrees is at best impossible on a small boat.

Two tables are provided:

Table 1—Course Corrections for Current

Table 2—Speed Corrections for Current

To illustrate the use of these tables, assume the following conditions: The drift of the current is 0.600 kts. The DR heading is 090 degrees. The set of the current is 030 degrees. The planned boat speed is 12.3 kts.

How to Use Table 1—Course Corrections for Current

To use Table 1, you need to know two facts:

1. The angle between your DR heading and the set of the current.
2. The ratio of drift to planned boat speed.

Follow these simple steps to determine your heading correction.

Step 1. Find the angle between your boat's heading and the set of the current. Subtract one from the other. If the answer is greater than 180, subtract 180.

Heading = 090; set = 030; 030 – 090 = 060

Step 2. Find the ratio of drift to planned boat speed. Divide your planned boat speed into the drift.

Planned boat speed = 12.300 kts; drift = 0.600 kts; 0.600 kts/12.300 kts = 0.049

Step 3. Using the angle and ratio, find the course correction from Table 1 (Figures 14.4a and b).

Angle = 060; ratio = 0.05; course correction from Table 1 = 002 degrees

Step 4. Add the heading correction to your DR heading when the current is striking your boat's starboard side. You always steer into the direction of the current.

| Table One | Heading Corrections Due to Current | | | | | | | | | Page 1 |

Angle	Angle	Ratio of Speed to Drift								
		0.01	0.02	0.03	0.04	0.05	0.06	0.07	0.08	0.09	0.10
000	180	0	0	0	0	0	0	0	0	0	0
001	179	0	0	0	0	0	0	0	0	0	0
002	178	0	0	0	0	0	0	0	0	0	0
003	177	0	0	0	0	0	0	0	0	0	0
004	176	0	0	0	0	0	0	0	0	0	0
005	175	0	0	0	0	0	0	0	0	0	0
006	174	0	0	0	0	0	0	0	0	0	0
007	173	0	0	0	0	0	0	0	0	0	0
008	172	0	0	0	0	0	0	0	0	0	1
009	171	0	0	0	0	0	0	0	0	1	1
010	170	0	0	0	0	0	0	0	1	1	1
011	169	0	0	0	0	0	0	0	1	1	1
012	168	0	0	0	0	0	0	1	1	1	1
013	167	0	0	0	0	0	1	1	1	1	1
014	166	0	0	0	0	0	1	1	1	1	1
015	165	0	0	0	0	0	1	1	1	1	1
016	164	0	0	0	0	1	1	1	1	1	1
017	163	0	0	0	0	1	1	1	1	1	1
018	162	0	0	0	0	1	1	1	1	1	1
019	161	0	0	0	1	1	1	1	1	1	1
020	160	0	0	0	1	1	1	1	1	1	1
021	159	0	0	0	1	1	1	1	1	1	1
022	158	0	0	0	1	1	1	1	1	1	1
023	157	0	0	0	1	1	1	1	1	1	2
024	156	0	0	0	1	1	1	1	1	1	2
025	155	0	0	0	1	1	1	1	1	1	2
026	154	0	0	1	1	1	1	1	1	2	2
027	153	0	0	1	1	1	1	1	1	2	2
028	152	0	0	1	1	1	1	1	1	2	2
029	151	0	0	1	1	1	1	1	2	2	2
030	150	0	0	1	1	1	1	1	2	2	2
031	149	0	0	1	1	1	1	1	2	2	2
032	148	0	0	1	1	1	1	1	2	2	2
033	147	0	0	1	1	1	1	2	2	2	2
034	146	0	0	1	1	1	1	2	2	2	2
035	145	0	0	1	1	1	1	2	2	2	2
036	144	0	0	1	1	1	1	2	2	2	2
037	143	0	0	1	1	1	1	2	2	2	2
038	142	0	1	1	1	1	2	2	2	2	3
039	141	0	1	1	1	1	2	2	2	2	3
040	140	0	1	1	1	1	2	2	2	2	3
041	139	0	1	1	1	1	2	2	2	2	3
042	138	0	1	1	1	1	2	2	2	3	3
043	137	0	1	1	1	1	2	2	2	3	3
044	136	0	1	1	1	1	2	2	2	3	3
045	135	0	1	1	1	1	2	2	2	3	3
046	134	0	1	1	1	1	2	2	2	3	3
047	133	0	1	1	1	1	2	2	3	3	3
048	132	0	1	1	1	1	2	2	3	3	3
049	131	0	1	1	1	1	2	2	3	3	3
050	130	0	1	1	1	1	2	2	3	3	3

Figure 14.4a   Table 1—Course Corrections for Current, Page 1.

Table One	Heading Corrections Due to Current									Page 2	
					Ratio of Speed to Drift						
Angle	Angle	0.01	0.02	0.03	0.04	0.05	0.06	0.07	0.08	0.09	0.10
051	129	0	1	1	1	2	2	2	3	3	3
052	128	0	1	1	1	2	2	2	3	3	3
053	127	0	1	1	1	2	2	2	3	3	4
054	126	0	1	1	1	2	2	3	3	3	4
055	125	0	1	1	1	2	2	3	3	3	4
056	124	0	1	1	1	2	2	3	3	3	4
057	123	0	1	1	2	2	2	3	3	3	4
058	122	0	1	1	2	2	2	3	3	3	4
059	121	0	1	1	2	2	2	3	3	4	4
060	120	0	1	1	2	2	2	3	3	4	4
061	119	0	1	1	2	2	2	3	3	4	4
062	118	0	1	1	2	2	2	3	3	4	4
063	117	0	1	1	2	2	3	3	3	4	4
064	116	0	1	1	2	2	3	3	3	4	4
065	115	0	1	1	2	2	3	3	3	4	4
066	114	0	1	1	2	2	3	3	4	4	4
067	113	0	1	1	2	2	3	3	4	4	4
068	112	0	1	1	2	2	3	3	4	4	5
069	111	0	1	1	2	2	3	3	4	4	5
070	110	0	1	1	2	2	3	3	4	4	5
071	109	0	1	1	2	2	3	3	4	4	5
072	108	0	1	1	2	2	3	3	4	4	5
073	107	0	1	1	2	2	3	3	4	4	5
074	106	0	1	1	2	2	3	3	4	4	5
075	105	0	1	2	2	2	3	3	4	4	5
076	104	1	1	2	2	3	3	4	4	5	5
077	103	1	1	2	2	3	3	4	4	5	5
078	102	1	1	2	2	3	3	4	4	5	5
079	101	1	1	2	2	3	3	4	4	5	5
080	100	1	1	2	2	3	3	4	4	5	5
081	099	1	1	2	2	3	3	4	4	5	5
082	098	1	1	2	2	3	3	4	4	5	5
083	097	1	1	2	2	3	3	4	4	5	6
084	096	1	1	2	2	3	3	4	4	5	6
085	095	1	1	2	2	3	3	4	4	5	6
086	094	1	1	2	2	3	3	4	5	5	6
087	093	1	1	2	2	3	3	4	5	5	6
088	092	1	1	2	2	3	4	4	5	5	6
089	091	1	1	2	2	3	4	4	5	5	6
090	090	1	1	2	2	3	4	4	5	5	6

Figure 14.4b   Table 1—Course Corrections for Current, Page 2.

Planned heading = 090 + 002 = 092 degrees
(This is the case for the example.)

Or subtract the heading correction from your DR heading
when the current is striking your boat's port side:

Planned heading = 090 – 002 = 088 degrees

You will find that trying to correct a heading change of 002 on a small boat is a very difficult task unless the weather is calm and there are not a lot of boats around making waves.

How to Use Table 2—Correcting Speed for Current

I think you will find that this is the table you will use most often. While heading corrections are minimal on a small boat over short distances, corrections to your predicted speed for drift are more meaningful for accurate piloting.

In order to use Table 2, you only need to know one fact: the angle between your DR heading and the set of the current.

Follow these simple steps to determine your heading correction:

Step 1.   Find the angle between your boat's heading and the set of the current. Subtract one from the other. If the answer is greater than 180, subtract 180.

> Heading = 090; set = 030; 030 – 090 = 060

Step 2.   Referencing the angle (060), find the speed correction factor from Table 2 (0.333).

Step 3.   Multiply the drift of the current by the speed correction factor from Table 2 (Figure 14.5).

> Drift of 0.600 × 0.333 = 0.200 kts

Step 4.   If the current is striking the forward half of your boat, subtract the result from your predicted speed. Current from this direction will be slowing your boat.

> Predicted speed = 12.3 kts – 0.200 kts = 12.1 kts
>   SOA

(Remember, if you are using tidal current charts, you must also factor the drift for the calendar date.) Or, if the current is striking the aft (rear) half of your boat, add the result to your predicted speed. Current from this direction is increasing the speed of your boat as is the case in our example.

> Predicted speed = 12.3 kts + 0.200 kts = 12.500 kts
>   SOA

Note: If you are using tidal current charts, remember to factor your drift before using Table 2.

Table Two   Correcting Drift

Use this table for the weaker currents—1.0 knots or less.
When the angle is less than 90 degrees, current is on the bow.
When the angle is more than 90 degrees, current is off the stern.

Angle	Angle	Corr %	Angle	Angle	Corr %
000	180	1.000	046	134	0.489
001	179	0.989	047	133	0.478
002	178	0.978	048	132	0.467
003	177	0.967	049	131	0.456
004	176	0.956	050	130	0.445
005	175	0.944	051	129	0.433
006	174	0.933	052	128	0.422
007	173	0.922	053	127	0.411
008	172	0.911	054	126	0.400
009	171	0.900	055	125	0.389
010	170	0.889	056	124	0.378
011	169	0.878	057	123	0.367
012	168	0.867	058	122	0.356
013	167	0.856	059	121	0.345
014	166	0.844	060	120	0.333
015	165	0.833	061	119	0.322
016	164	0.822	062	118	0.311
017	163	0.811	063	117	0.300
018	162	0.800	064	116	0.289
019	161	0.789	065	115	0.278
020	160	0.778	066	114	0.267
021	159	0.767	067	113	0.256
022	158	0.756	068	112	0.245
023	157	0.744	069	111	0.233
024	156	0.733	070	110	0.222
025	155	0.722	071	109	0.211
026	154	0.711	072	108	0.200
027	153	0.700	073	107	0.189
028	152	0.689	074	106	0.178
029	151	0.678	075	105	0.167
030	150	0.667	076	104	0.156
031	149	0.656	077	103	0.145
032	148	0.644	078	102	0.133
033	147	0.633	079	101	0.122
034	146	0.622	080	100	0.111
035	145	0.611	081	099	0.100
036	144	0.600	082	098	0.089
037	143	0.589	083	097	0.078
038	142	0.578	084	096	0.067
039	141	0.567	085	095	0.056
040	140	0.556	086	094	0.045
041	139	0.544	087	093	0.033
042	138	0.533	088	092	0.022
043	137	0.522	089	091	0.011
044	136	0.511	090	090	0.000
045	135	0.500			

Figure 14.5   Table Two—Speed Corrections for Current.

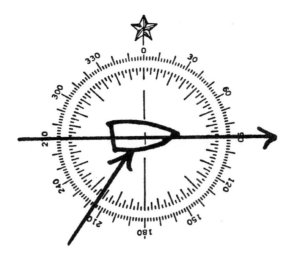

Figure 14.6 Current quadrant *(F. J. Larkin).*

As an aid to view how the current is striking your boat, draw a diagram similar to Figure 14.6. It is easy to see that the current is striking the port quarter with this quadrant.

CORRECTING PREDICTED SPEED
FOR WEIGHT CHANGE

The weight of your boat at the time when you ran your speed curve is called the base weight of your boat. Your speed curve is only valid at this base weight. Changes in a boat's base weight cause changes in the speed of the boat. Loss of base weight increases the speed of your boat while additions of weight slow your boat. Weight changes are most evident on smaller boats. To use an existing speed curve when your boat's base weight has changed, you must learn to correct your predicted speed for the change. Here are the rules of thumb:

- The percentage change in boat speed is equal to approximately one-half of the percentage change in the weight of the boat.
- The loss of weight increases the speed of a boat.
- The addition of weight decreases the speed of a boat.

For example, a weight decrease of 425 pounds (75 gallons of gasoline) produces a 10% weight change in a boat weighting 4,250 pounds. Half of 10% equals 5%, which will be the increase in boat speed due to this weight loss. If your predicted speed was 12.3 knots, the speed increase would be 0.615 knots (i.e., 12.3 kts × 0.05 = 0.615 kts).

In this situation, you would need to correct your predicted speed upward by 0.615 kts to 12.915 kts due to this 425-lb loss of weight

(12.300 kts + 0.615 kts = 12.915 kts). Your only other alternative is to rerun your speed curve at the new boat weight.

Computation of Fuel Consumption Rate

The most common weight loss on a boat is due to the consumption of fuel while underway. Here is a simple procedure for calculating this correction.

Step 1. Establish your boat's base weight with full fuel tanks (e.g., 4,350 lbs).

Step 2. Make a long run with your boat over a measured course at your normal running speed. This run should be at least 25 to 50 nautical miles in length (e.g., 50 miles).

Step 3. Refill your fuel tanks noting the gallons purchased (e.g., 25 gallons).

Step 4. Compute your nautical miles per gallon (e.g., 2 NMPG). Divide the nautical miles run by the gallons purchased:

50 miles/25 gallons = 2 NMPG

Step 5. Compute your fuel consumption rate by dividing the nautical miles per gallon (2 NMPG) into your planned speed (i.e., 12.3 kts):

12.3 kts/2 NMPG = 6.15 gallons per hour

Computation of Fuel Consumption Weight Loss and Predicted Speed Correction

When you need very accurate speed predictions, always compute weight lost due to fuel consumption. This procedure works for any addition or loss of weight such as when you add extra guests or remove equipment from your boat. The secret to accurate navigation is to maintain your boat's weight as close as possible to its weight when you ran your speed curve—your boat's base weight.

Step 1. Determine your time under way:

Depart time = 09:00:00

Current time = 10:52:12

Travel = 01:52:12 or 1.87 hours

Step 2. Calculate your fuel consumption by multiplying the time under way by your fuel consumption rate.

> Fuel consumption rate of 6.15 × 1.87 hr = 11.5 gallons used

Step 3. Figure the weight of the fuel lost by multiplying the gallons used by 5.667 lbs per gallon (weight of a gallon of gasoline).

> 11.5 gals × 5.667 lbs/gal = 65.2 lbs

Step 4. Determine the percentage of weight lost by dividing the weight lost by the base weight of your boat.

> 65.2 lbs/4,350 lbs = 0.015 or 1.5%

Divide the percentage by 2.

> 0.015/2 = 0.0075 or 0.75%

Step 5. Compute the predicted speed change by multiplying the percentage of weight lost by the predicted speed.

> Predicted speed of 12.3 kts × 0.0075 = 0.092 kts

Step 6. Develop the corrected speed prediction. If the weight is decreased, add the predicted speed change to the predicted speed.

> 12.300 kts + 0.092 kts = 12.392 kts

If the weight is increased, subtract the predicted speed change from the predicted speed.

To make the weight problem more realistic, suppose you add two additional guests weighing a total of 410 pounds to the 65.2-pound weight loss due to fuel consumption (410 lbs added, minus 65.2 lbs lost equals a 344.8-pound increase). The percentage of weight gained would be 7.93% and the predicted speed would change to 11.813 knots because the increased weight will slow your boat. Assume your boat's base weight is 4,350 lbs.

> 344.8 lbs/4,350 lbs = 0.0793/2 = 0.0396 × 12.300 kts = 0.487 kts – 12.300 kts = 11.813 kts

You can see from these weight calculations that the impact on predicted speed on small boats can be significant. To become a serious navigator, pay attention to these suggestions:

- Develop an awareness for things that affect the weight of your boat.

- Run tests to verify the relationship between changes in boat weight and the actual speed of your boat.

- Using your speed curve and the formula, produce a table that shows the relationship between RPMs and weight changes. Start with 100-lb changes.

Things to Consider When Establishing Your Boat's Base Weight

	SAMPLE WEIGHTS	
Fixed weight factors:		
Hull weight. Your dealer should provide this figure.	3,750	
Engine(s) weight. Your dealer should provide this figure.	525	
Batteries. Ask any marine store.	50	**4,325**
Variable weight items:		
Capacity/weight of fuel tanks (125 gallon – gas @ 5.667 lbs/gal).	709	
Capacity/weight of water tanks (20 gallon @ 8.3 lbs/gal).	167	
Capacity/weight of holding tanks (10 gallon @ 8.3 lbs/gal).	83	**959**
(Gas weighs 5.667 lbs per gallon; diesel weighs 7.2 lbs per gallon; water weighs 8.3 lbs per gallon.)		
Weight of gear:		
Spare engine oil.	20	
Anchor and chain.	45	
Anchor rode.	25	
Lines.	25	
Cushions.	45	
Bed blankets and sheets.	15	
Boat cover/canvas.	40	**215**
Other equipment:		
Electronic equipment.	15	
First aid kit.	10	
Tool kit.	13	
PFDs.	15	
Manuals.	12	
Fishing gear.	30	
Refreshment cooler.	15	
Ice and drinks.	15	
Food.	10	**135**
Captain, crew, and guests:		
Skipper.	250	
Mate.	150	
Guests (1) (or ballast).	125	**525**
Total		**6,159**

You can easily load your boat with a lot of extra weight. The unloaded weight of my boat is 4,325 lbs. I got these figures from a boat dealer. Most dealers have a book with all this good information. The base weight of my boat is around 6,160 pounds. When I need to be extremely accurate with my predicted speed such as during a predicted log race, I use the following checklist to ensure that my boat's base weight is the same as when I ran my speed curve.

___ Fill the fuel tanks.
___ Fill the water tank.
___ Fill the head water tank.
___ Carry one extra gallon of
    oil as a spare.
___ Fill the oil reservoir.

___ Carry 12 cans of soda and
    2 bags of ice.
___ Carry one food cooler.
___ Set trim angle to one bar
    on indicator.
___ Pump bilge dry.

CORRECTING PREDICTED SPEED FOR DEPTH OF WATER

Oddly enough, I have discovered that the depth of the water can have an effect on your piloting predictions. Depths under 18 feet will change your boat's speed. The effect depends on whether your boat has a planing hull or a displacement hull. Planing boats increase in speed over shoal water, while a displacement boat's speed decreases. The rules of thumb for the depth element are as follows:

- Boat speed changes approximately 0.125 knot for each foot difference of depth under 18 feet of water depth.

- Displacement vessels are dragged deeper in the water by the bottom so that they slow down.

- Planing vessels are pushed up by the water so that they increase in speed.

Here is a simple technique for correcting your boat's predicted speed for water depths under 18 feet.

Step 1. Determine the depth of water along your course from a nautical chart (e.g., 12 ft).

Step 2. Calculate the height of tide for the time period when you will be transiting along your course line. A simple method is to draw a tide graph. Refer to Chapter 13. Assume the depth change is 3.5 feet.

        12 ft + 3.5 ft = 15.5 ft

Step 3.   Determine the depth below 18 feet by subtracting the height of tide from 18.

$$15.5 \text{ ft} - 18 \text{ ft} = 2.5 \text{ ft}$$

Step 4.   Compute the speed change due to depth by multiplying the depth below 18 by 0.125 kt.

$$2.5 \text{ ft} \times 0.125 \text{ kts} = 0.313 \text{ kt}$$

Step 5.   Correct your predicted speed. If you have a displacement vessel, subtract the speed change from your planned speed because your boat will be slowed.

$$12.3 \text{ kts} - 0.313 \text{ kt} = 11.987 \text{ kts}$$

Or, if you have a planing vessel, add the speed change to your planned speed because your boat will increase in speed.

$$12.3 \text{ kts} + 0.313 \text{ kt} = 12.613 \text{ kts}$$

Note that at slower speeds, every planing vessel operates in a displacement mode. When this occurs, treat your planing vessel as if it was a displacement vessel. A table is provided below to help you determine when your boat transitions from displacement to planing modes.

Computation of Start of Planing

Planing begins at a speed equal to 1.34 times the square root of the waterline length of your boat. A vessel is said to be truly planing at two times the square root of the waterline length.

WATERLINE LENGTH (ft)	START OF PLANING (kts)	TRULY PLANING (kts)
15	5.2	7.7
16	5.4	8.0
17	5.5	8.2
18	5.7	8.5
19	5.8	8.7
20	6.0	8.9
21	6.1	9.2
22	6.3	9.4
23	6.4	9.6
24	6.6	9.8
25	6.7	10.0
26	6.8	10.2
27	7.0	10.4

WATERLINE LENGTH (ft)	START OF PLANING (kts)	TRULY PLANING (kts)
28	7.1	10.6
29	7.2	10.8
30	7.3	11.0
31	7.5	11.1
32	7.6	11.3
33	7.7	11.5
34	7.8	11.7
35	7.9	11.8

CORRECTING PREDICTED SPEED FOR WIND

A continuous wind can produce a current that is deflected about 20 to 30 degrees to the right in the Northern Hemisphere due to the Coriolis effect. As a rule of thumb, the drift of this current is approximately 0.2 knot for a 10-knot wind. The drift increases by 0.1 knot for each increase of 10 knots of wind speed.

Waves are the result of this wind effect. By noting the direction of the waves, you can determine the set of the current created by the wind. This current phenomenon is found offshore and is not generated in inshore locations due to lack of fetch. *Fetch* is the distance that the wind blows in a fixed direction without encountering any land masses to block its effect.

Since it is virtually impossible to predict wind in advance, you should learn to make wind speed corrections while under way. Your major problem will be estimating wind velocity. The best source is the national weather broadcasts on your VHF radio. (See Figure 14.8 later in this chapter for a method for reading current from buoys while under way.) Here is a quick technique to correct your speed for wind.

Step 1.   Estimate the velocity of the wind (e.g., 16 knots).

Step 2.   Determine the angle between your boat's heading and the direction of the wind. This is accomplished by using angles relative to your heading. Assume your boat is heading 000 degrees and then estimate the wind's direction from that point (e.g., 045 degrees relative to the boat's heading).

Step 3.   Referencing the angle, look up the speed correction factor in Table 2 (0.500). (See Figure 14.5 Table 2—Speed Corrections for Current.)

Step 4.   Look up the rate of drift in the wind drift correction graph (Figure 14.7) referencing the estimated wind velocity.

Wind speed = 16 knots – rate of drift downwind
= 1.18 knots

Step 5.   Factor the rate of drift by the speed correction factor.

1.18 knots × 0.500 = 0.590 kt

Step 6.   If the waves are striking on the forward half of your boat, decrease your predicted speed by the factored rate of drift. Recompute your ETA.

12.3 kts – 0.590 kt = 11.710 kts

Or if the waves are striking your boat on the aft (rear half), increase your predicted speed by the factored rate of drift. Recompute your ETA.

12.3 kts + 0.590 kt = 12.890 kts

Step 7.   If your boat is equipped with a tachometer that reads each RPM, you can decrease your engines RPMs to correct for the loss in predicted time, or you can adjust your predicted speed and recompute your ETA.

Note: The data used to make the drift correction graph of Figure 14.7 was taken from the *U.S. Coast Guard SAR Manual.* This data is the result of the compilation of many SAR incidents involving boats of various sizes which were grouped into this small cabin cruiser category. The drift correction graph may not fit your boat exactly. It is presented as a baseline only. Work out your own tables for your boat.

ESTIMATING THE SET AND DRIFT OF A CURRENT FROM BUOYS

Figure 14.8 presents a series of representations of the action of water as it strikes buoys. The direction of the downstream ripple is the set of the current. The characteristics of the water as it strikes the buoy along with the attitude of the buoy provide an estimate of the drift of the current. Use these illustrations to double-check your current predictions. They will provide a reality check to your arithmetic and tabular calculations of set and drift. They are also very useful for those areas that have no published current predictions. Again, it will take practice to learn to use them quickly and efficiently.

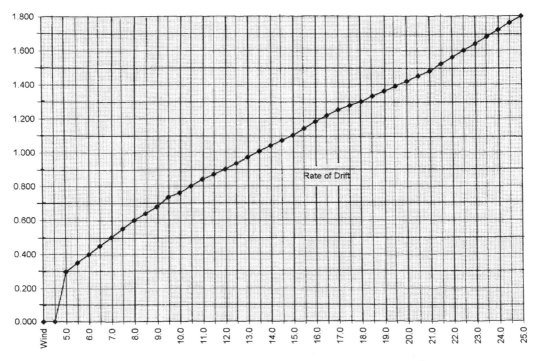

Figure 14.7   Wind drift correction graph for small cabin cruiser
(F. J. Larkin).

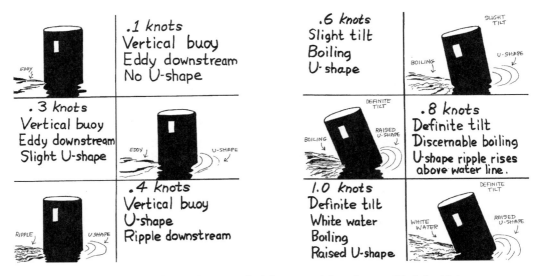

Figure 14.8   Estimating speed of the current from buoys *(F. J. Larkin).*

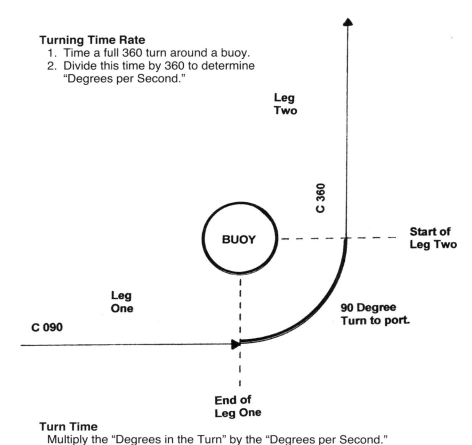

Turning Time Rate
1. Time a full 360 turn around a buoy.
2. Divide this time by 360 to determine "Degrees per Second."

Turn Time
Multiply the "Degrees in the Turn" by the "Degrees per Second."
90 degrees × 0.1 = 9 seconds.

Figure 14.9 Turning time rate *(F. J. Larkin).*

COMPUTING TURNING TIME

Each time that you make a turn around a buoy, either inside or outside, you add travel time to the next leg of your trip. Figure 14.9 demonstrates the problem. Take, for example, a 90-degree turn around a buoy. The first leg is ended when your boat is abeam of the buoy at the end of the leg. Then, you make a 90-degree turn and the next leg starts when you are abeam of the buoy on your new heading. The turn time is the travel time expended from the end of the first leg until you reach the starting point of the next leg.

To compute the turn time, measure the time that it takes your boat to complete a full circle—360 degrees—at your boat's normal speed. It is best to make the circle around a buoy and note the distance that you are off the buoy. Keep this same distance off buoys when you make your regular turns. Assume that it took 35 seconds to make the circle. Divide the time by 360 (e.g., 35 / 360 = 0.0972 seconds per degree).

To predict a time for a turn, multiply the seconds-per-degree time by the number of degrees in the turn (e.g., 90 × 0.0972 = 8.748 or 9 seconds). This is a simplistic solution for dealing with turning times but it works.

While most boat operators won't do turn computation, it is important that you know that turning time exists. Predicted loggers will want to pay particular attention to turning time if they want to be competitive.

Reader Progress Note

All of these calculations may be a lot to internalize at one time. It took me many years to figure out the effect of these elements on my boat. If you want to take up predicted logging, you will need to keep your predicted speed errors under 1%—that's under 36 seconds of error for every hour run. However, it doesn't take long to become an expert if you practice the art of navigation. I find that it takes away any boredom on long trips and makes each leg of the trip a game of competing against the clock. At some point along the way, you just may become a highly skilled navigator.

How to Check the Installation Accuracy of Your Compass and Install a Steering Post

Compass installation errors are a common cause of steering problems on pleasure boats. For every degree of compass installation error, your boat will be approximately 250 feet or 80 yards off course for every nautical mile that you travel. Therefore, you want to be sure that your compass is installed correctly. Compasses are generally mounted in front of the helm or steering station on a boat. During installation, follow these simple steps to avoid steering problems. Figure AP1.1 graphically explains the procedure.

Step 1

- Measure the width of your boat at the point where your compass is installed. You can use a tape measure. Divide the width by two.

- At this same point, measure from the same edge to the center of your compass.

- Subtract this measurement from the first to get the distance that your compass is installed from the center line of your boat. For example, the width of your boat measures 120 inches. Divide by 2 to get 60 inches. The measurement to the center of your compass is 32 inches. Your compass is installed 28 inches from the centerline of your boat (60 – 32 = 28).

Step 2

- Double the length that the center of your compass is located from the centerline of your boat (28 × 2 = 56).

- Set the tape measure or string to this width (56 inches) and find the point on your port and starboard bow rails that is exactly this width. It is important for this crossing line to be at a right angle (90 degrees) to the keel line of the boat. Check this by measuring back to the center of the rail at the bow. Place a mark on the bow rail side in front of your compass.

- This is the position for your steering post. I placed a burgee staff at this position.

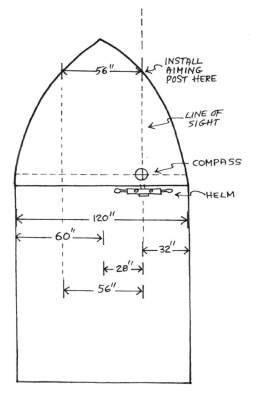

Figure AP1.1   A compass installation procedure diagram *(F. J. Larkin).*

Step 3

- Sight along the center of the compass card and the lubber line that is scribed into the compass housing toward the aiming post or point. Your line of sight should be centered on the aiming post for your compass to be parallel to the keel.

- Make any adjustments to correct the alignment of the compass.

By performing this check, you have accomplished two objectives. You have corrected the installation of your compass and you have provided a proper aiming post for steering your boat. Many skippers erroneously use the center of the bow as a steering point when their helm and compass are installed off-center. This practice introduces steering error into their headings and causes their boat to move along an arc rather that a straight course line, which has a negative effect on their ability to predict an ETA accurately.

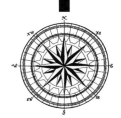

How to Check Your Compass for Built-in Error

Built-in compass error is a fault that is generated inside your compass and not from an outside magnetic influence. It is important to understand this type of error because it can usually be adjusted with a little work and planning. When a compass can't be completely adjusted free of compass error, you need to know the extent of this error in your compass so that you can compensate for it in your compass heading calculations.

This procedure applies to your boat's compass as well as any handheld or portable compasses.

Step 1. Find a convenient location ashore that fits the following standards:

  • There is no local magnetic influence in the area. Stay away from large iron masses, metal rails, or large metal tanks.

  • The location is positioned on a line of position (LOP) formed by two fixed objects that are charted on a nautical chart and form a natural range to your chosen accessible land position. Figure AP2.1 illustrates an ideal location.

Step 2. Using a plotting instrument, determine the true bearing of the LOP from your position toward the fixed objects that form the natural range.

Step 3.   Using the TVMDC formula, convert the true bearing to a magnetic bearing. Record this bearing for reference on a Navigation Worksheet.

Step 4.   Sight your compass along the range and record the compass bearing.

Step 5.   Compare the magnetic bearing to the compass bearing.

Your compass has no built-in error when the magnetic bearing equals the compass bearing. When your compass bearing is *greater* than the magnetic bearing, you have *westerly* compass error. When your compass bearing is *less* than the magnetic bearing, you have *easterly* compass error.

If your compass has significant compass error (more than 3 degrees), you should:

1.   Adjust it according to the manufacturer's instructions which are usually included in the literature that is packed with your compass when purchased.

2.   Take the compass to your dealer and have it adjusted professionally. If you don't know what you're doing, this is always your least expensive alternative.

When a compass cannot be adjusted to read absolutely perfect, record the compass error near or even write it on your compass. Always show whether the error is westerly or easterly. This will remind the helmsperson to correct the course for the built-in steering error.

Since hand-held compasses should normally be used in a magnetic-free location on your boat, a deviation table is not required. Record any built-in compass error on the compass's housing to remind you to correct all readings taken with this compass for the built-in error.

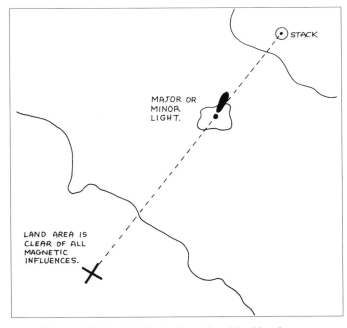

Figure AP2.1   An illustration of an ideal land range
(F. J. Larkin).

APPENDIX THREE

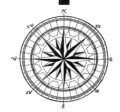

How to Develop Data for a Deviation Table Using Multiple Ranges and Your Boat's Compass

A deviation table is needed to correct your compass heading for magnetic influences found aboard your boat. These magnetic influences are caused by ferrous metal (iron) objects and their magnetic fields, which can be generated from wiring, transformers, electrical motors, and speaker magnets installed near your compass. You can minimize these influences on your compass by installing electrical equipment and wiring at least 3 feet away from your compass and by twisting all wires located near your compass. Twisting wires helps to offset their magnetic fields.

Evaluate the magnetic influence of each piece of electrical equipment mounted near your compass. Start by turning off all electrical appliances located in the area. Next, switch on each electrical device one at a time while you observe the needle of your compass. Record the number of degrees that the compass needle swings. Any electrical appliance with a speaker magnet or electrical motor can influence your compass. Isolate, shield, or reinstall any problem appliances. Windshield wiper motors should always be checked. You normally only use windshield wipers during poor weather conditions and you want to be assured that they will not cause compass error. Lay your radio mike beside your compass and observe how dramatically the needle of your compass is deflected. Mount your radio and microphone well away from your compass. Continue this checking process until you have eliminated all magnetic influences on your compass.

You will also want to review the handling procedures for portable appliances, especially portable radios. Visualize a globe, 3 feet in diameter, surrounding your compass. Establish the practice of not using this area for storage or the installation of any electrical appliances.

In some instances, you may not be able to remove the magnetic influence by moving or shielding the cause. If the error is small (less than 5 degrees), record it as part of your deviation table.

CAUTION: *Equipment-generated compass error changes when the appliance is in operation or off. Make special notes on your deviation table about this type of magnetic influence on your boat.*

Follow these simple steps to develop data for your deviation table:

Step 1.

- Using a nautical chart, find charted objects in your area that form natural ranges.

- Watch out for shoal areas along the LOP formed by the range.

- Discard ranges with shoals or other obstructions because you will need to operate your boat in these areas to complete Step 6.

Only use objects that are identified with the chart symbol of a circle with a center dot. These are surveyed positions and are accurate for use in obtaining position fixes in navigation. You need at least 10 to 12 ranges on various points of the compass to develop an adequate deviation table. An ideal deviation table will have 24 points.

Step 2.

- Using the Deviation Planning Sheet found in Appendix 7, write in the names of the charted objects that you have selected as your ranges on Column 1, Objects. For example, Stack and Tower.

Step 3.

- Using your plotter, determine the true bearing of each range.

- Record the bearing toward the object. You will use these bearings later in Step 7. For example, 065 degrees True.

- Write your bearings in Column 2, True Heading, on the Deviation Planning Sheet. You will have a different heading for each range that you select.

Step 4.

- Select the variation from the compass rose nearest to the range on the nautical chart.

- Enter the variation in Column 3, Variation, on the Deviation Planning Sheet. For example, 004° West.

Step 5.

- Compute the magnetic heading.

- You are proceeding from true to magnetic in the TVMDC formula so add westerly error and subtract easterly error in making your computation.

True heading	060
Variation	004W
Magnetic heading	064

Step 6.

- Take a trip on your boat and align your boat's keel line on a range line or LOP.

- Allowing time for the compass needle to settle, record the compass reading. It will be difficult to get accurate readings when the sea is up or when boating traffic is heavy in the area. For example, 065 degrees.

- Enter the compass reading in Column 6, Compass Heading, on the Deviation Planning Sheet.

Step 7.

- Compute the deviation for each entry on the Deviation Planning Sheet by comparing Column 4, Magnetic Heading, to Column 6, Compass Heading.

- If the compass heading is larger than the magnetic heading, you have westerly deviation error.

- When the compass heading is less than the magnetic heading, you have easterly deviation error.

Magnetic heading	064 degrees
Compass heading	065 degrees
Deviation	001 West

(Compass heading is larger than the magnetic heading.)

Magnetic heading	125 degrees
Compass heading	123 degrees
Deviation	002 East

(Compass heading is less than the magnetic heading.)

Refer to Figure 9.1 for a diagram that visually explains how this deviation calculation is accomplished.

How to Develop Data for a Deviation Table Using One Range and a Pelorus

The purpose of this procedure is to develop corrections to your compass for magnetic influences found at various headings of your boat. To perform this exercise, you need an instrument called a pelorus and someone to assist you. One person operates the boat and observes the boat's compass headings. The other person operates the pelorus and takes the relative bearings along a predefined range. You will need a calm sea to accomplish this task on a small boat. Don't forget your constant need for vigilance and lookouts while you are under way.

Set up the pelorus so that it is aligned along your boat's keel similar to your boat's compass. Aim the 000 degree point on the pelorus' compass card at the bow of your boat. Any reading on your pelorus will now be relative to the reading on your boat's compass.

Step 1.
- Find objects on your nautical chart that form natural ranges.
- Watch for shoal areas along the LOP formed by the range and reject them since you will need to align your boat on each range in Step 6.
- Only use objects that are identified with the chart symbol of a circle and a center dot on your chart. These are surveyed positions and are accurate for use in navigation.

Step 2.

- Using the Deviation Planning Sheet found in Appendix 7, write in the names of the objects on the range that you have selected.
- Enter this data in Column 1, Objects.

For this procedure, you are using a single range to complete your deviation table. All bearings will be taken along this single range.

Step 3.

- Using your plotter, measure the true heading for the range.
- Use the direction from your boat toward the range.
- Write the true heading in Column 2, True Heading, on the Deviation Planning Sheet.
- This heading will be the same for all entries planned in this procedure. This is the direction that your pelorus will be aimed in Step 6.

Step 4.

- Select the variation from the compass rose nearest to the range.
- Enter the variation in Column 3, Variation.
- The variation in this exercise will be the same for all entries.

Step 5.

- Compute the magnetic heading for each entry on your Deviation Planning Sheet and post in Column 4, Magnetic Heading.
- You are proceeding down the TVMDC formula so add westerly error and subtract easterly error.

Step 6.

- Take the range bearings with the pelorus. Maneuver the boat so that the pelorus is aligned along the range.
- Figure AP4.1 illustrates this technique.
- The pelorus operator calls out "Mark" for each reading and records the relative bearing from the pelorus.
- The boat operator, upon hearing the "Mark" command, reads and records the boat's compass heading.
- Record the compass bearings in Column 7, Boat's Heading, on the Deviation Planning Sheet.

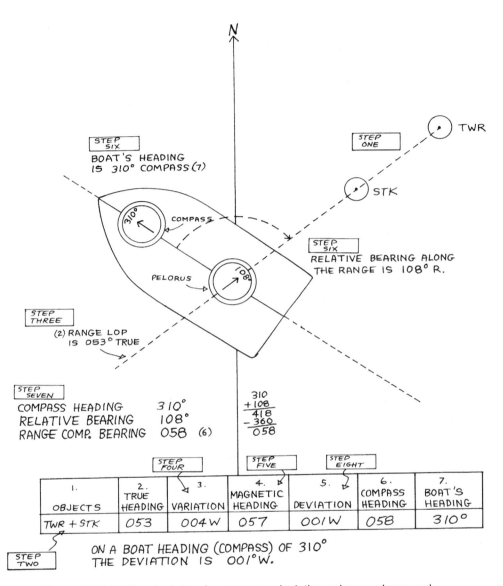

Figure AP4.1 How to determine compass deviation using a pelorus and relative bearings *(F. J. Larkin).*

- The deviation that you calculate with this procedure is associated with this compass direction on your boat (not the direction in which the pelorus is pointing).
- Repeat this process until 12 to 20 readings are obtained as the boat is maneuvered around the 360-degree arc of the compass.

Step 7.

- Convert the relative bearings to range compass bearings.
- To convert a relative bearing to a compass bearing, add the relative bearing to the compass bearing:

Compass bearing	090 degrees
Relative bearing	+ 030 degrees
Converted relative bearing	120 degrees

- When your answer is larger than 360 degrees, subtract 360 to obtain the correct converted relative bearing.
- Record the converted relative bearings in Column 6, Compass Heading, on the Deviation Planning Sheet.

Step 8.

- Compute the deviation using the TVMDC formula.

What you have calculated is the deviation for a single compass heading on your boat. Continue this same procedure through 12 to 20 points of the compass and you will develop the data for plotting a deviation table for your boat.

How to Plot Deviation on a Deviation Plotting Sheet

The purpose of the Deviation Plotting Sheet is to graph your deviations prior to the finalization of the deviation table for your boat. A blank Deviation Plotting Sheet is provided in Appendix 7 for use in this procedure.

You need to plot two graphs: one for magnetic headings and one for compass headings. Plot one category at a time so you won't become confused by an excess of plotting points on your graph. I suggest that you use different color pencils for each deviation curve.

The Deviation Plotting Sheet has two scales:

1. *The vertical scale:* The vertical scale (at the left-hand side of the graph) is divided to reflect easterly and westerly error by a zero error line. Plot easterly error below the zero line. Plot westerly error above the zero line.

2. *The horizontal scale:* The horizontal scale (at the bottom of the graph) is divided into 10-degree segments and is labeled in 30-degree intervals.

HOW TO PLOT MAGNETIC HEADING DEVIATIONS

Deviation on this graph refers to the magnetic headings found in Column 4, Magnetic Headings, on the Deviation Planning Sheet and will be the reference point for the heading column on your deviation table.

Step 1.

- Referencing your Deviation Planning Sheet, plot all the data found in Column 5, Deviation, in the Deviation Plotting Sheet's vertical scale (left side of the graph) in relationship to your magnetic headings found in Column 4, Magnetic Heading, in the graph's horizontal scale (bottom of the graph).

Note: If you are using relative bearings, as explained in Appendix 4, you must calculate the magnetic heading for the boat's heading using the TVMDC formula.

T

V

M   Calculate using TVMDC formula rules.

D   Take from Column 5, Deviation.

C   Take from Column 7, Boat's Heading.

Step 2.

- Draw a line through all of the points that you have plotted so that you approximate a curve.
- In other words, round the line through the plotted points rather than just connecting the dots.

Step 3.

- Develop your deviation table by reading the data from the deviation curve you drew on your graph.
- Read up the scale from a selected compass heading on the horizontal scale to the place where your line intersects with the deviation curve.
- Read across to your left from this intersecting point to the deviation error scale.
- Record the deviation error for the selected compass heading on a Deviation Table form supplied in Appendix 7.

HOW TO PLOT COMPASS HEADING DEVIATIONS

The reference point for your compass graph is Column 6, Compass Heading, on the Deviation Planning Sheet.

Step 1.

- Referencing your Deviation Planning Sheet, plot all the data found in Column 5, Deviation, against the vertical scale in relationship to the headings found in Column 6, Compass Heading, on the horizontal scale.

- Note that if you are using relative bearings as explained in Appendix 4, use the data from Column 7, Boat's Heading, to complete the horizontal scale.

Step 2.

- Draw a line through all of the points that you have plotted so that you approximate a curve.

- In other words, round the line through the plotted points rather than just connecting the dots.

Step 3.

- Develop your deviation table by reading the data from the deviation curve you drew on the graph.

- Read up the scale from a selected compass heading on the horizontal scale to the place where your line intersects with the deviation curve.

- Read across to your left from this intersecting point to the deviation error scale.

- Record the deviation error for the selected compass heading on a Deviation Table form, which is supplied in Appendix 7.

How to Develop a Speed Curve

An integral part of any navigational package is an accurate speed curve. The smaller your boat, the more difficult it is to develop and use a speed curve. The principal problem will be the weight that you carry on your boat. As explained in Chapter 16, small boats are greatly affected by any weight difference compared to their base weight. The more frequent weight problems are related to fuel consumption, number of guests aboard, and changes in the amount of equipment that you carry on a trip. Your speed curve is only valid for the weight aboard your boat at the time when you ran the speed trials to develop your speed curve. I call this the boat's *base weight*. For accuracy in your piloting predictions, you must compensate your predicted speed for any change in weight from your base weight. Otherwise, your predictions will be invalid. Note that this is not as serious a problem on heavy displacement cruisers.

Here are a few of the main reasons that can invalidate a speed curve:

- Fuel consumption on a trip or half full fuel tanks. These computations are explained in Chapter 14.

- Additional guests.

- Extra equipment aboard. It's amazing how much junk accumulates aboard a boat as the season progresses. You will get a strong feeling for this situation if you can remember back to the day that you unloaded your boat last year.

- Marine growth on your hull. Any grass growing on your hull will slow your boat considerably.

- Bilges full of water. Remember to pump the bilge before you start out on any trip. Excess water slows your boat and sometimes can change the stability of your boat.

- Hull weight. If you have a wooden boat, let your boat sit in the water for a week or two before you calculate your curve. This allows time for the wood to absorb water. This water absorption adds weight to your boat. A wooden boat is much heavier at the end of the season than at the start if it is hauled annually. Wooden boats will be much slower at the end of the season.

EQUIPMENT YOU WILL NEED

Tachometer.   Your boat must be equipped with a decent tachometer. Most standard analog and digital tachs read in 100-RPM increments. This means that the tach is averaging the readout to 100-RPM increments. Note that 50 RPMs can have an effect on your speed predictions.

When your boat has twin engines, use only one tachometer as your primary controlling instrument. Synchronize the other engine to your primary engine. Rarely will two tachs agree precisely, even when the engines are synchronized.

Stop Watch.   Your watch should have the ability to time multiple legs.

Speed Curve Worksheet.   A copy of a suggested speed curve worksheet is provided in Appendix 7, Navigation Forms.

Tide Graph.   A copy of this form is available in Appendix 7, Navigation Forms.

HOW THE DATA COLLECTION PROCESS WORKS

This simple step-by-step procedure will help you to develop a speed curve for your boat.

Step 1.   Find a natural or measured mile range on your chart. Be sure that the water depth is over 18 feet and that current influence is minimal. If there are no measured mile runs in your area, try to find two fixed aids to navigation. Measure the distance between the fixed aids. The distance doesn't have to be exactly a mile (see Figure AP6.1).

Step 2.   Approach the starting point of your selected measured course with your engine set at a planned RPM setting on the tachometer. As you pass the starting line, start your

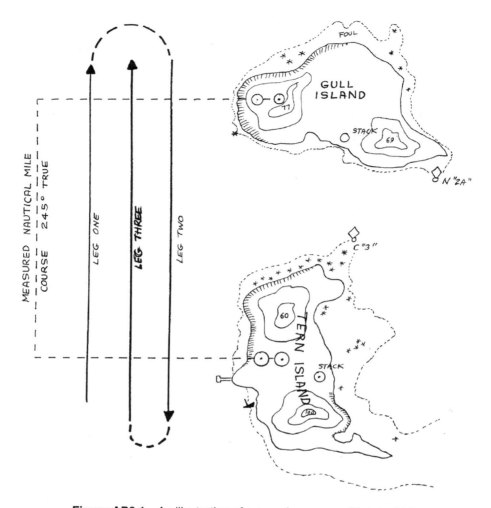

Figure AP6.1   An illustration of a speed curve run *(F. J. Larkin).*

stop watch. Hold this RPM setting for the entire run. Steer as straight as possible. It is best to make these timing runs when boating traffic is light, the weather is calm, and the current is at slack.

Step 3.   As you cross the finish line, stop the watch. Record the running time on the Speed Curve Worksheet (Appendix 7). Make a triple run, repeating steps 1, 2, and 3, down (S1), back (S2), and down (S3) the measured course.

Step 4.   Compute the speed made good for each of the three runs at each selected RPM, using the DR formula: $60 \times D = S \times T$.

Step 5. Average the speed of the runs, not the times. Average S1 to S2. Average S3 to S2. Then, average the speed of your two answers. It is more accurate to use seconds than minutes in your formula. Here is an example of a triple run with calculations. Use either the regular DR formula ($60 \times D = S \times T$ in minutes) or ($3600 \times D = S \times T$ in seconds).

RUN	TIME	SECONDS	SPEED @ 3,000 RPM	AVERAGE SPEED	SPEED
S1	4 m 28 s	268 s	13.432 kts		
				14.033 kts	
S2	4 m 06 s	246 s	14.634 kts		14.150 kts
				14.267 kts	
S3	4 m 19 s	259 s	13.900 kts		

Repeat this process at different RPM settings. Use intervals of 500 RPM. Record all the data on a Speed Curve Worksheet for future reference. Allow yourself plenty of time to complete all of the runs needed to finish the speed curve.

Step 6. Using a Tide Graph sheet (Appendix 7), label the vertical and horizontal scales. The vertical scale is on the left-hand side of the graph. Starting at the bottom, label upward at 500-RPM increments. The horizontal scale is at the bottom of the graph. Starting at the left, label to the right in 1-nm increments.

Step 7. Plot the data from your Speed Curve Worksheet onto the graph. Figures AP6.2 and AP6.3 provide an illustration of speed curve data and a plotted speed curve.

Note that displacement and planing boats will have a different curve. The displacement boat's speed curve will be more linear (a straight line), while a planing boat's curve will look more like an "S." The planing boat starts out as a displacement boat. As speed increases, it starts to come up on plane. As it reaches plane, the curve will flatten—smaller increases in RPMs cause larger increases in boat speed. As you apply more speed, it tends to become linear again. Figure AP6.3 shows a typical speed curve for a planing boat.

USE OF A SPEED CURVE OR RPM TABLE

The primary purpose of a speed curve is to predict the speed you intend to travel on a leg of a trip. For example, you may want to travel at a speed of 15 knots. You would use the DR formula to calculate your ETA.

Speed Curve Worksheet

Date:	15-Aug-98	Boat: Idyle Time			Run Length:	1.0	
	Time (min)	(60 x D)/T					
RPM 0500	Leg 1	60	1.00				
	42.30		42.30 =	1.418	Avg Leg 1 & 2		
	Leg 2	60	1.00		1.480		Avg Speed
	38.90		38.90 =	1.542	Avg Leg 3 & 2		1.5
		60	1.00		1.466		
	43.20		43.20 =	1.389			
RPM 1000	Leg 1	60	1.00				
	21.00		21.00 =	2.857	Avg Leg 1 & 2		
	Leg 2	60	1.00		2.967		Avg Speed
	19.50		19.50 =	3.077	Avg Leg 3 & 2		2.9
	Leg 3	60	1.00		2.927		
	21.60		21.60 =	2.778			
RPM 1500	Leg 1	60	1.00				
	13.10		13.10 =	4.580	Avg Leg 1 & 2		
	Leg 2	60	1.00		4.899		Avg Speed
	11.50		11.50 =	5.217	Avg Leg 3 & 2		5.0
	Leg 3	60	1.00		5.088		
	12.10		12.10 =	4.959			
RPM 2000		60	1.00				
	7.00		7.00 =	8.571	Avg Leg 1 & 2		
	Leg 2	60	1.00		9.841		Avg Speed
	5.40		5.40 =	11.111	Avg Leg 3 & 2		9.7
	Leg 3	60	1.00		9.503		
	7.60		7.60 =	7.895			
RPM 2500	Leg 1	60	1.00				
	6.10		6.10 =	9.836	Avg Leg 1 & 2		
	Leg 2	60	1.00		10.687		Avg Speed
	5.20		5.20 =	11.538	Avg Leg 3 & 2		10.7
	Leg 3	60	1.00		10.769		
	6.00		6.00 =	10.000			
RPM 3000	Leg 1	60	1.00				
	5.20		5.20 =	11.538	Avg Leg 1 & 2		
	Leg 2	60	1.00		11.652		Avg Speed
	5.10		5.10 =	11.765	Avg Leg 3 & 2		11.3
	Leg 3	60	1.00		10.967		
	5.90		5.90 =	10.169			

Number of people aboard:	2	Equipment Weight	2300.0
Gallons of fuel:	120	Gallons of water:	20.0

Figure AP6.2   A speed curve worksheet with data *(F. J. Larkin)*.

However, you must use your speed graph (RPM table) to determine which RPM setting to use to achieve the 15-knot speed on the leg.

Another typical reason is the need to travel at a certain speed in order to reach a destination point at a specific time. Your speed graph tells you the RPMs needed to attain the desired speed.

Things are constantly changing on your boat so you will need to check the accuracy of your speed curve. By using a Trip Log (provided in Appendix 7) for recording information about your trip, you will have the data necessary to validate your speed curve. Make checking your speed curve a standard practice after each trip.

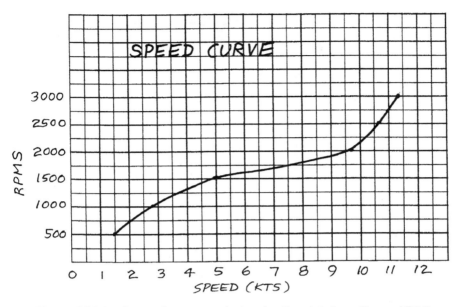

Figure AP6.3 A speed curve graph showing the plots from Figure AP6.2
(F. J. Larkin).

If your boat is slower than your speed curve:

- Did you have fewer people on board when you calculated your speed curve?
- Were you carrying any extra equipment?
- Were you towing a dinghy?
- Is there marine growth on the hull?
- Were you experiencing heavy weather or adverse currents?
- Did you have anything in your propeller, or is your propeller slipping or damaged?

If your boat was faster than your speed curve:

- Did you have more people on board when you calculated your speed curve?
- Have you taken any heavy equipment off your boat?
- Have you recently tuned up your engine(s)?
- Were you experiencing favorable currents or winds?

As you can see, nothing's perfect in the game of navigation. You must constantly observe what is happening to your boat versus what you are predicting will happen. I find the fun of navigation is trying to figure out what has gone wrong when things don't turn out exactly right and why.

APPENDIX SEVEN

Navigation Forms

Eight forms you will find useful as you work with this book or in actual practice on your boat are provided on the following pages:

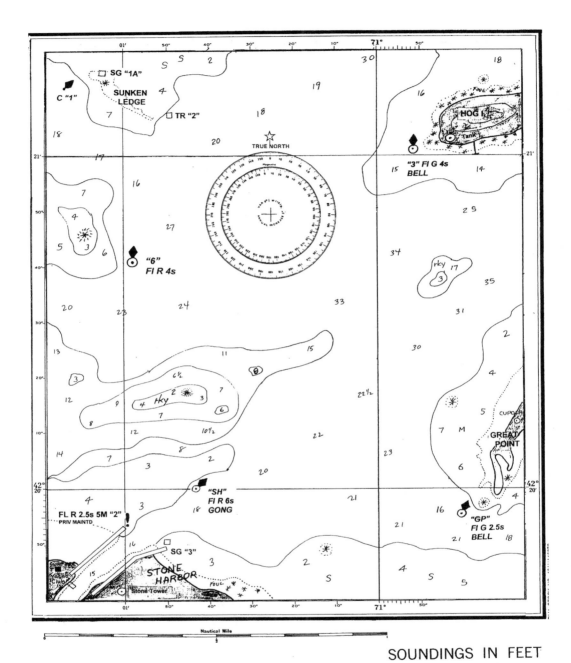

Form 1: Navigation Practice Chart *(F. J. Larkin).*

Navigation Worksheet | 60D=ST | TVMDC Add West Down |

Date:	Trip Name:

Leg_____

Dist: _____ nm   Speed _____ kts.

60 x D = S x T

T _____   DEP ___:___:___

V _____   TURN ___:___:___

M _____   TOT ___:___:___

D _____   ___ ___:___:___

C _____   ETA ___:___:___

Leg_____

Dist: _____ nm   Speed _____ kts.

60 x D = S x T

T _____   DEP ___:___:___

V _____   TURN ___:___:___

M _____   TOT ___:___:___

D _____   ___ ___:___:___

C _____   ETA ___:___:___

Leg_____

Dist: _____ nm   Speed _____ kts.

60 x D = S x T

T _____   DEP ___:___:___

V _____   TURN ___:___:___

M _____   TOT ___:___:___

D _____   ___ ___:___:___

C _____   ETA ___:___:___

Leg_____

Dist: _____ nm   Speed _____ kts.

60 x D = S x T

T _____   DEP ___:___:___

V _____   TURN ___:___:___

M _____   TOT ___:___:___

D _____   ___ ___:___:___

C _____   ETA ___:___:___

Leg_____

Dist: _____ nm   Speed _____ kts.

60 x D = S x T

T _____   DEP ___:___:___

V _____   TURN ___:___:___

M _____   TOT ___:___:___

D _____   ___ ___:___:___

C _____   ETA ___:___:___

Leg_____

Dist: _____ nm   Speed _____ kts.

60 x D = S x T

T _____   DEP ___:___:___

V _____   TURN ___:___:___

M _____   TOT ___:___:___

D _____   ___ ___:___:___

C _____   ETA ___:___:___

Form 2:   Navigation Worksheet *(F. J. Larkin).*

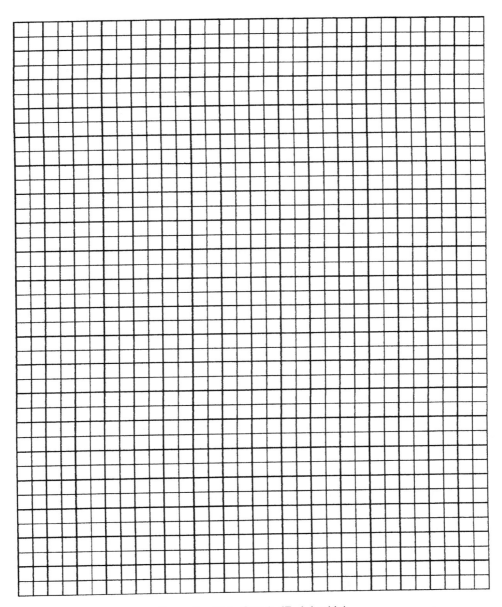

Form 3:   Tide Graph *(F. J. Larkin).*

DEVIATION PLANNING SHEET

DATE_____ BOAT NAME_____PREPARED BY_____

1. Objects (Range)	2. True Heading	3. Variation	4. Magnetic Heading	5. Deviation	6. Compass Heading	7. Boat's Heading

Form 4: Deviation Planning Sheet *(F. J. Larkin).*

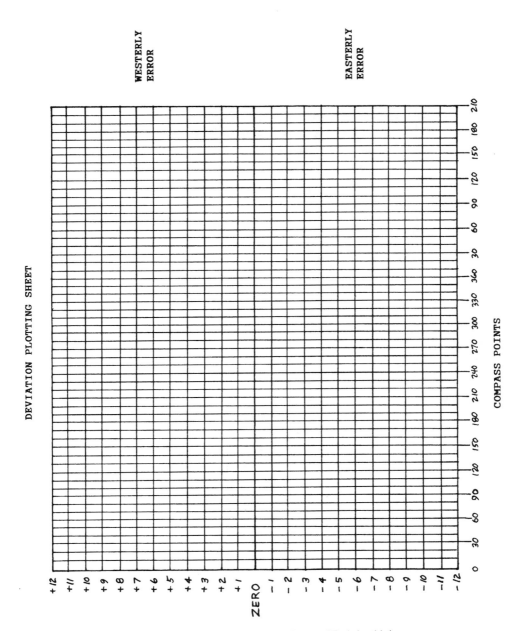

Form 5: Deviation Plotting Sheet *(F. J. Larkin).*

DEVIATION TABLE

BOAT NAME _____ DATE _____

PREPARED BY _____

Heading	Magnetic Deviation	Compass Deviation	Notes
000			
015			
030			
045			
060			
075			
090			
105			
120			
135			
150			
165			
180			
195			
210			
225			
240			
255			
240			
255			
270			
285			
300			
315			
330			
345			

Form 6:   Deviation Table *(F. J. Larkin).*

Speed Curve Worksheet

Date:		Time (min)	(60 x D)/T	Boat:		Run Length:	
RPM	Leg 1		60 =		Avg Leg 1 & 2		Avg Speed
	Leg 2		60 =		Avg Leg 3 & 2		
	Leg 3		60 =				
RPM	Leg 1		60 =		Avg Leg 1 & 2		Avg Speed
	Leg 2		60 =		Avg Leg 3 & 2		
	Leg 3		60 =				
RPM	Leg 1		60 =		Avg Leg 1 & 2		Avg Speed
	Leg 2		60 =		Avg Leg 3 & 2		
	Leg 3		60 =				
RPM	Leg 1		60 =		Avg Leg 1 & 2		Avg Speed
	Leg 2		60 =		Avg Leg 3 & 2		
	Leg 3		60 =				
	Leg 1		60 =		Avg Leg 1 & 2		Avg Speed
	Leg 2		60 =		Avg Leg 3 & 2		
	Leg 3		60 =				
RPM	Leg 1		60 =		Avg Leg 1 & 2		Avg Speed
	Leg 2		60 =		Avg Leg 3 & 2		
	Leg 3		60 =				

Form 7: Speed Curve Worksheet *(F. J. Larkin).*

TRIP LOG		Date:				Page		Boat:		
Leg/ WPT	To	TRUE Heading	DIST nm	SPEED KTS / RPM	TOT hr:min:sec	DEP hr:min:sec	Turn Time hr:min:sec	ETA hr:min:sec	COMP Heading	Actual DEP / ETA
Start Point										
LEG 1										
Notes										
LEG 2										
Notes										
LEG 3										
Notes										
LEG 4										
Notes										
LEG 5										
Notes										
LEG 6										
Notes										

Form 8:   Trip Log *(F. J. Larkin).*

APPENDIX EIGHT

Coast Guard Districts and Addresses of District Commanders

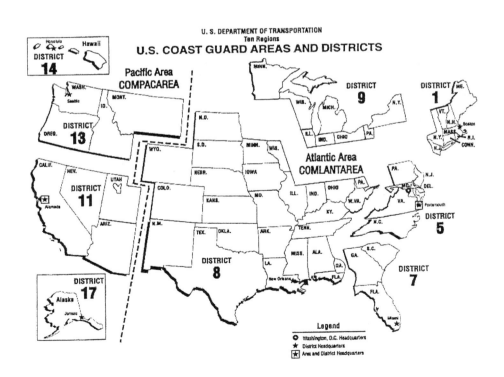

U. S. DEPARTMENT OF TRANSPORTATION
Ten Regions
U.S. COAST GUARD AREAS AND DISTRICTS

Coast Guard Districts and Addresses of District Commanders

DISTRICT	ADDRESS	WATERS OF JURISDICTION
FIRST	408 Atlantic Avenue Boston, MA 02110-3350 PHONE: DAY 617-223-8338 NIGHT 617-223-8558	Maine, New Hampshire, Massachusetts, Vermont (Lake Champlain), Rhode Island, Connecticut, New York, to Shrewsbury River, New Jersey.
FIFTH	Federal Building; 431 Crawford Street Portsmouth, VA 23704-5004 PHONE: DAY 757-398-6486 NIGHT 757-398-6231	Shrewsbury River, New Jersey to Delaware, Maryland, Virginia, District of Columbia and North Carolina.
SEVENTH	Brickell Plaza Federal Building 909 SE 1s tAvenue; Rm:406 Miami, FL 33131-3050 PHONE: DAY 305-415-6730 NIGHT 305-415-6800	South Carolina, Georgia, Florida to 83°50'W, and Puerto Rico and adjacent islands of the United States.
EIGHTH	Hale Boggs Federal Building 501 Magazine Street New Orleans LA 70130-3396 PHONE: DAY 504-589-6277 NIGHT504-589-6225	Florida westward from 83°50'W, Alabama, Mississippi, Louisiana, Texas, the Mississippi River System except that portion of the Illinois River north of Joliet, Illinois.
NINTH	1240 East 9th Street Cleveland OH 44199-2060 PHONE: DAY 216-902-6060 NIGHT 216-902-6117	Great Lakes and St .Lawrence River above St. Regis River.
ELEVENTH	Coast Guard Island Building 50-6 Alameda, CA 94501-5100 PHONE: DAY 510-437-2976	California.
THIRTEENTH	Federal Building 915 Second Avenue Seattle, WA 98174-1067 PHONE: DAY 206-220-7270 NIGHT206-220-7004	Oregon, Washington, Idaho, and Montana.
FOURTEENTH	Prince Kalanianaole Federal Bldg. 300 Ala Moana Blvd 9th Floor,Room 9139 Honolulu, HI 96850-4982 PHONE: DAY 808-541-2315 NIGHT 808-541-2500	Hawaiian, American Samoa, Marshall, Marianas, and Caroline Islands.
SEVENTEENTH	P.O. Box 25517 Juneau, AK 99802-5517 PHONE: DAY 907-463-2262 NIGHT 907-463-2004	Alaska.

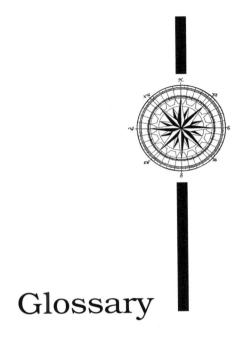

Glossary

Absolute accuracy: A term used to describe LORAN and GPS position accuracy when traversing an area for the first time. In LORAN-C, absolute accuracy decreases as a boat approaches shore and coastal bays.

Adrift: Afloat but unattached in any way to the shore or seabed.

ATON: Aid to navigation.

Base weight: The weight of a boat when the speed curve is being prepared.

Bearing: The horizontal direction of a line of sight between two objects on the surface of the earth. *Beam bearing:* A beam bearing is a relative bearing, which is taken at a 90-degree angle from the heading of your boat. (It is assumed that your boat is traveling along its plotted DR track line.) *Relative bearing:* A bearing taken in relation to the heading on your compass. Relative bearings are usually taken with an instrument called a pelorus.

C&GS: NOAA Coast & Geodetic Survey.

CMG: Course made good, the net direction of the actual path of your boat.

Coast Pilot: A nautical publication that enhances and expands on the data provided on a nautical chart.

COG: Course over the ground. The course calculated by your GPS.

Compass: A magnetic navigational instrument used to measure the heading of a boat.

Compass card: A card showing a 360-degree arc on a compass.

Compass rose: A printed compass card found on a nautical chart that indicates the direction of true north and magnetic north, shows the variation error for the area and the rate of change of this error.

Current: The movement of water. Usually, it is expressed in terms of direction (set) and speed (drift).

Current triangle: A graphic using a triangle where one side represents the set and drift of the current, one side represents your boat's DR course, and the third side shows the actual track of the boat.

Datum: A reference point for data. A vertical datum on a chart could be mean low water. A horizontal datum for a chart could be NAD27.

Dead reckoning: Deduced reckoning. A procedure for calculating your position from a known starting point using time, speed, and distance.

DEP: Depart or departure point.

Deviation: Deviation is a magnetic influence on your compass originating on your boat. This error is solved by developing a deviation table.

Deviation table: A curve or list of compass errors for the full arc of your compass due to magnetic influences aboard your boat.

DTG: Distance to go.

DGPS: Differential GPS.

Dividers: A two-armed instrument used in navigation to measure distance on a nautical chart.

DMAHC: Defense Mapping Agency Hydrographic Center.

DR: *See* Dead reckoning.

DR position: A position calculated by dead reckoning procedures.

Draft: The measurement from the lowest point protruding below your boat up to the waterline.

Drift: The speed of current.

ETA: Estimated time of arrival.

Fix: A position obtained by two or more LOPs. Considered to be more accurate than an estimated position and a DR position.

Flashing: A light characteristic in which the total duration of light is shorter than the total duration of darkness.

Geographic range: The greatest distance at which an object can be seen due to the curvature of the earth from a particular height of eye without regard to luminous intensity or visibility conditions.

GPS: Global Positioning System.

Great circle bearing: The Equator and meridians of longitude are great circle bearings. Bearings produced by GPS are great circle bearings.

Heading: The direction in which your boat's bow is pointed.

IALA: International Association of Lighthouse Authorities.

ICW: Intracoastal Waterway.

ISO: Isophase light characteristic. The duration of the light and the darkness cycle are equal.

Junction: The point at which a channel divides when proceeding seaward. The place where a tributary separates from the main stream.

Keel line: A line drawn fore and aft along the center of your vessel.

Lateral system: A system of aids to navigation in which the characteristics of buoys and beacons indicate the sides of the channel or route relative to a conventional direction of buoyage (usually upstream or from seaward).

Latitude: The lines that run horizontally across a nautical chart. Latitude is measured north and south from zero degrees at the equator to 90 degrees at the poles.

Leg: A single segment of a trip. The distance between two buoys.

Light: The signal emitted by a lighted aid to navigation. The illuminating apparatus used to emit the light signal. A lighted aid to navigation on a fixed structure.

Light List: A publication of the U.S. Coast Guard that lists all of the aids to navigation in an area.

LLNR: *Light List* number reference.

LNM: *See* Local Notice to Mariners.

Local Notice to Mariners: A written document issued by each U.S. Coast Guard district to disseminate important information affecting aids to navigation, dredging, marine construction, special marine activities, and bridge construction on the waterways within the Coast Guard district.

Longitude: The vertical lines that run north to south on a nautical chart. Longitude is measured east and west of the prime meridian at Greenwich, England.

LOP: Line of position.

LORAN-C: An electronic aid to navigation system that measures the time differences (TDs) of radio signals from land-based transmitters to a LORAN receiver on a boat to determine position.

LORAN-C chain: A series of LORAN-C transmitting stations.

Lubber line: A mark scribed on a compass housing to indicate the direction in which the bow of the boat is heading.

Magnetic north: The position on the earth's surface that attracts the needle of your compass.

Mark: A term for a buoy or day mark. An aid to navigation.

Mercator projection: A charting technique that projects the earth's spherical shape on a cylinder. Most nautical charts on the East Coast of the United States are Mercator projections.

Meridian: Vertical line on a nautical chart. Also called a meridian of longitude.

MHW: Mean high water.

MOB: Man overboard.

NAD83:   North American Datum of 1983. The newest horizontal datum for nautical charts of the United States and its territories.

NIMA: National Imagery and Mapping Agency.

NLT: No less than.

NMT: No more than.

NNME: National Electronics Association.

NOAA: National Oceanic and Atmospheric Administration.

NOAA-NOS: National Oceanic and Atmospheric Administration–National Ocean Survey.

Nominal range: The maximum distance that a light can be seen in clear weather (meteorological visibility of 10 nautical miles). Listed in the *Light List* for all lighted aids to navigation except range lights, directional lights, and private aids to navigation.

NOS: National Ocean Survey located at Rockville, MD.

Occulting: A light flash in which the total duration of light is longer than the total duration of darkness.

Parallel: Horizontal line on a nautical chart. Parallel of latitude.

Parallel rules: An instrument for measuring course angles in navigation.

Pelorus: A nonmagnetic navigational device for taking bearings relative to your compass heading.

Pilotage: A Coast Guard term for the rules of using a pilot in a port.

Plotter: An instrument for measuring course angles in navigation.

POD: Print-on-demand chart.

Polyconic projection: A flat chart projected from a cone.

Port: The left side of a boat when facing forward.

Prime meridian: Vertical line on a nautical chart that traverses Greenwich, England. Assigned the value of zero. Longitude is measured east and west from this point.

RACON: An electronic signal that is activated by radar.

Reference station: A fixed tide station where daily predictions of high and low water are provided in the *Tide Tables*.

Repeatable accuracy: Using LORAN or GPS, it is the navigator's ability to return to a position where prior electronic position readings were taken.

Retroreflective: A material that reflects light.

Route: A group of waypoints used in GPS for navigation.

SA: Selective availability error.

SC: Small craft. Used as a suffix on Small Craft Charts, i.e., 12345 SC.

Scale: Usually refers to the standard to which the distances on a nautical chart are referenced, i.e., 1:2500 where one inch on the chart refers to 2500 inches on the earth's surface.

Set: The direction of current.

SMG: Speed made good, the net rate of travel along a track.

SOA: Speed of advance, the planned rate of travel along an intended track line.

SOG: Speed over the ground.

Sounding: A depth of water.

Speed curve: A series of measurements of speed over the ground in relation to the RPMs of the boat's engine plotted on a graph in the form of a curve.

Starboard: The right side of a boat facing forward.

Substation: A fixed location referenced in Table 2 of the *Tide Tables* for which corrective data are supplied in relation to a reference station.

Towage: A term used by the Coast Guard that indicates the rules and/or the availability of resources that supply boat towing services in an area.

TR: Abbreviation for track.

Track: The direction of your calculated track line using a current triangle.

True north: The north at the top of the nautical chart. The point where the earth spins on its axis at the North Pole.

TTG: Time to go.

TVMDC: Formula for converting true courses to compass courses.

Variation: Variation is a predictable magnetic influence on your compass, which is directly related to the position of the magnetic North Pole, the true North Pole, and the position of your boat.

USWMS: Uniform State Waterway Marking System.

UTC: Universal Time Coordinates.

WAAS: Wide Angle Augmentation System.

Waypoint: A LAT/LON position used in GPS for navigation.

WGS84:   World Geodetic System of 1984. A horizontal datum used for the Pacific Island territories of the United States.

XTE: Cross-track error.

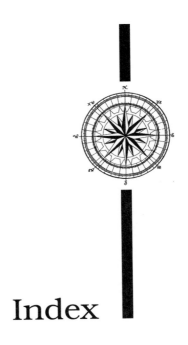

Index

Other books of interest from Sheridan House

BASIC COASTAL NAVIGATION
by Frank J. Larkin
"An excellent self-teaching textbook.... His approach is straightforward and his sense of humor refreshing." *The ENSIGN*
"Every navigator would benefit from having this comprehensive reference book available as a refresher or for new skills." *Ocean Navigator*

CELESTIAL NAVIGATION IN A NUTSHELL
by Hewitt Schlereth
"Every concept is explained in straightforward language and illustrated with clear diagrams. [Schlereth] covers everything you need to know to become an expert celestial navigator." *Cruising World*
"...tackles the nuts and bolts of modern celestial navigation...in clear, concise language that makes it very easy to follow." *Sailing*

READY FOR SEA!
by Tor Pinney
"...an easy read, packed with good advice. Even experienced cruisers will pick up a thing or two from this one." *Latitudes & Attitudes*
"...presents clearly and concisely what it takes to provision a boat and sail it confidently..." *SAIL*

BOAT INTERIOR CONSTRUCTION
by Michael Naujok
This bestselling guide to do-it-yourself boatbuilding will prove extremely useful to any owners not completely happy with the layout of their production boat and those who want to fit out a new or renovated hull.
"As useful to the beginner as the experienced amateur...with this you'll have the information and inspiration to fit out a boat." *Sailing Today*
"...very clear and detailed..." *Sailing & Yachting (SA)*

MOTORBOAT ELECTRICAL & ELECTRONICS MANUAL
by John C. Payne
Following the international success of *Marine Electrical and Electronics Bible*, Payne turns his talents from sailing boats to powerboats.
This complete guide, which covers inboard engine boats of all ages, types, and sizes, is a must for all builders, owners, and operators. Payne has put together a concise, useful, and thoroughly practical guide, explaining in detail how to select, install, maintain, and troubleshoot all electrical and electronic systems on a boat.
Contents include: diesel engines, instrumentation and control, bow thrusters, stabilizers, A/C and refrigeration, water and sewage systems, batteries and charging, wiring systems, corrosion, AC power systems, generators, fishfinders and sonar, computers, charting and GPS, radar, autopilots, GMDSS, radio frequencies, and more.
"... tells the reader how to maintain or upgrade just about every type of inboard engine vessel." *Soundings*

America's Favorite Sailing Books
www.sheridanhouse.com